YES, 1 ACRE IS ENOUGH!

A Guide to Sustainable, Respectful and Ethical Livelihood

SANGAM

ABSTRACT

We live in a world where humans are Alpha. But amongst the 8 billion of us, a mere 810 million / 81 crore people hold 85% of the total wealth. This is the same world where the bottom 4 billion/400 crore own 1% of the total wealth. How will we sustain like this?

A potential solution for a sustainable and honorable existence.

This effort of mine is dedicated to my grandparents

Mrs Namita Sinha & Late Mrs Majidan Begum

Late Mr Anath Bandhu Sinha & Late Sahibzada Muhammad Iliyas

Table of Contents

Table of Contents

Prologue

Education

My educational journey has been shaped by the freedom my parents granted me to make my own decisions. However, this wasn't without its challenges. I pursued the sciences in my higher secondary education, even though it wasn't my passion. Yet, through this experience, I gained valuable knowledge that later helped me in my career and life.

I completed my engineering in computer science, a field that I initially struggled to connect with but ultimately excelled in. This education gave me the foundation for my work in the IT industry, but it wasn't until later in life, while pursuing my MBA and now my PhD, that I found my true calling. This book is part of my ongoing research and development of a sustainable land project—a model designed to help marginal farmers create self-sustaining businesses and achieve financial stability.

Drive

What drives me is a deep sense of dissatisfaction with the growing inequalities and divisions in the world. Everywhere I've traveled, I've observed a widening gap between the rich and the poor. This divide has led to a world where millions struggle to survive, while a few hold unimaginable wealth. My drive comes from a desire to address this imbalance by providing practical, actionable solutions. I believe that when people have the resources to sustain themselves—through food, shelter, and employment—they can focus on bettering their lives and contributing to society. This drive is at the heart of this book: to offer a pathway for families with limited land to become self-reliant and create a better future for themselves.

Passion

Passion isn't inherent or tied to talent—it is something that grows over time and can become a powerful force for change. My passion for this project stems from my desire to bridge the gap between rich and poor by creating a model that turns land, education, and hard work into sustainable livelihoods. When people have the ability to support themselves, they have the opportunity to live with dignity and purpose. This passion drives me to ensure that the solutions I propose in this book will help people lead balanced, fulfilling lives.

Determination

Determination has been the driving force behind this book and the project it describes. From conceptualizing the idea to testing it in real life, every step of this journey has required overcoming obstacles. The biggest challenge was time—balancing a demanding career with the development of this project. I found support in Anusha Khan, who helped document my thoughts and bring structure to the project. Bringing the idea to life was the next challenge. I knew that the theory alone wasn't enough—I needed to test it. That's why I raised goats myself, built sheds, and experimented with sustainable farming techniques. This hands-on experience provided the practical insights that make this project feasible for others to implement.

Final Outcome

The final outcome of this land project goes beyond financial stability – it's about creating a legacy of self-reliance and sustainability. The model aims to generate an annual income of $30,000 to $60,000 (INR 24-48 lakhs) for a family of 10-15 members. This income ensures a lower-middle-class lifestyle, but more importantly, it engages every family member in meaningful work that contributes to their collective future.

The project is designed to be sustainable across generations, with every member of the family playing a role in its success. It provides employment, education, and a pathway to a dignified life, all while nurturing the land and fostering community. By following the principles in this book, families can create a self-sustaining farm that will continue to support them for years to come, providing not just financial security but a meaningful legacy.

Acknowledgments

To my teachers – Sir Rakesh Khandelwal, Mr Navneet Verma, Mr Mudit Khetan, Mr Sunil Jose & Mr Anil Yadav – You all were there to bring me back from a point of no return... Thank you for being the light that every growing kid deserves.

I would like to extend my deepest gratitude to my parents for teaching me the power of questioning. My father, Mr. Prince Salim, always used reasoning to guide me to answers. While it was often a longer journey, it always led me to the truth. One of my earliest questions was about why stars twinkle, and another memorable one was about the Nile River and the civilization that thrived on its banks. I still remember writing a four-page answer in my 7th standard exam, covering everything from river floods to alluvial soil and minerals essential for cultivation. Although the teacher gave me a zero, my father—who holds an MA in Geography—was proud of my thoroughness. His pride in that moment is something I carry with me, and it's one of the reasons I've developed a solid foundation of knowledge. Thank you, Babba!

Mummy, thank you for everything. You were always there saving me from trouble, supporting me through my worst moments, and bailing me out when I needed it most. Your unwavering strength has been a cornerstone in my life. I can't understand the fact that you're getting old; it's hard for me to comprehend. Words can't express my feelings, ma.

Dear Rumani, you and Rahul are pillars of inspiration and strength in my life. I have the confidence to experiment with my ideas because I know we are a team, and you are always there to support and enable me when needed. I'm incredibly proud of who you've become and everything you've achieved.

Sagnik – waiting for your happily ever after! Your dedication to theater and your ability to balance it with your work is truly inspiring.

Sumit – you and I are like opposite poles, but it's that very contrast that keeps me positively charged and energized. Your unique perspective inspires me to keep my focus. I wish someday we will work together and make Buli Maasi proud.

Acknowledgments

Dear Anusha, thank you for your incredible research and analysis for this book. It wouldn't be possible to complete this project in the time it took without your efforts. We do make a great team!

Ishita – kudos to you for the beautiful artwork and design on the cover of this book. I wish you all the success in your future endeavors.

To Notion Press, thank you for your unwavering support and for bringing a professional touch to this book's publication. You've helped bring to life my dream 'Dauraiwala', and I look forward to continuing this journey beyond just this book.

– Sangam
MBA, B.E Hons. Computer Science

Whispers in the Wind: A Tale of Loss and Hope

A VILLAGE IN the early hours of dawn. The sun has not risen yet, but there are already people shuffling around in the darkness, getting ready for the day – farmers. Their shadows move along the unpaved roads of the village as they leave their homes to work in the fields, where they will remain until sunset.

Mukesh is a farmer, the youngest among his 4 brothers and 2 sisters. He inherited 2 acres of land from his father; this land is his sole source of earning and livelihood.

(Imagine) You are Mukesh, making your way toward the field around 6 in the morning. Sunrays cover everything in a soft orange hue. The fields of wheat stand tall, gently swaying in the morning breeze, radiating a golden light, indicating that they are ready to harvest.

Just 4 months ago, these long stalks of wheat had been mere seeds that you had planted. Now, seeing how well the wheat had grown, you let out a sigh of relief. The money from the sale of this harvest is going to be your family's support until the next crop season. You also had to repay the loans you took from the bank and the local moneylender to buy fertilizer and good quality seeds.

You worked hard for the next few days to harvest the wheat. After reaping, the crop had to be cleaned; until then, it would stay in the field. There was no visible harm in keeping the harvested crop in the open fields until it was cleaned; however, fate had other plans.

It rained. It started as a gentle pitter-patter, and you thought it would stop soon. After all, it was not supposed to rain at this time of year. Even with the advanced radar and remote sensing information shared by the meteorological department, which predicted a light shower, the unpredictable happened. The rain didn't stop and soon turned from a light drizzle to a heavy downpour.

Your harvest, the potential earnings, and hard work of the past 4 months were drenched by a single rain shower. Moist grains are useless. High humidity/moisture content leads to rot, and threshing is no longer possible.

You stand over the harvest, heaps and heaps of unsellable crop, angry and cursing. Next, you get worried about how you will feed your family for the next few months, how you will pay back loans, and how to deal with the social stigma of being a failure.

The pressure keeps mounting and mounting. You lose foresight and get surrounded by the darkest of thoughts. You withdraw into a shell, not able to share your burden with anyone because no one can help. This is not only your disaster but scores of people come to your mind who have the same fate as you. You look right and left to the other fields and find your siblings and neighboring farmers, their faces as if reflecting your own thoughts, everyone seems to be staring endlessly into nothing.

Next day newspapers and TV channels report the untimely rain showers and cite the unpredictability of mother nature. Some even state that perhaps the gods were angry, while the rest blame climate change. Very few people talk directly about the meteorological department's failure at being more accurate. In a small column in the newspaper, they report the untimely demise of many farmers, including you, who had committed suicide under the pressure of crop failure and mounting loans.

In the quiet hours before dawn, the village stirs to life as farmers tread along the dim paths, greeting the day's toil.

Mukesh, the youngest of seven, walks toward his golden promise, the sun's first rays casting hope over his fields.

Amidst the sway of golden wheat, Mukesh stands, a soft sigh escaping him, a blend of pride and relief for the harvest ahead.

Dark clouds gather uninvited, spilling the first drops of despair on Mukesh's labor, a harbinger of the storm to come.

Amidst the wreckage of his hopes, Mukesh sits, engulfed by the loss, as the rain mocks the ruins of his hard work.

Silent solidarity in despair, as faces across the fields mirror Mukesh's turmoil, a community united in their defeat.

Words on paper and echoes on air, speaking of rain and nature's whims, yet silent on the plight of those who feed the nation.

In the quiet that follows the storm, a flame flickers in the night, a somber tribute to lost souls swallowed by their toil.

The Last Harvest – Father, Son & a Long-Lost Dream

A hot July day during summertime in a small village of Rajasthan (an arid Indian state). The village roads stand deserted as most people have retired into their homes or under cool shades of trees to protect themselves from the heatwave (locally referred to as 'Loo'). A lone person is seen working in the field, under the burning sun, preparing the soil to sow seeds. This is you, an agricultural laborer hired to cultivate. You have been promised half of the yield or half of the money procured post sales of the harvest as payment. Even though the work is very demanding and extremely tedious, you still go on with this job. Being landless, you do not have many alternatives; this is all you know.

Upon your return home, while you rest a bit, seeing your state, your father repeats a story that he has spoken about endless times. The glorious history of your ancestors. In the past, your bloodline was not so poor and had bountiful land which provided for your great-grandfather and his 6 children. The land was then equally divided among his children, and your grandfather received 4 acres of land. He also equally divided this land among his four children, and your father received 1 acre of land. Your ancestors were just, but perhaps not foresighted.

Your father boasts of being the wise one, only having 2 kids and doing justice by equally giving half an acre of land to both of you. You ponder for the nth time about how to feed the upcoming generation and your now retired father and ailing mother. And what to leave as inheritance for your son and daughter. Having studied till the 10th standard, you do the basic mathematics that in 4 generations your family had declined from being landlords, having 24 acres of land, to becoming marginal farmers where you have to work on the fields of others to make ends meet. As the land kept getting divided among siblings, each generation got less and less. By the fourth generation, which is yours, 24 acres had been reduced to half an acre per descendant, a size so small that it is no longer possible to sustain a family solely on it, being the reason why you have sought employment as an agricultural laborer during the crop season and a daily wage laborer during the off-season, to support your family.

If these stories sound heart-breaking to you, then imagine what it would be like when it becomes the reality of a person. Stories like these are the actual truth of farmers in our nation.

A scorching July day in Rajasthan; the village roads lay deserted under the wrath of the 'Loo' The empty roads are surrounded by a few trees that offer little shade.

Alone in the fields, a laborer toils under the relentless sun, sowing seeds on the landowner's field

Back home you sit near a window for some cool air. Your father, an old man with a face showing wisdom and hard work, sits opposite you, starting to tell a story you've heard before.

A look back at fertile fields. It starts with your great grandfather and his six children on a large land. Land is divided among his children, each generation receiving lesser and lesser.

Using a pen and paper, the person figures out how much land has been divided over time. From 120 acres to not even 1 acre per person.

With not enough land to cultivate, the farmer is forced to become an agricultural labourer and work on the fields of others.

In the off season he works as a daily wage labourer, doing unskilled labor.

Worried and frustrated, the farmer thinks about how to provide for the family and what to leave for the kids."

What is a mind map?

A mind map is a visual representation of a thought or idea. It has a central theme, which can be divided into sublevels, and each sublevel can be branched further into sublevels. It helps to understand a complex idea by breaking it down into smaller levels and analyzing how sublevels are associated with the central theme. In simple language, it helps us to 'connect the dots'.

How to read a mind map?

A mind map has a theme at its center. Focus on the theme first.

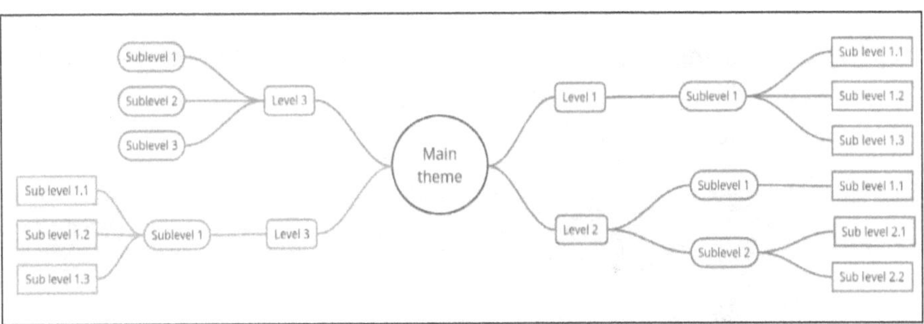

Starting at the center, begin reading clockwise. So, the first sub-level you will read is the one situated at the top-right corner, which is Level 1. Each level is further divided into branches. In the diagram, the numbering after each level indicates the order in which to read them.

You will notice that the mind map consists of different shapes. The purpose of shapes is to differentiate between the different components of the map. Here is a breakdown of the different shapes used in the mind map and its components:

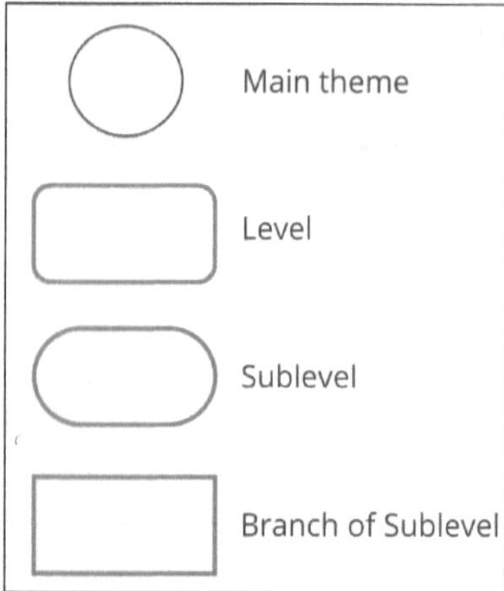

There are 3 ways to make associations in the branches of the sub-level:

1. **General to specific**

    In this approach, the reading order is left to right. As you progress further, a general idea becomes more specific. It can be understood as breaking down a structure into smaller parts to analyze each part individually. So, the deeper you go, the more specific the details become. For example, look at the following diagram:

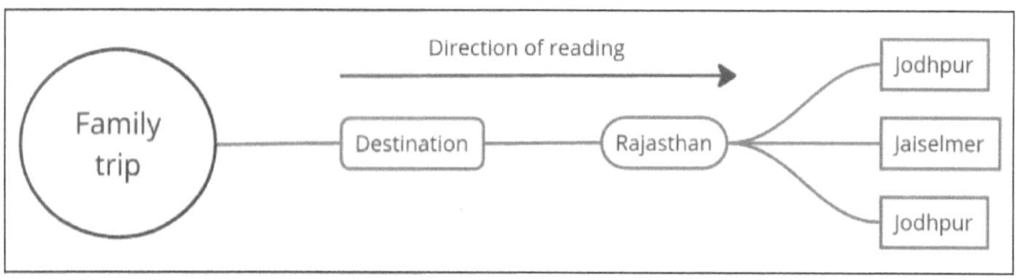

2. **Abstract to Concrete**

    In this approach, the reading order is from right to left. As you read the branches backward, a previously abstract idea takes on a more concrete shape. It can be understood as assembling the pieces of a jigsaw puzzle where the smaller parts add up to form a concrete picture.

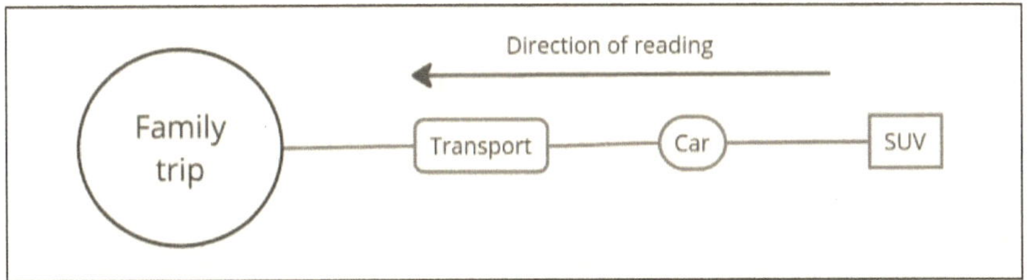

So, this can be read as, an SUV is a car, a car is a means of transport for the family trip.

Whole to parts

In this approach, a whole is divided into parts. You can either read from left to right, that is, the whole divided into branches, or from right to left, that is, the branch is a part of the whole.

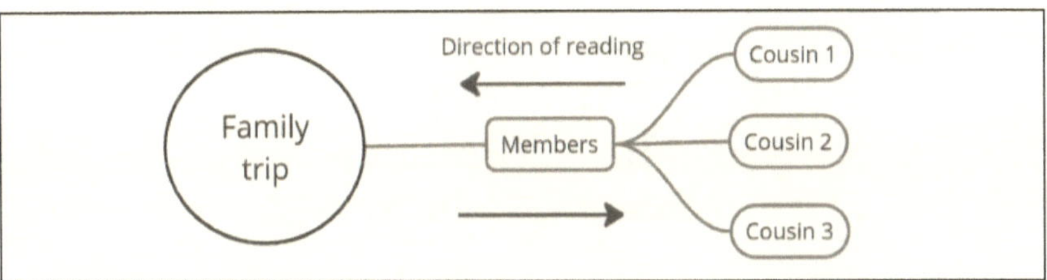

So, you can either read it as members of the family – Cousin 1, 2, and 3 or read it as Cousin 1 is a member of the family.

Mind maps are provided at the start of each chapter for the reader's ease. They will provide a summarized idea of the topics covered in the chapter.

Coming up...

Low yield
Growing population
Less land per capita
Intensive agriculture
Using chemical fertilizers
Mounting loans
Land fragmentation
Land degradation
Less profits
Increasing capital investment
The predicament of marginalized farmers
Man made instability
Lack of efficient irrigation systems
Rising inflation rates
Global warming
Limited freshwater
Using inland saline water
Low yield
Changing climate
Wasted in traditional irrigation systems
Soil salinization
Low income
Flood irrigation
High prices of basic necessities

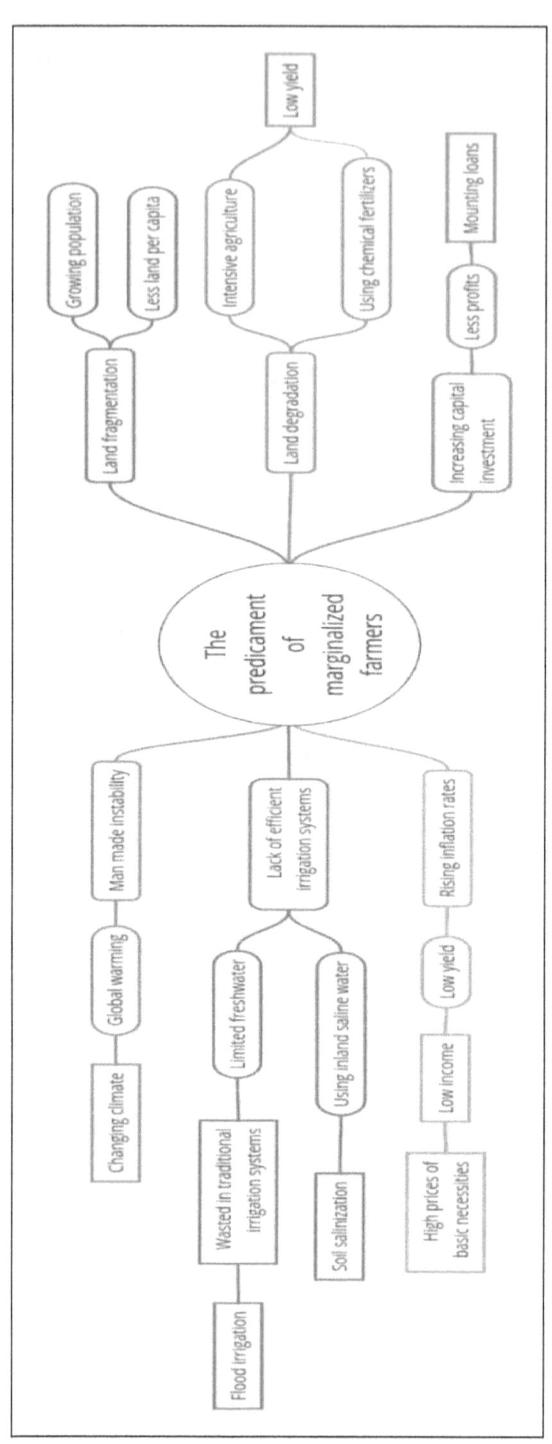

CHAPTER 1

The Predicament of Marginalised Farmers

A LAND WHERE earth and grain are a common thread binding more than half of the country's population – This is India, where the rhythm of life is dictated by the seasons and the harvest. India, a country where stories of grit, resilience and transformation are a daily phenomenon, occurring in fields of gold and green. Being a country that has a large agrarian economy, we can say that India relies on agriculture as its main source of income and economic activity.

In an agrarian economy such as India, a large portion of the population is involved in farming, raising livestock, and producing food crops, which are critical for the livelihood and survival of individuals.

The significance of agriculture for India and its people can be better understood by looking at the numbers revealed in the last census report. The last census conducted in 2011[1], around 13 years ago, highlighted a stark reality: 54.6%[2] of the country's population was engaged in agriculture and allied activities, which means 5 out of every 10 people were dependent on agriculture for their livelihood.

Needless to say, agriculture, with its allied sectors, is the largest source of livelihood here. This continues to be the case even today. Considering a 15% decline, we will still have 41.6% of India's population, which would be roughly 58 crore or 582 million Indians who are employed or engaged in this field. This cannot be refuted, period!

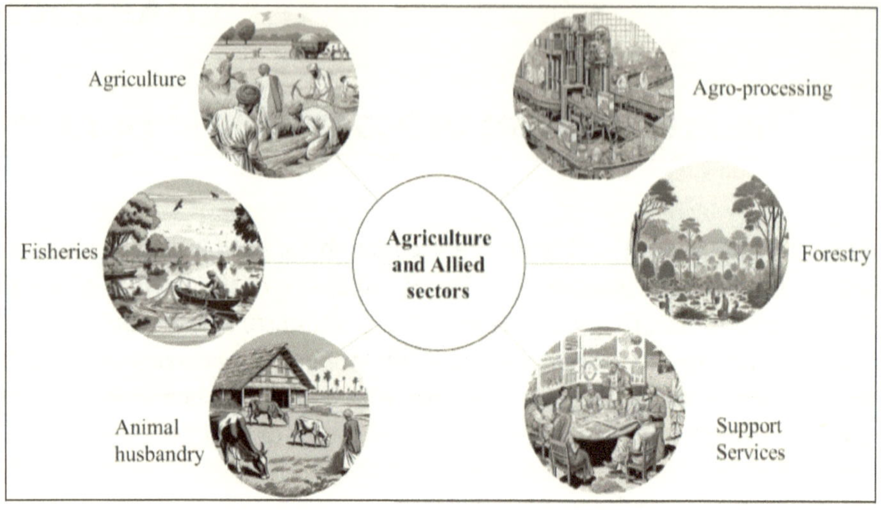

Figure 1: Agriculture and Allied Activities

This is not just a tale of numbers but of faces, families, and futures intertwined with the earth they till. The land of this country reflects the hard work of the people who cultivate it.

Statistics show that cultivation tops the list when it comes to land use. This indicates that agriculture owns the biggest portion when we talk about the various ways in which land is used in our country.

Figure 2 illustrates the vast scale of agriculture in India. It is not just an important part of the economy but also a way of life for millions of people, or should we say close to 600 million people.

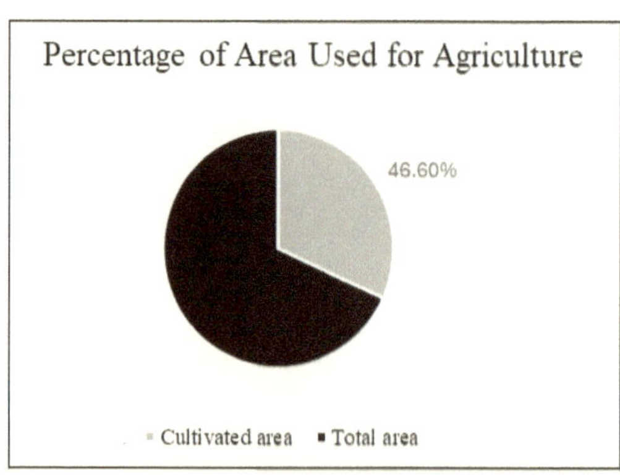

Figure 2: Illustration of the area cultivated out of the total area

Farming is at the heart of India's traditions, its economy, and the daily lives of a significant portion of its population. It shapes the rhythms of rural life, dictates the patterns of migration, and influences the country's dietary staples and food culture.

The large areas of land dedicated to agriculture highlight the strong connection between Indians and their land, a bond that supports, feeds, and sometimes tests them as they work toward a better living.

The magnitude of the previous statement can be better understood when we compare the percentage of agricultural land in India to that of other countries. Figure 3 is a graph showing the percentage of agricultural land use country-wise:

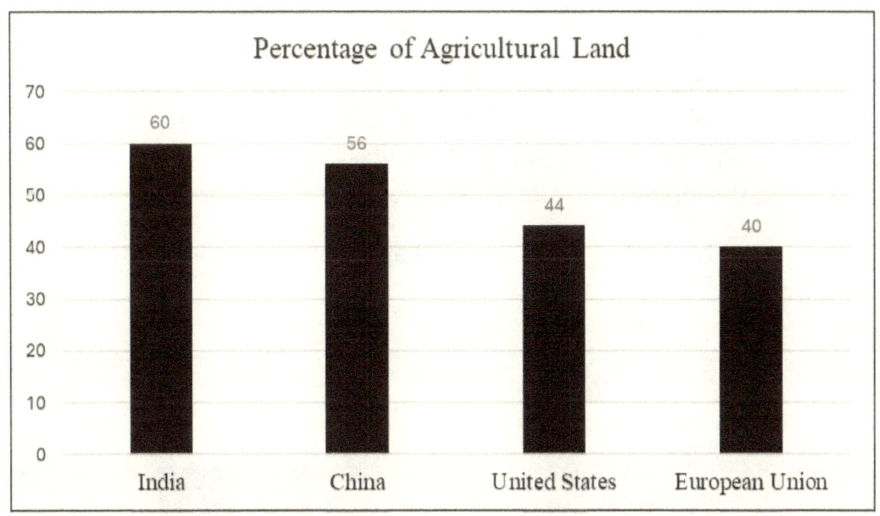

Figure 3: Agricultural Land Use

The graph shows land use in broad terms as agricultural land is a broad category that includes all land used for agricultural purposes. This encompasses:

- **Arable Land**: Land used for crops that are replanted after each harvest (e.g. wheat, rice, vegetables).
- **Permanent Crops**: Land with crops that do not require replanting after each harvest (e.g., fruit trees, spices, and plantation crops).
- **Permanent Meadows and Pastures**: Land used for grazing livestock.

Now let us narrow down the area of inspection and consider only the land used for cultivation. There are 2 parameters to consider here-

1. ***Total Cropped Area***: This includes all the planting activities throughout the year. If the same piece of land is used to grow multiple crops in different seasons, each crop cycle is counted separately.
2. ***Net Sown Area***: This refers to the total area of land on which crops are grown and harvested during a single agricultural year. Each plot of land is counted only once, regardless of the number of crops grown in a year.

We can better understand the difference between these 2 parameters with the help of an example. Suppose a farmer has 1 acre of land, which they cultivate 2 times a year. The Net Sown Area here will be 1 acre, since we are only considering the land and not the cropping activity.

The Total Cropped Area will be 2 acres since the farmer is cultivating the land twice a year. So, while the NSA (Net Sown Area) tells us the total area of land cultivated on a broad scale, TCA (Total Cropped Area) shows detailed data about the intensity of cultivation.

Let us analyze India's cultivable land and cropping activity in the light of this example.

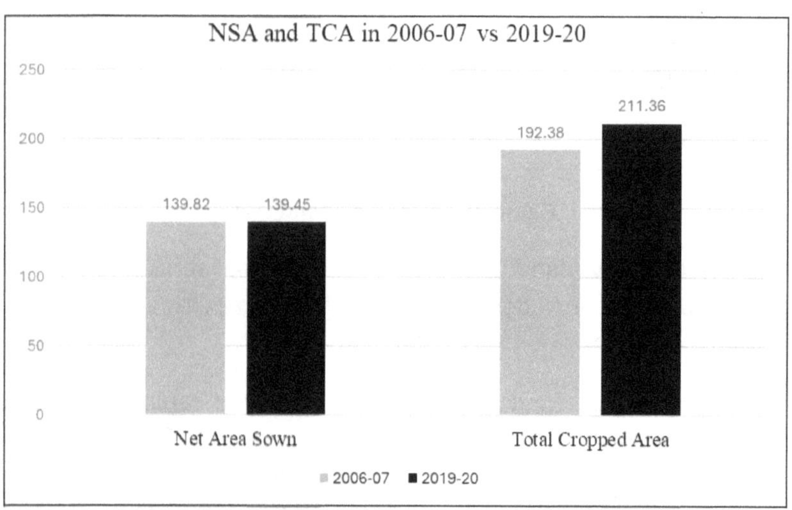

Figure 4: Net Sown Area and Total Cropped Area in 2006-07 and 2019-20

As of 2020, the Total Cropped Area in India stood at 211.36 million hectares. This was a 9.8% increase since the year 2006 when it stood at 192.38 million hectares.

Meanwhile, the Net Sown Area stood at 139.45 million hectares in 2020, with a mere increase of 0.26% since the year 2006 when it stood at 139.82 million hectares.

What does this figure tell us? While the NSA has barely increased in 13 years, the TSA has increased by 9.87%. This indicates that the amount of times the same land is being cultivated has increased over the years.

This points toward intensive agriculture practiced by farmers. The area of land being cultivated has not increased, but the number of times it is cultivated has.

What could be the possible reasons for this spike in cultivation? From a nation's point of view, it could be a way to fulfill the increasing food demand for its exponentially growing population. From a farmer's point of view, it could be a way for them to earn more money from the sales of 2 or 3 crops instead of one. After all, they too have a family to feed.

With a huge portion of its population and land engaged in agriculture, and being one of the leading food producers in the world, one would expect the farmers of India to be well off; however, the reality is far from this assumption. The farmers, who are the backbone of this nation, often find themselves grappling with hardships.

While the vast area of land dedicated to agriculture in India might suggest abundance, it's crucial not to be misled. On the surface, the huge percentage of cultivable land paints a very utopian picture of rich farmers and lush fields spanning acres. But just below the surface is the cruel reality of small patches of land that cannot produce an output enough to feed even the family of the farmer.

In the grand picture of being the topmost country in the world for having the highest amount of land dedicated to agriculture, we fail to see the ground reality of how much land a farmer actually owns. And that, dear reader, is how we fail to see reality.

The truth of the matter comes to light when we consider the per capita availability of agricultural land (that is how much land is available per person or specifically a farmer for cultivation).

The per capita availability of agricultural land in India is a mere 0.12 ha (0.29 acres) as opposed to the world per capita agricultural land, which is 0.29 ha (0.71 acres). [3]

If we calculate this in the local unit of measurement i.e. bigha[4], 0.29 acres do not amount to even half a bigha (specifically 0.29 acres is about 0.468 bigha).

Why is it important to consider the factor of per capita availability? Because it shows us the actual reality of farmers in this nation. Let us understand this through an example.

Imagine we have a group of 5 individuals with the following incomes:

- Person A, B, C: ₹200
- Person D: ₹50
- Person E: ₹500

If we calculate the average income of this group, it will be ₹230. Why? Because the income of one person in the group who earns ₹500 increases the average considerably.

On the surface, this group has a shiny average income of ₹230. But when we consider per capita income, 3 out of 5 people are earning below the average, and 1 of them is barely making ends meet. This is why it is necessary for us to consider the per capita parameter.

The readers are requested not to react, but rather absorb first.

Expanding on this reality, we found that, as of 2019, a staggering 89.4% of farming households were working with less than 2 hectares (5 acres) of land[5].

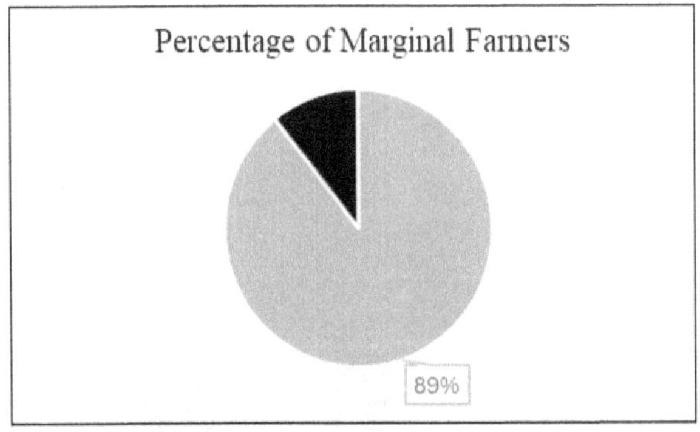

Figure 5: Percentage of marginal farmers in 2019

When we say 2 hectares, it can be a bit misleading. After all, 2 hectares is no small piece of land. But we should remember that this is the upper limit of land per capita. When we say less than 2 hectares (5 acres) of land, it could mean any number from 0.1 hectare (0.2 acre) to 2 hectares (5 acres). In other words, it could range from the size of 32 cricket pitches (22 yards in length and 10ft wide) to 3.7 football fields (2 hectares).

What is the threshold of land one must own to be considered marginal, medium, or large farmer?

Table 1 will establish better the distinction between the different categories of farmers on the basis of land ownership.

Table 1: Area of land owned by different categories of farmers

Category	Size Class
Marginal	Below 1.00 hectare (below 2.5 acre)
Small	1.00-2.00 hectare (2.5-5 acre)
Semi – Medium	2.00-4.00 hectare (5-10 acre)
Medium	4.00-10.00 hectare (10 – 25 acre)
Large	10.00 hectares and above (25 acre or above)

The percentage of marginal and small farmers in India has seen a steep increase in recent years. At the same time, the percentage of medium and large farmers has been declining over time.

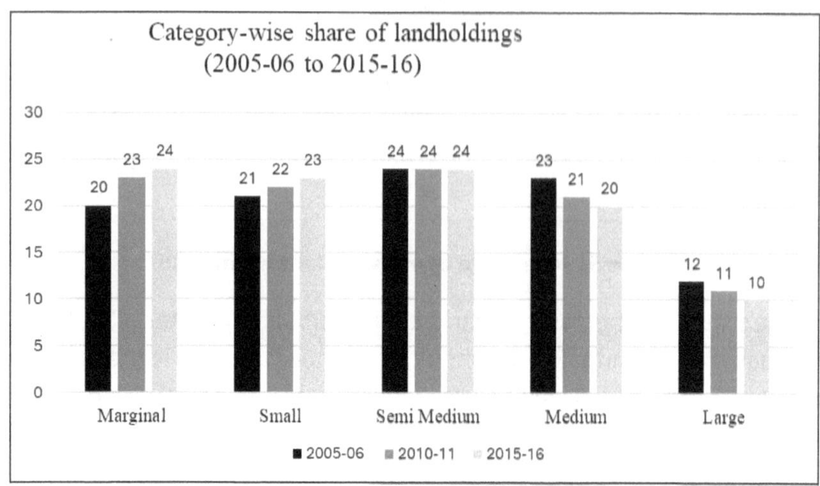

Figure 6: Category-wise share of landholdings (2005-06 to 2015-16)

What is the reason for this change?

Whether it be an increase (in the size of landholdings) or a decrease (in the number of medium and large farmers)? The answer to this question is one of the most worrying phenomena seen in farmer families of India today. We will pick this up again later in the chapter; until then, we would advise the reader to keep these statistics in mind as it will be easier to connect the dots later.

With decreasing land comes increasing poverty. Landholdings of sizes as small as 0.12 hectares (0.29 acres) cannot even fulfill the basic needs of a family, much less maintain a standard of living. The result? A huge percentage of the population falls under the tag of Below Poverty Line or BPL.

The poverty line is the threshold line that defines the minimum requirement of income required by an individual to fulfill basic necessities. The current poverty line in rural regions is ₹1,059 per month, while in urban areas it is ₹1,286. According to the 2022 "Agricultural Statistics at a Glance 2022" report published by the Directorate of Economics and Statistics (Department of Agriculture and Farmers Welfare, Ministry of Agriculture and Farmers Welfare), around 22% of the rural population, which predominantly includes farmers, is below the poverty line.

Let us convert this percentage into numbers to emphasize the gravity of this situation. As of 2022, the rural population stood at 90 crores (900 million)[6]. Which means 19.8 crore (198 million) were surviving on less than ₹1,059 per month.

The person reading this might be a farmer, a student, an employed or an unemployed person. Whatever your identity may be, you, like everyone else, also need some basic necessities to live. Food, clothes, shelter – these are basic needs.

Ask yourself this: what can you buy with ₹1,000 in your hand?

In today's world, could you survive for 30 days with ₹1,000, which is ₹33 per day (~40 cents)?

Forget 3 meals a day, do you think you could afford even one meal a day for 30 days?

The farmers of our nation are caught in this bottomless pit of despair!

It is both ironic and distressing to see that the very people who work all year round to provide us with food are spending hours in the field in every type of weather, be it scorching heat, heavy downpour, or even during bone-chilling winters. The very same people have been reported sleeping on an empty stomach. Remember Latur...

In Rajasthan, an arid state of India, you can see farmers preparing the fields for the upcoming Kharif season in the scorching heat of summers (June-July) where temperatures can go up to 50 degrees in some areas. The paddy cultivators of West Bengal transplant paddy saplings during the monsoon, drenched from head to toe.

Many of us are privileged enough to not think about how to survive another day or how to get food on the table for our family, but the farming population of our country is not so fortunate. Nobody in this country works as hard as the farmer toiling for long hours just to put a little bit of food in his children's mouths.

They are not aware of the modern techniques in farming such as aquaponics and hydroponics, which could make their lives easier because they are not considered worthy by the people who decide their fate.

It is easy for the upper section of society to have 3 hearty meals a day without a single thought about how they got there. For example, pulses are not grown in arid regions, yet they are available in markets of dry states such as Rajasthan. Similarly, green vegetables which are brought in summer (as frozen food) or winter fruits like apples and oranges are still available during the summer season. These are definitely not produced locally but transported from faraway regions.

The next time you sit down to eat a meal, take some time and think about how many farmers worked hard to bring even the smallest morsel of food to your plate. While we eat a scrumptious meal made out of all kinds of fresh vegetables, there is no food on the plate of the person who actually grew those.

The plight of the Indian farmer goes beyond the mere numbers of statistics and graphs. The infographics can only depict the material information, but what it fails to present is the real-life hellish loop of poverty the farmer is stuck in.

Therefore, while it's important to study figures and reports to gain a better understanding of the problem, we must remind the readers that the numbers on paper have actual consequences in the physical world. There are real people with real problems who are, in truth, living the nightmare that the graph is trying to depict. When talking about the reduced standard of living of farmers, it would be impossible not to bring up inflation in the conversation. It is one of the primary reasons why farmers cannot break out of the cycle of poverty.

The following graph shows the inflation rate in some basic food commodities over the span of 10 years (2012-2022).

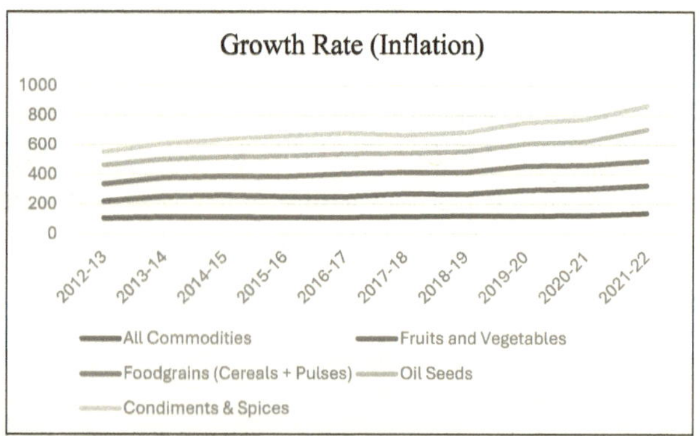

Figure 7: Growth rate (Inflation) [7]

It might be difficult for some readers to relate to the graph and the rate at which prices have shot up in recent years. We can better understand this with some real-world examples.

Search for a coin from the year 2000 or before. Look at the size and metal used and now get the same denomination coin from the current year or the near past. You would find 2 instances-

1. The said denomination might not have existed in the year 2000 (for example – a 20-rupee Indian coin was non-existent in 2000).
2. The 2-rupee Indian coin of today (2024) is smaller and lighter than the 1-rupee coin of 2000.

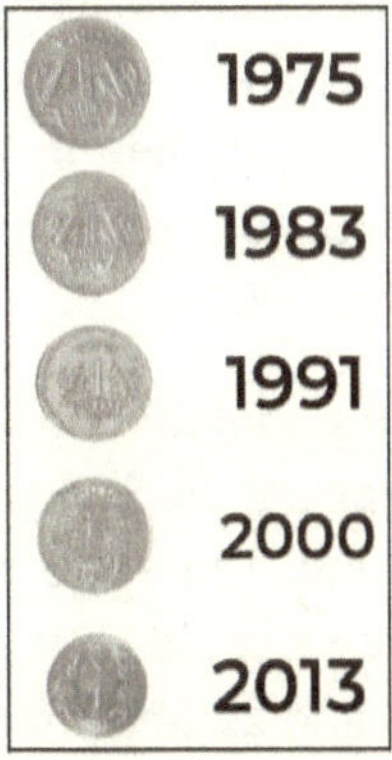

Figure 8: 1-rupee Indian coin over the past 40 years

Figure 9: New denomination of 20-rupee coin

What conclusions do we draw from this observation? Over time, things have become more expensive, and money itself has lost value. The reader will find that with the same amount of money, the things you could buy 10 years ago and now have significantly decreased.

Talk to someone in your family who is 30-40 years old or older, such as your parents or grandparents. Ask them about the things they used to buy when they were kids. You will find out that they used to have denominations that don't even exist now, like anna and paisa. In those times, a 1-rupee coin was equal to 16 annas or 64 paisa. This means that the 1-rupee coin could be broken down into smaller currencies, and one could buy so many things with 1 rupee.

However, with time, numbers do change. And the change at which inflation rates have risen in the past few years is truly unprecedented.

Let us consider another point of view – why do we talk about percentages and not numbers when comparing the past and present? Because comparisons require the denominator to be constant.

If the population were either stagnant or growing at a slow rate, then it would be easy to simply cite numbers. For example, we could have said 50 lakh farmers were below the poverty line in 2000 and 55 lakh farmers are below the poverty line in 2024. By looking at these numbers, someone might conclude that poverty has increased.

But when we compare the population in 2000 vs 2024 (hypothetically), almost 40 crore people have been added. But only 5 lakhs are the total increase in farmers below the poverty line. Therefore, if the same were explained in the form of a percentage, then we could have said that 25% of farmers were below the poverty line in 2000 and 22.5% of farmers were below the poverty line in 2024. This means that we have reduced the number of farmers below the poverty line by 2.5%.

Therefore, we can say we have progressed. Because even though the number of farmers below the poverty line has increased, the population of India has increased as well.

This is just an example to show why a percentage is a better option for measuring change instead of numbers. Numbers are absolute but only when the denominator is static.

Now that we have understood some basic concepts like how important agriculture and farmers are for the economy of this country, about the increasing number of marginal farmers, rising rates of inflation and consequently rising poverty; we can now move on to deeply analyze the 'predicament of marginal farmers.'

To have a deeper understanding of the farmer's predicament, we must examine it from grassroots levels. We will be focusing on the following areas:

1. Fragmentation of land over generations
2. Land degradation
3. Poor farming practices
4. Lack of proper irrigation system
5. Rising inflation
6. Mounting loans

If we had to simplify it, it would come down to problems related to:

1. Land
2. Food
3. Water
4. Capital (money)
5. Man-made instability (greed)

Let us dissect these reasons to properly understand the plight of our food cultivators. Our goal is to assist you in understanding these problems so that we can all collectively work on a practical solution.

LAND FRAGMENTATION

Let us start with the most basic and yet the most significant of the issues – fragmentation of land. Previously, in the chapter, when we were discussing Figure 6, we raised a question about the steady percentage decline in medium and large-scale farmers.

What is the reason for this change: an increase (in the size of landholdings) or a decrease (in the number of medium and large farmers)?

Why is this the most prominent problem in an agrarian society like India?

Agrarian societies prefer to stay together, either in joint families or in close proximity to each other. Often, this is due to the need for cheap labor to grow crops in a sizable area, as well as the necessity of having a single decision-maker.

However, once the head of the family passes away, the land is divided among the next generation and the kids become heads of their respective families. This is done in order to have freedom of choice as well as decision-making and to avoid confrontation. This is also the law of the land for property that is inherited.

Every generation of farmer families will divide their land so that each of their children has some land to cultivate. But this is a bane rather than a boon because even though they have the choice and freedom, eventually the size of the land shrinks generation by generation.

Division of land is bound to hit a dead end sooner or later. We predict that it will not go beyond 2 generations from now and will reach a critical stage by 2050.

We can better understand this with the following flowchart:

Time scale (year)
Suresh – 1960
Child – 1990
Grandchild – 2020
Great-grandchild – 2050
Great-grandchild's child – 2080

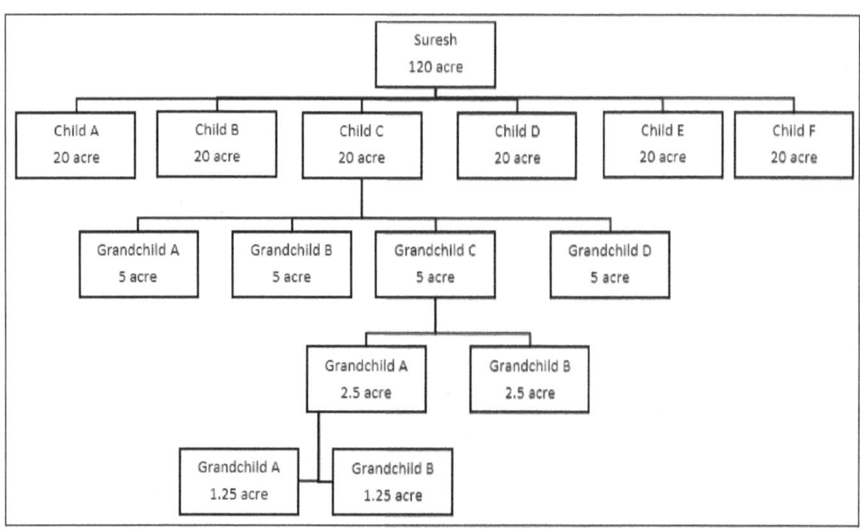

Figure 10: Family chart depicting decreasing area of land per capita

You will note that we optimistically considered 1960 as the starting year when Suresh was given 120 acres of land (a considerable amount). Now see what happens to Suresh's great-grandson's child in 2080.

One grasps the gravity of the situation when we realize that neither the starting year nor the size of Suresh's land is the norm. Many people might have acquired land later in the 90s or 2000s, and it could have been 1 acre or even smaller than that.

The norm is fragmentation. Whether it's a family that owns 120 acres of land or a family that owns 1 acre, they will all go through the process of fragmentation. Some will become landless sooner than others, but it's a destination that everyone will arrive at unless they change their trajectory.

As depicted in the flow chart, even a person who owned 120 acres of land in the 1960s, which is a considerable amount, has descendants who own merely 1 acre in 2080. The rapid decrease in the size of landholdings is more terrifying when one realizes that this happened over just 4 generations.

As per the latest information available from *Agriculture Census*[8], the average size of operational holdings in India has decreased from 2.28 hectares (5.63 acres) in 1970-71 to 1.84 hectares (4.54 acres) in 1980-81, to 1.41 hectares (3.48 acres) in 1995-96, and to 1.08 hectares (2.66 acres) in 2015-16.

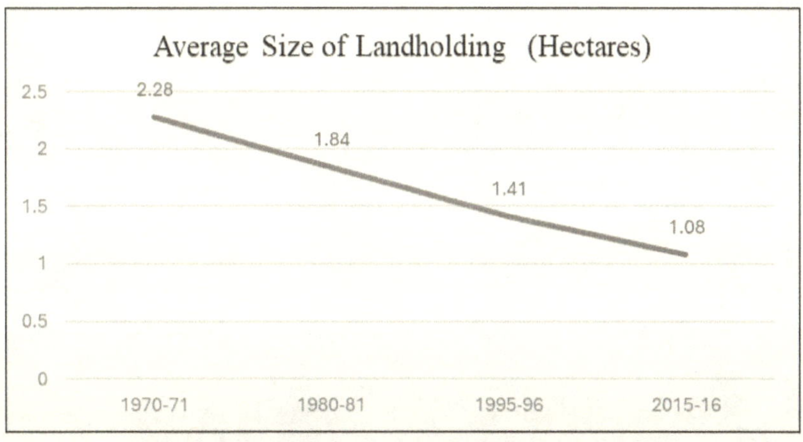

Figure 11: Average size of land holdings (1970-2015)

The upcoming generations will not even have land to sustain themselves and will end up as unskilled laborers, forced to survive on a minimum daily wage. Our education system is of no help here.

With fragmentation of landholdings and the rise in population over the past several decades, the number of farm holdings has increased while the area under farming has declined. The primary reason is that each landowner also needs a house, which will be built either on the agricultural land or by selling the agricultural land to buy residential land. This is what people fail to understand – **land is not growing like the population**. Every year, the number of people employed in the agriculture sector rises while the size of the land remains the same. Thereby increasing the number of laborers compared to the number of landowners. This is also a direct result of India becoming the most populous country in the world as of today.

The estimated population of India at present is on the higher side of 1.4 billion, and it will continue expanding until the year 2080[9].

With this source data, now reconsidering Suresh and putting into perspective the graph below, there is 95% accuracy that Suresh's great-grandchild will get 1 acre of land or less.

India also has one of the youngest populations globally, with 68% of its population aged 15-64.

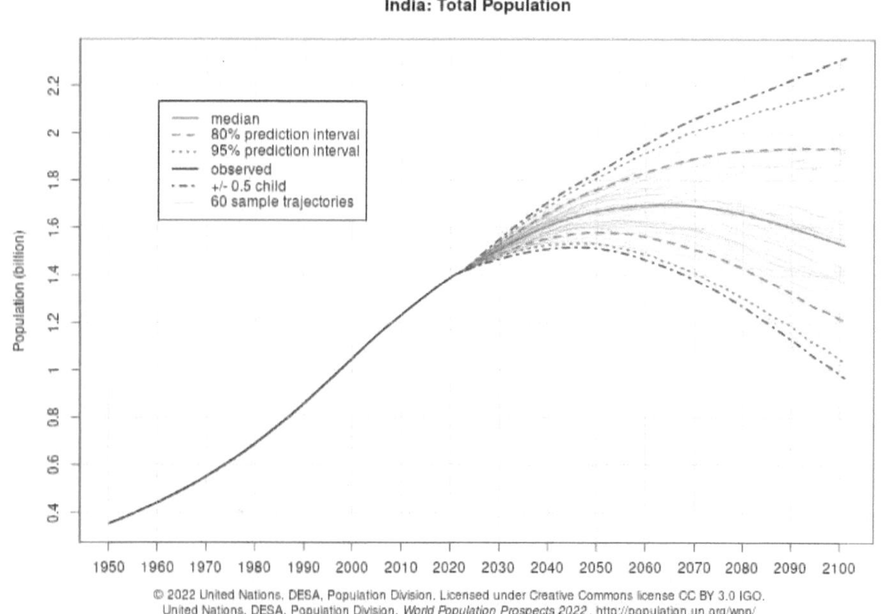

Figure 13: Population of India by age group (2023)[10]

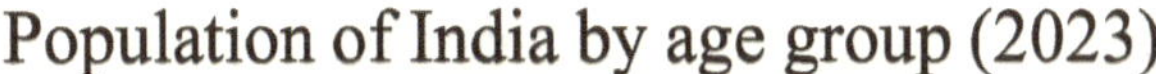

Population of India by age group (2023)

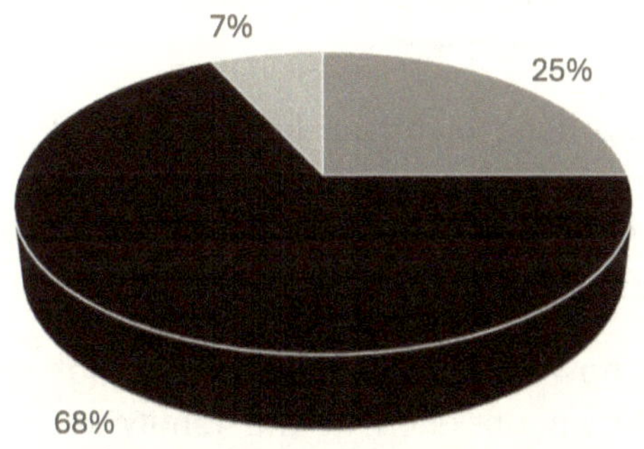

Table 2: Population demographics[11]

Total population in millions, 2023	1,428.6
Population annual doubling time, years, 2023	75
Population aged 0-14 per cent in 2023	25
Population aged 10-19, percent, 2023	18
Population aged 10-24 per cent, 2023	26
Population aged 15-64 per cent in 2023	68
Population aged 65 and older, percent, 2023	7
Total fertility rate per woman, 2023	2
Life expectancy at birth in 2023 for males	71
Life expectancy at birth in 2023 for females.	74

Having a young population means that the nation should provide its youth with ample employment opportunities; however, without proper training, most of the rural youth end up being unskilled laborers.

We are appalled to see how the youth are being misled or the youth themselves are misleading peers by spending an average of over 3 hours daily on social media. They are mostly creating content that is in no way economically benefiting the present or future of the masses.

As the majority of agricultural households are undereducated or uneducated, the only means they know of earning an income is either farming or unskilled labor. When we say undereducated, we refer to education that does not lead to skill development.

The farmers who don't own land become agricultural laborers in the fields of land-owning farmers or agricultural corporations. They do not have the knowledge or the resources to invest in education or in learning skills to upgrade their living standards.

Only knowing how to read and write but not understanding the concepts, they remain unskilled in the family trade. You would see scores of them standing daily at the main chowk of your town, waiting to be hired as daily wage earners or seasonal labor on hire. Another employment opportunity provided to them by the government is through *The Mahatma Gandhi National Rural Employment Guarantee Act 2005 (MGNREGA)*.

The MGNREGA, launched in 2006, was a law that guaranteed employment to people living in rural India. The Act gives a legal guarantee of a hundred days of wage employment in a financial year to adult members of a rural household who demand employment and are willing to do unskilled manual work[12]. As of today, it can be comfortably said that in the era of MGNREGA, many farmers (hypothetically) prefer to make money by participating in MGNREGA and not by working in fields.

As of 2022 **a total of 11.37 Crore households availed employment under MGNREGA[13]. In Rajasthan, as of 13 May 2024, over 114 lakh job cards[14] were issued, and the approved labor budget for the fiscal year 2024-25 was ₹2000 lakhs.**

The share of landless agricultural laborers in total agricultural workers has increased over the years from 28% in 1951 to 55% in 2011, while the share of cultivators has correspondingly reduced from 72% to 45% during the same period.

This is a direct consequence of land fragmentation. As the land size decreases with each generation, it becomes increasingly difficult to sustain a family on such a small patch of land. The added troubles of investing capital, land degradation and decreasing yields force the farmer off his own land, and they end up as either agricultural laborers or daily wage earners.

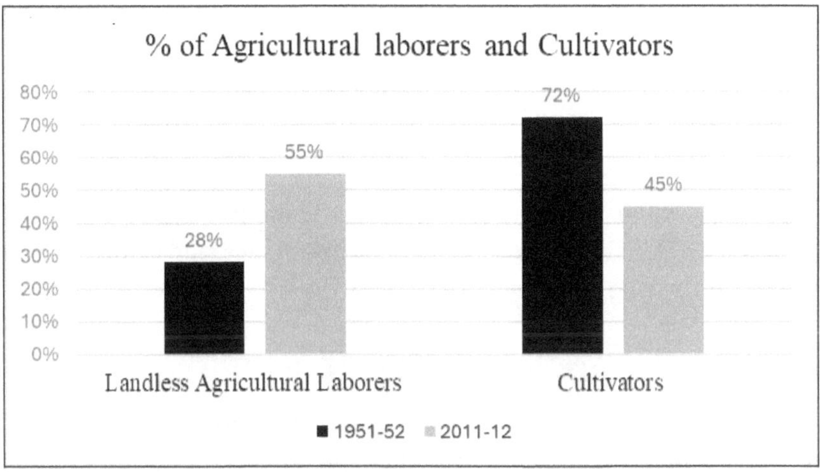

Figure 14: % of Agricultural laborers and Cultivators (1951-2011)[15]

Unfortunately, we cannot cite data beyond the year 2011 because the census of 2021 has not been done yet. But luckily, the author has been a business analyst and has some semblance of forecasting and probability. So here we go.

In 80 years, the percentage of landless agricultural laborers has doubled between 1951 and 2011. This growth corresponds to an annual growth rate of approximately 1.13%. Hypothetically speaking, if the same trend continued, this 55% would have become 61.5% in 10 years, i.e. in 2021.

That would be a 12% growth in the percentage of landless agricultural laborers per decade. This means that landless agricultural laborers would comprise more than half of the people employed in the agriculture sector. In the next 10 years, if the same trend continues, this percentage would reach an astounding 69%.

This is where the farmers of our nation are heading with the current trend of land fragmentation and cultivation becoming increasingly capital-intensive, and that's why the author is extremely concerned.

What's the irony, you ask? In a nation with an agrarian economy, with more than half of its population employed in the agriculture sector, more than two-thirds of people would be landless. Connect the dots; it's just like asking for more drivers and fewer owner drivers.

The problem of land fragmentation is not an isolated phenomenon affecting only India. It does not just affect farmers in India but farmers worldwide. To understand how this is a global problem, we must go back to the initial statement – **Land is not growing like the population.**

It is a limited resource forced to fulfill the unending demands of our species. This problem is bound to hit a dead end sooner or later, and with the current trends of intensive agriculture and consequent land degradation, the end is closer than we could imagine.

GROWING POPULATION AND FOOD DEMAND

The global population is increasing at an exponential rate. Look at the following graph representing the increase in world population in the last 10 years.

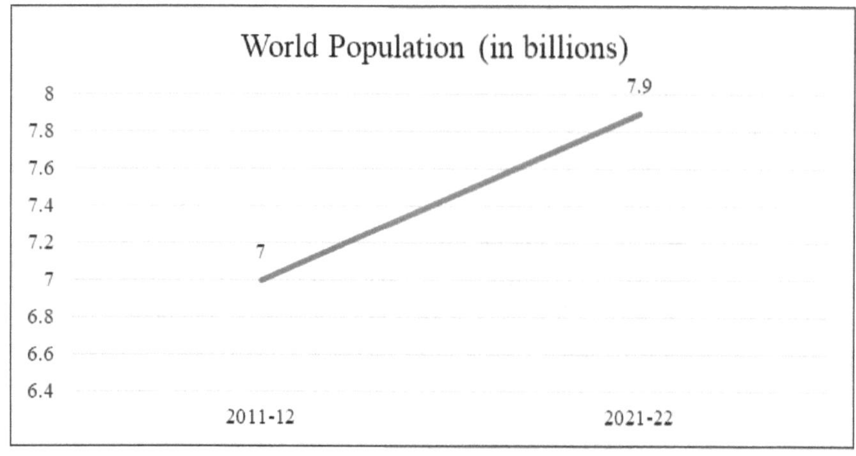

Figure 15: World population (2011-2021)

The steep slope of the graph explains why we used the word 'exponential'. Our population is increasing by folds every year. Just in 10 years, it has increased with a growth rate of 12.8%. Hypothetically, sans pandemic, we might be worse than now.

Earth's population is projected to reach approximately 9.7 billion by 2050. This estimate is based on current growth trends and demographic analyses. By the 2080s, it is expected to reach about 10.4 billion.

Do you think the Earth could even accommodate 10.4 billion people? Even at present with a population of 7.9 billion people, there are millions of people in the world struggling to survive, deprived of basic needs. There are 653,104 homeless citizens in the USA as of 28th March 2024, as per the Department of Housing and Urban Development (HUD).

As the population increases, so does the food demand. More people mean more mouths to feed. The problem is the cultivable area. Why? To answer this question, let us take a look at the population of some of the densest cities in the world.

Consider Shanghai, China, with a population of 29.87 million (2.99 crore) or Tokyo, Japan, with a population of 14 million[16] (1.4 crore) people or New York, USA, with a population of 8.80 million[17] (88 lakhs). These are Tier 1 cities in terms of population.

(India has some of the most populous cities in the world like Delhi, Mumbai, and Bangalore; however, since the last census was done in 2011, the data available cannot represent the current population of these cities. Hence, we are not citing these cities as an example.)

Examples of Tier 2 cities include Singapore with a population of 5.92 million[18] (59.2 lakh) or Boston with a population of 675,647[19] (6 lakh) which is not even one million.

Who is feeding the mega populations of these megacities? They do not have enough agricultural land of their own. Housing complexes and/or infrastructure account for a huge portion of land use in these cities. Their food is sourced from rural areas/villages or imported.

In other words, they are consumers, not producers. Or to be more accurate, they can <u>only be consumers</u>; they do not have the capacity to produce. The mega population of these cities is dependent on the farmers to provide them with the most basic, primal need of all – i.e. food.

The same farmers who are struggling to produce enough for even their own family. With the cultivable area shrinking due to land degradation and building activities, and farmers losing their land, food production becomes more prone to worldwide shortages.

And the woes barely start. According to the *Food and Agriculture Organization of the United Nations*, the total agricultural land area worldwide stands at roughly 5 billion hectares, representing around 37 percent of the Earth's land surface. Of this, approximately one-third (equivalent to 12% of the global land surface) is dedicated to cropland, with the remaining two-thirds serving as meadows and pastures for livestock grazing.

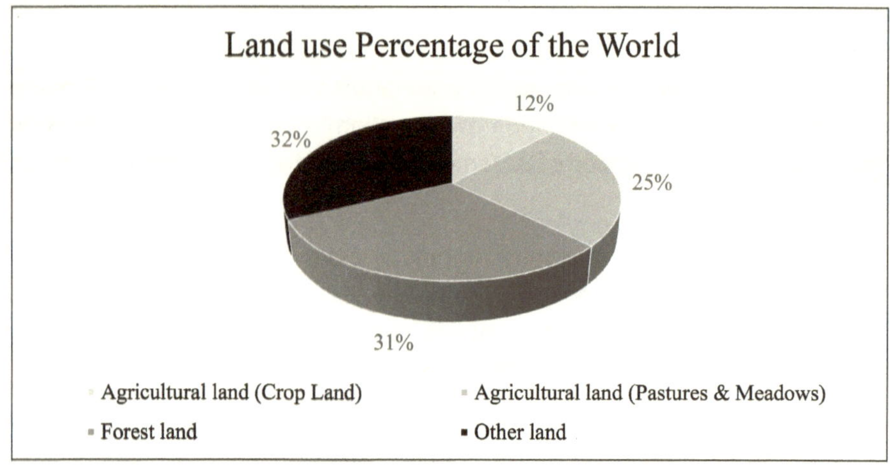

Figure 16: Land use percentage of the world[20]

The following statement of the *Food and Agriculture Organization (FAO) of the United Nations* gives us a harsh reality check about our current circumstances-

"As the global population continues to grow, with the number of people in the world more than doubling between 1961 and 2016, the strain on land, which is a limited resource, has also grown."

Global cropland area per capita has decreased continuously over the period between 1961 and 2016: from about 0.45 hectares (1.11 acres) per capita in 1961 to 0.21 hectares (0.51 acres) per capita in 2016[21]."

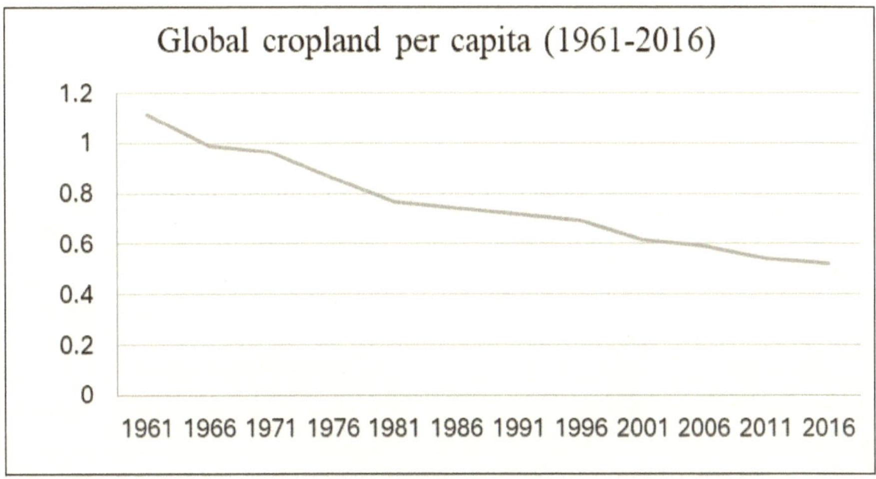

Figure 17: Decreasing area of cropland per capita (acre/capita) over the last 55 years[22]

Notice how we went from a person having more than 1 acre of land during the 1960s to a person having half the size, 0.5 acres of land in the 2010s and we can guarantee that this has not improved in the 2020s.

The natural questions to ask now would be:

1. Is the world equipped to feed its growing population?
2. Can Earth afford full stomachs for everyone with the current land size and agricultural practices?
3. In a rapidly changing world, can we guarantee a stable income source for our farmers?
4. Can agriculture, with its current methods, ensure an uninterrupted supply of food?
5. The most important question of all: can we solve the problem of increasing fragmentation of cultivable land?

Please ponder on these questions before reading further and even better, write them down for future use. They say hindsight is always 20/20, and maybe your written words will help you in the future.

This space is for you to jot down your thoughts.

LAND DEGRADATION

Up to now, we have discussed the fragmentation of land, decreasing area of land per capita, and how it will affect the farmers and the increasing food demand of the world. We have understood the basic concepts of where the problem starts, so let us untangle and analyze each thread of this issue.

We would assume that you have your own opinions based on the previously mentioned facts as well as additional information provided. The first thread to untangle in this knot is land degradation.

Previously, we stated that the land available for cultivation is shrinking. What happens when the land available for cultivation starts becoming uncultivable? And not due to natural causes but because of degradation caused by human practices? Degradation that can be managed and stopped if we steer ourselves away from intensive practices and toward a more sustainable approach.

Soil is a non-renewable resource (once destroyed, it takes 500 years to regenerate, which is way beyond a human's lifespan).

As the name suggests, non-renewable resources will cease to exist at some point in time even if used moderately, for example, fossil fuels like coal and petroleum, mineral ores like silver and iron, etc.

Rapid human consumption has increased the speed of exhaustion of these resources manifold. To put things in perspective, imagine a person having 1000 (₹/$) to spend every month. Now they could spend 900 (₹/$) in the first few days and spend the rest of the month in crisis mode.

Or they could budget 25 (₹/$) for each day and save 250 at the end of the month. It all depends on careful planning and systematic execution. At present, we have spent most of our income, and we still have many days to go before the month end. Rapid consumption by present generations will leave no resources for future generations. At this rate, the things that we take for granted today would become rare commodities in the future.

We need to learn to value and preserve for our tomorrow. A legacy is always created; it is not something that will build by itself. It is very easy to gift a depleted/degraded/difficult future rather than a bright/happy/radiant one. Is that what you want the future of this planet to look like?

The dirt beneath our feet is one of the most essential resources of life and supports countless ecosystems. Our existence wouldn't be possible without it (unless merpeople exist in the underwater city of Atlantis[23]).

However, humans are rapidly degrading it through various unsustainable practices, with one of the most significant being intensive farming.

What exactly is intensive farming? The word 'intensive' can be defined as – constituting or relating to a method designed to increase productivity by the expenditure of more capital and labor rather than by an increase in scope.

Intensive farming uses higher inputs and advanced agricultural methods to increase the overall crop yield. This is possible through the high-level use of inputs such as capital, labor, fertilizers, insecticides, pesticides, weedicides, etc., which results in increased crop yield per hectare.

In this intensive system, the use of inputs is comparatively higher than traditional methods.

To understand this with a simple example: Imagine you want to make chocolate milk. Typically, you would use 20 grams of chocolate to achieve the desired flavor. However, to make your milk more chocolaty and enhance the taste faster, you decide to mix in 50 grams of chocolate instead. Initially, this results in a richer and more intense chocolate flavor. But if you continue to increase the chocolate amount beyond a certain point, the milk will become overly bitter and unconsumable. For tea lovers, you can replace chocolate with tea leaves.

Similarly, in intensive farming, there is a threshold for the optimal use of inputs. Beyond this point, the excessive use of fertilizers, pesticides, and other resources will lead to diminishing returns and negative effects such as soil degradation, pollution, and reduced crop quality. Because of increasing food demand (a direct consequence of the increasing population), the practice of intensive agriculture has become widespread. And there are major drawbacks to this practice. The aim of intensive agriculture is to mass produce on a small area of land by increasing the number of inputs in farming.

This will require the farmer to invest more capital. After all the hard work, they get a bountiful amount of produce, but in the long-term, this boon becomes a bane. Mass production of a crop will drive down its market price as one of the aims of intensive agriculture is to make food affordable and cheap for the consumer.

In the process of ensuring that it is available to the consumer at an affordable price, the producer faces financial loss, and farmers often have to sell their produce at low profits. In today's age, any business which is cost-intensive and labor-intensive will prove to be disadvantageous to the producer.

Gradually, this process of investing more capital for more produce becomes a loop. The farmer must continuously invest more money after every harvest while making little profit. At the same time, the farmer is bleeding money, their soil is losing its vitality.

Intensive agriculture has disastrous effects on the quality of soil in the long run. How? Remember the milk that became bitter and unconsumable? Something similar happens to the soil when we use excessive amounts of chemical fertilizers and pesticides for a long time.

Soil has a natural cycle to restore its nutrients after a crop has been harvested; it's a slow process and can take any amount of time from 3 months to 3 years depending on several factors, including the type of soil, the previous crop, environmental conditions, and the presence of organic matter.

The practice of intensive agriculture does not wait for much time. It requires immediate replenishment, continuously, causing the farmers to use chemical fertilizers to force-feed nutrients to the soil.

To further delve in, consider the statement-

'Nature is ever evolving. Thus, all elements in nature can be considered as variables, while some change rapidly, others change gradually.'

But to a human, nature seems constant. The reason is that nature brings about change at an incredibly slow rate. When change is brought slowly, things have time to accept and adapt to the change. But humans have completely thrown this principle out of the window. We have changed the landscape of the earth by rapid technological developments.

Principally, we would conclude that from an existential perspective, **any change that is sudden or radical is not sustainable.**

At present, our world is changing radically, and neither nature nor our species has the time to adapt to these changes. This will lead to a dead-end situation sooner or later.

CHEMICAL FERTILIZERS

Chemical fertilizers and pesticides are the driving force of intensive agriculture. The purpose of a fertilizer is to increase the amount of nutrients in the soil and make it more fertile and friendlier to plant growth. Typically present in fertilizers are one or more of the macronutrients – nitrogen, phosphorus, and potassium, or NPK.

However, chemical fertilizers manufactured in factories are a far cry from the natural fertilizers that actually replenish soil nutrients. Organic fertilizers made from natural elements contain organic matter and nutrients of all kinds. Contrary to them, chemical fertilizers can be customized to be rich in only one type of nutrient, like nitrogen or phosphorus, which is not natural. Additionally, they add no organic matter to the soil.

So, what happens when you feed the soil with only factory-made processed nutrients and deprive it of organic matter? The soil will die slowly. Every year, the amount of organic matter, which holds the soil together and helps in water and nutrient retention, will decrease. With no organic matter to feed on, the helpful microorganisms in the soil will die. Gradually, the soil will not be able to hold water or nutrients and thus will not be able to support plant growth.

The end result? Barren land and no yield.

When used in excessive amounts, as is done by most farmers today, chemical fertilizers destroy the natural balance of the soil, resulting in low yields. Foolishly, the farmer takes it as a sign that the soil needs more fertilizer. It does, but not the chemical ones.

Low levels of soil nutrition require even more use of fertilizers to grow crops. The farmer uses increasing amounts of chemical fertilizers until it becomes a loop that ends in extreme soil degradation.

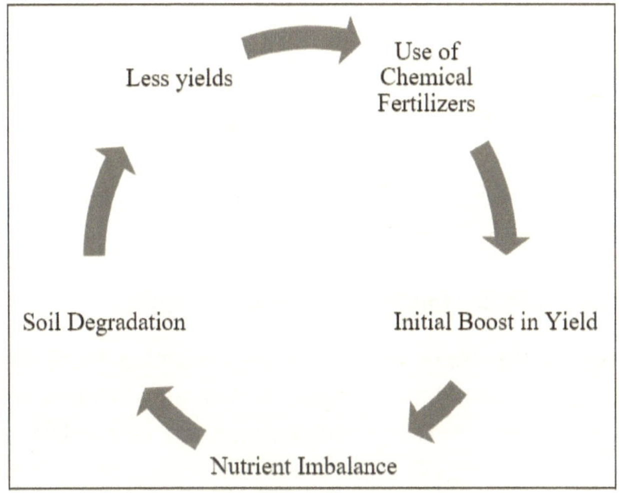

Figure 18: Cycle of soil degradation

Imbalance in the use of fertilizers in soil results in a loss of fertility. Chemical fertilizers can make the topsoil acidic. The ideal pH[24] for maximum plant growth and crop yield is between 5.5 and 8. If the soil is too acidic (pH lower than 5.5), it will yield fewer crops.

Let us take the example of wheat production, a staple crop, in India. According to *Agriculture Department, Uttar Pradesh*, for every hectare of rain-fed wheat farming, 40 kg nitrogen (N), 30 kg phosphorus (P), and 30 kg potash (K) are required for optimum productivity (a total of 100 kg of fertilizer used).

With intensive agriculture, deficiency of essential nutrients has also become widespread. According to the work conducted under PwC India, deficiency of Zn, Fe, Cu, Mn and B has been observed in 36.50%, 12.80%, 4.20%, 7.10% and 23.40% of soils of India, respectively[25].

Use of chemical fertilizer coupled with the practice of intensive agriculture leads to rapid soil degradation. Huge capital investment together with soil degradation pushes the farmer into a corner. Farming becomes too expensive for the farmers to afford while receiving less yield every year because of intensive farming practices.

Farmers suffer from stagnated agricultural production while their expenditure on agricultural inputs increases over time.

From a human's perspective, we still do not know the genetic modifications that the lack of natural minerals and added chemicals would cause in our biological systems. After all, nature changes slowly, and we are a part of nature (no Botox or plastic surgery can solve this problem).

Not to forget, the introduction of high-yield genetically modified seeds might also hold some unkind news for our progeny.

INCREASING CAPITAL INVESTMENT AND DEBT

This brings us to the issue of agriculture becoming increasingly capital-intensive and consequently the rising poverty among farmers. Agriculture in the 21st century has become increasingly dependent on modern technologies and as of today, technology is used rather required by every farmer in some way or another.

Cultivation has become highly capital-intensive, and while big farmers can afford it, small farmers either cannot or break their backs trying. Farmers' poverty is mainly concentrated in countries and regions with large numbers of poor people, such as India, Bangladesh, Pakistan, Sri Lanka, and Indonesia, Myanmar, etc. Another important focus is on areas with poor natural conditions, such as arid areas, mountainous areas, and areas with frequent natural disasters.

In arid areas, typically located in North Africa and West Asia, low soil fertility and soil degradation are directly linked to low productivity and rural poverty. Similarly, in such vulnerable areas that are particularly sensitive to climate change (e.g. heatwaves, sea level rise, destruction of coastal zones, and water shortages due to drought), farmers faced elevated poverty risks in the past and will remain subject to this risk in the future.

Marginal and small-scale farmers are at the highest risk of being pushed below the poverty line due to increasing capital investment in agriculture. Since they have a small area of land, higher levels of investment are not possible for them. Take the example of India where the majority are marginal farmers and let us cover the following factors from their standpoint – Profits, Capital investment, and Debt.

How does this cycle of poverty come to be and what keeps it running? Let's analyze the cost of cultivation and the net return from the produce to answer this question.

Table 3: Cost of wheat cultivation in India (For 1 acre)[26]

Cost Variables	Amount
Seed Material (₹1,200 + 200)	₹1,200 ($14)
Land preparation	₹1,400 ($17)
Sowing + weeding (₹600 + ₹800)	₹2,200 ($27)
Fertilization	₹1,500 ($18)
Plantation	₹1,200 ($14)
Harvesting and threshing (₹700 + ₹500)	₹300 ($4)
Transportation cost	₹1,900 ($23)
Miscellaneous cost	₹11,100 ($134)
Total Cost of Wheat Cultivation	₹12,210 ($147)

Assume the following for the financial year 2023 in India:

Table 4: Investment and profits from cultivating wheat on 1 acre of land in India

Minimum support price for wheat (As of 2023)[27]	₹2,275 (~USD $27)
Total output from 1 acre of land[28]	15 Quintals (1 Quintal = ~100 kg) = ~1,500 kg
Total Gross Earnings from 1 acre	₹2,275 x 15 = ₹34,125 = ~$409
Net Cost	₹12,210 (~ $151)
Total Net Earning Total Earnings minus Net Cost equals Net profit	₹34,125 − ₹12,210 = ₹21,915 (~$262)

As shown in Table 4, the total profit the farmer can earn from cultivating wheat on 1 acre of land is about ₹21,915 (~$262), as against the invested sum of ₹12,210 ($147) (within 3-4 months).

It is clear from the example given above that the farmer does not earn as much as he spends on cultivation. The net cost and net profit may vary from state to state, but to have a general idea, let us look at data from *Ministry of Statistics and Program Implementation (MOSPI)*. According to the MOSPI data, the average monthly income of agricultural households was Rs 10,218 in 2018-19[29], as shown in Table 5.

Table 5: Average Monthly Income for an Agri Household, India[30]

Financial Year	Average Monthly Income for an Agricultural Household
2002-03	₹2115 (~$44 at an exchange rate of 48 INR / USD)
2012-13	₹6426 (~$122 at an exchange rate of 53 INR / USD)
2015-16	₹8059 (~$122 at an exchange rate of 66 INR / USD)
2018-19	₹10,218 (~$143 at an exchange rate of 71 INR/USD)
2022-23	Data not available in the public domain

Meanwhile, as of December 2019, half of all agricultural households are indebted, with an average outstanding loan of Rs 74,121. See the following data sourced from *PRS*.

Table 6: Percentage of agricultural households in debt and average loan amount

Year	Agricultural household count (in Lakh = 100 thousand)	% of indebted households	Average outstanding loan in INR
2003	894	49%	₹12,585 (~$ 244)
2013	902	52%	₹47,000 (~$ 887)
2019	930	50%	₹74,121 (~$1044)
2022	Data not available in the public domain	-	-

When we did the above analysis, our reaction was 🤦 (facepalm).

The numbers here paint a very worrisome picture of how the cultivators are pushed into a loop of poverty. It is important for the reader to understand it at the grassroots level in order to constructively figure out a long-term and beneficial solution.

It is saddening that the Government of India has failed to conduct the 2021 census. As a result, the government reports provided do not have the updated data since the year 2011 when the last census was conducted.

IMPROPER USE OF LAND

There is a term called 'optimum' which means the most favorable situation or level for growth, reproduction, or success. When we talk about the ways in which land is used for agriculture in India, it is sub-optimal at best.

What does that mean?

In spite of having fertile land resources, outdated agricultural practices and norms in our country have restricted the land from reaching an optimal state. That is, the land is not able to reach its highest capacity of production.

Let us analyze how agricultural land is used in India. It would not be harsh to state that there is a lot of scope to optimize and make land use more efficient. Till date, hard work has been considered more fruitful and satisfying because it's a time-tested strategy – *'Hard work always pays.'*

Farmers break their backs on their fields doing hard work but have a bias to adapt techniques/ technologies which reduce efforts, thinking about the one-time expenses they have to incur. This results in the low yield of crops and therefore the same area of land produces different amounts of yields depending on hard work versus smart work.

To explain this with a real-world example, look at this graph of the top 10 countries in the world in terms of cropland, i.e. land used for growing crops.

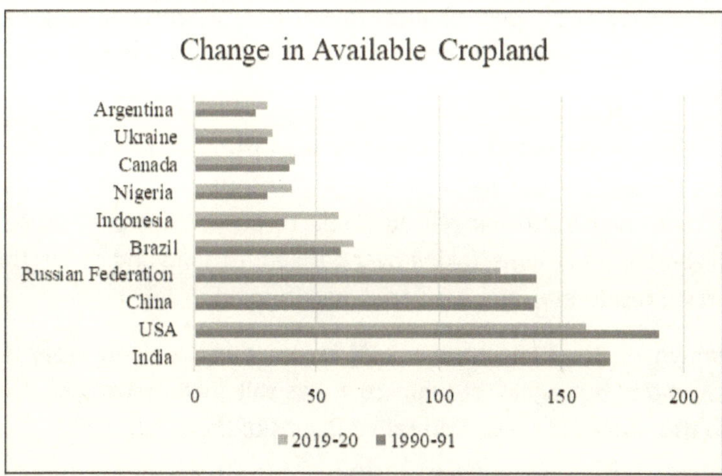

Figure 19: Change in cropland area between 1990-2019 in the top 10 countries of the world[31]

As you can infer from the graph, as of 2019, India had the largest total cropland area in the world, with nearly 170 million hectares. Additionally, compared to other countries, there has not been any change in the available cropland in the case of India. It is the same as it was 30 years ago.

India was closely followed by the United States of America (160 million ha), China (about 140 million ha), the Russian Federation (125 million ha), and Brazil (nearly 65 million ha).

Over the period 1990–2019, the top 10 countries by the extent of cropland showed diverse trends. In India and China, the cropland area remained constant or showed little variation. The area of cropland declined in the United States of America (-15 percent) and the Russian Federation (-8 percent). Conversely, large increments were recorded in Brazil (+13 percent). Before we proceed to our discussion of the optimal use of cropland, let us first analyze this trend of increase and decrease in the area of cropland.

Changes in the area of cropland, whether increasing or decreasing, are concerning. Why? Because it raises the following questions-

Question 1 – At what cost is the cropland area increasing?
Question 2 – At what cost is the cropland area decreasing?

Question 3 – If we are still trying to increase the area of cultivable land after decades of technological inventions, then what progress have we made in the agricultural sector or whether pondering over this is even worthwhile?

According to the *American Farmland Trust (AFT)*, farmland in the United States decreased by 31 million acres, a territory equivalent to the state of New York, over a 20-year period (1992 to 2012). This is because of the expanding cities and towns, taking over agricultural land and converting it for commercial, residential, and industrial development.

Meanwhile, Brazil recorded a 13% increase in cropland area, which is a huge number, but again, at what cost was this increment made? Brazil is home to the Amazon Forest, also called *'Lungs of the Earth'.*

These forests are being cut down and converted into pastures or cropland. In 2000, 26 million hectares were used for cropland; that area grew to 46.5 million hectares by 2014, at the expense of forests.

Forests are not just trees that can be replanted elsewhere. They are entire ecosystems and take decades and centuries to come into existence. Once gone, they are gone forever.

Coming back to the discussion of optimal use of land, it seems natural that since India has the largest land area for crop production, it should also be the country with the highest yield. However, as you can see in the figure, India's crop yields do not match the amount of land under cultivation. Despite having the largest area under cropland, India's yield of major crops is significantly lower than in other leading food-producing countries.

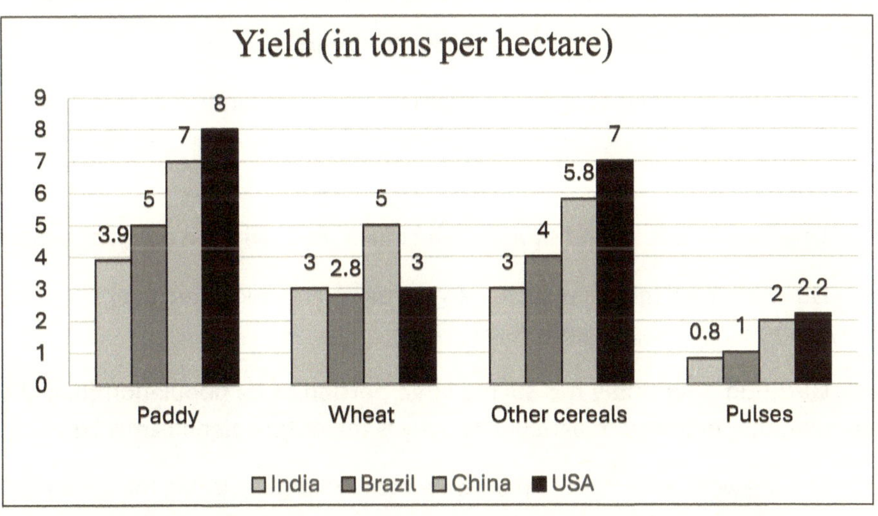

Figure 20: Yield in different countries in 2014-15 (in tons per hectare)[32]

It appears that the farmers in India are not practicing efficient techniques to increase their yield and, as a result, they are unable to reach the optimal level of production.

Take maize, for example, the third most important food crop in India. The global average for the productivity of maize is 4.92 tons per hectare (1.98 tons per acre). The country with the highest maize productivity is the USA, and it produces > 9.6 tons per hectare (3.8 tons per acre), which is double the global average. Meanwhile, India produces only 2.43 tons per hectare (0.98 ton per acre), which is half the global average.

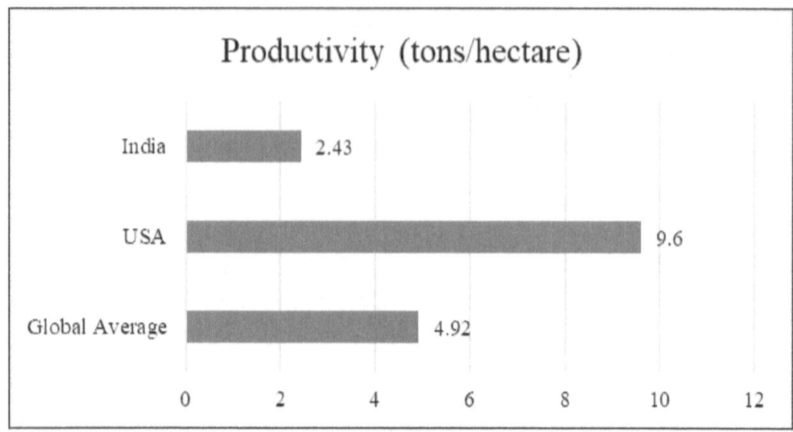

Figure 21: Maize production (tons/hectare)

This clearly shows that for the same amount of land (1 hectare), India produces significantly less than its competitors. The natural questions to ask here would be-

Question 1 – More land should mean more yield. Why is it not happening?

Question 2 – If India has such a large area of land dedicated to agriculture, why is the output significantly less?

Question 3 – If India has such a large portion of its population (half the population) dedicated to agriculture, why is the output significantly less?

The answer lies in the initial probe we conducted regarding the increasing number of marginal farmers in India.

More than half of the landholdings in India belong to marginal farmers. With a small area of land, they do not have:

1. Enough capital to invest.
2. Modern Farming equipment
3. They require credit for short-term uses such as:

   a. Purchasing inputs
   b. Weeding
   c. Harvesting
   d. Sorting
   e. Transporting

4. They require credit for long-term uses such as:

    a. Investing in agricultural machinery
    b. Investing in agricultural equipment
    c. Irrigation

In the absence of credit, they cannot cultivate the field to its maximum potential and thus cannot reach the highest level of yield. The government has taken initiatives to provide support; however, the government is also fighting the constraints of increasing population, unemployment, and above all the influence of capitalism.

IRRIGATION

When we talk about the many resources not available to marginal farmers, water for irrigation tops the list. Why?

Water is an essential input required in cultivation, and while it is a non-renewable resource, it is not abundant. Out of all the available water on Earth, only 2.7% is freshwater. The other 97.3% is saline water and cannot be used for cultivation. We could say that freshwater is a fast-depleting resource.

For good measure, it should be used meticulously to avoid overconsumption leading to a drought-like situation. As per *International Commission on Irrigation and Drainage, Annual Report 2014-15*, the highest share of irrigated area is by emerging/ developing countries (78%), followed by developed countries (16%), and in the least developed countries (6%).

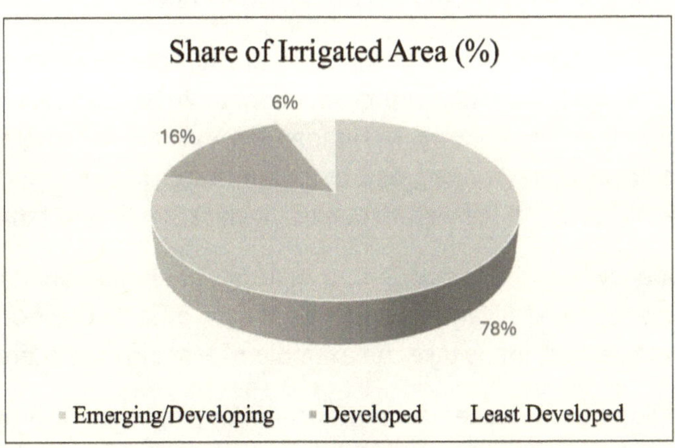

Figure 22: Share of irrigated area in the world

On a regional basis, the highest irrigated area is in Asia (72%), followed by the Americas (15%), Europe (8%), and Africa (5%)[33].

Some parts of the world are in more need of water than others. In the arid and semi-arid regions of the world such as the Arabian Peninsula, Iran, central Asia, northern Africa, Australia, and western North America, irrigation is crucial for crop production.

These are also the regions where water availability is rapidly becoming scarce and will pose major problems for crop production in the future. If not used properly at present, water scarcity will become the leading reason for crop failure in these areas.

Even in areas under temperate climate conditions like the eastern United States, Canada, western and central Europe, additional irrigation is used on high-value crops, such as maize, to compensate for rainfall variability during the growing season.

To conclude:

1. Freshwater is a limited resource.
2. It is an absolute necessity for growing food.
3. Rising temperatures are leading to higher evaporation rates, and it does not rain at the same place.
4. Traditional irrigation systems are suboptimal and lead to considerable water wastage.
5. Traditional irrigation methods are labour-intensive.
6. Groundwater is depleting at an alarming rate.

India is a country dependent on annual rainfall, specifically the monsoon, as the fresh water source for crop production. In 2012-13, 53% of the sown agricultural area in the country was dependent on rain-fed irrigation, while 47% of the sown area was irrigated by groundwater sources (such as wells and tube-wells) and surface water sources (such as canals and tanks)[34].

Dependency on the monsoon, a natural phenomenon, is a major disadvantage to the small farmers who do not have other sources of irrigation. To better understand, let us take the example of Maharashtra (Central India).

This region heavily depends on monsoon for irrigation. Ironically, it also has the highest suicide rates of farmers in the whole country. To be more specific, the prominent arid region of the state, Marathwada, which consists of 8 districts—Aurangabad, Jalna, Beed, Parbhani, Nanded, Osmanabad, Hingoli, and Latur.

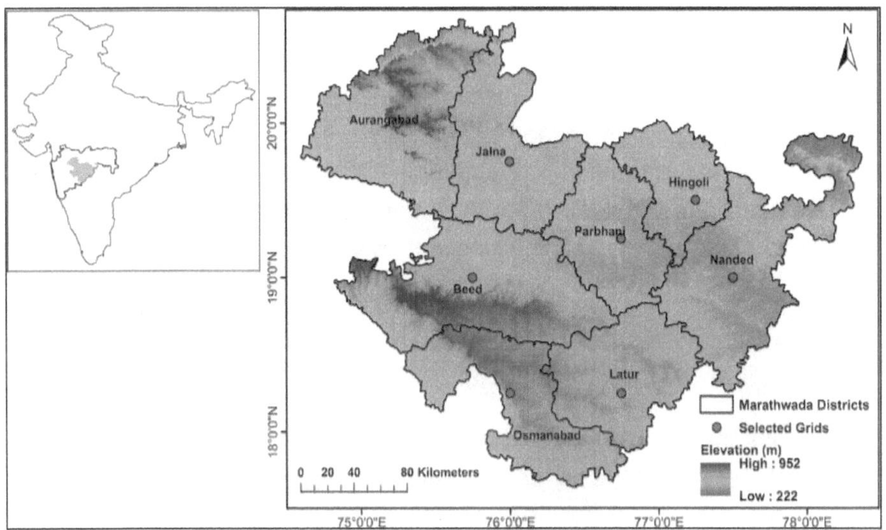

Figure 23: Marathwada on the map of India[35]

One can easily say that the monsoon is the lifeblood of agricultural life here, yet the region is situated at a precarious junction of the monsoon winds.

These winds rise from the Arabian Sea and the Bay of Bengal, bringing moisture with them, which they then pour off throughout the country during the months of June to September.

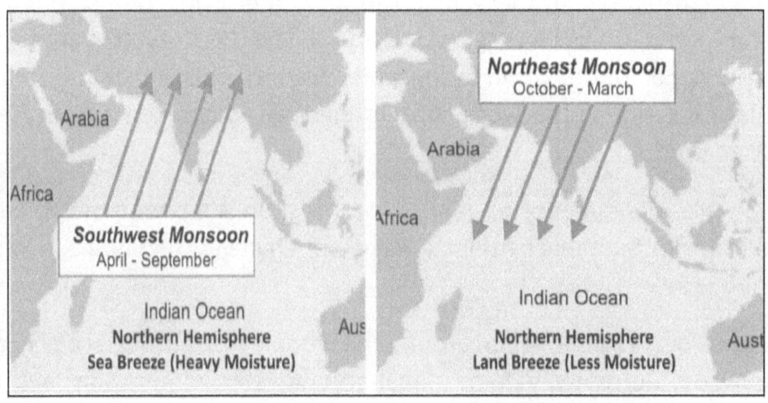

Figure 24: Monsoon winds[36]

The region of Maharashtra can be understood as the central point of a peninsular triangle. Since it is at the center, by the time the monsoon reaches here from either side, it has already lost most of its moisture.

Year after year of low rainfall leads to increasing water scarcity, as water consumption rises while water resources are not replenished on time. Small farmers dependent on monsoon showers for growing crops face failure after failure as the fate of their crops and their lives is solely dependent on the rain. The use of groundwater for irrigation is also ruled out as the region does not receive enough rainfall to replenish water levels.

It is worth mentioning that in some tehsils of Latur, there is no water even 304 meters below the ground. Just in one year (2015 – 16) the water table in Latur has gone down by 3.5 to 4.0 meters[37].

To bring this into perspective, imagine this – it would take the fastest man at present, Michael Johnson (Olympic athlete with a record of running 400m in 43.49 seconds) 33.15 seconds (more than half a minute) to reach the level of depletion from the surface. Or if you start walking at a normal pace of let's say 1.39m per second, then it would take you 219.42 seconds or 3 minutes 39 seconds to reach the point of depletion.

As per a report from the *Divisional Commissioner's office* here, 685 cultivators have ended their lives between January 1 and August 31, 2023, in the region, and 294 of these deaths took place in the 3 monsoon months alone (June to August)[38].

The hardship tale of the Maharashtrian farmer is just one among many. This story is not just of one region, it is and will be the story of every arid and semi-arid region in the world facing water scarcity. This will be the future of most farmers around the world if an immediate action plan and strategy is not taken up.

However, dependence on rainfall for irrigation is a phenomenon limited to countries in Southeast Asia like Pakistan, Thailand, Cambodia, Vietnam, and Indonesia.

Major sources of irrigation around the world consist of surface water and groundwater. Currently, 70% of global groundwater withdrawals, and even more in arid and semi-arid regions, are used in the agricultural production of food, fibers, livestock, and industrial crops.

Ironically, agriculture is also a major source of water pollution because of the use of chemical fertilizers, pesticides, and other contaminants, which, when unmanaged, can lead to significant social, economic, and environmental costs.

The main reason for the alarming dips in groundwater levels is that it is not being valued (mostly subsidized/provided for free).

As an open-access resource employed by individuals, groundwater is difficult to regulate and monitor, and the legal basis for this is often absent. The farmers overusing groundwater do not understand the great implications it will have in the future. After all, their concern is how to feed their family in the near future. They do not have an assurance or guarantee of a good lifestyle in the short-term. Groundwater overuse at present will also lead to less groundwater available for agriculture in the future, thus causing even more pressure on agricultural production.

SOIL SALINIZATION

The utilization of inland saline water poses a significant challenge in irrigation, leading to the issue of soil salinization. Soil salinization is a serious ecological threat affecting the agricultural output of more than 100 countries across the world.

Salinization causes the worldwide loss of ~1.5 million hectares of arable land per year, affecting about 16% of all agricultural lands[39]. The primary inland saline areas across the globe are located in arid, semi-arid, and low-lying regions with inadequate drainage, leading to the accumulation of high concentrations of salts in the soil.

This phenomenon, known as primary salinization, is a result of insufficient rainfall, leading to inadequate leaching of soluble salts or constrained drainage. The extensive use of underground saline water for agricultural irrigation has converted once-fertile lands into unproductive wastelands.

Take the state of Gujarat, India, for example. It is the state most affected by soil salinity.

'Of the 6.73 million hectares of land affected by salinity in India, Gujarat constitutes 2.23 million hectares.' – *The Times of India*[40].

So, approximately 33.17% of the 6.73 million hectares of land affected by salinity in India are in Gujarat. It is one of the most intensively irrigated regions in India; water availability is a concern because groundwater irrigation contributes more than 90% of the overall livelihoods of the farms.

Water is an essential requirement for agriculture, but many farmers do not have access to freshwater. As the demand for food keeps rising, the farmer must explore alternative irrigation methods to ensure a consistent supply, leading to the utilization of brackish groundwater.

Prolonged use of brackish water results in land degradation. In a matter of a few years, the once-fertile land turns barren, failing to produce adequate yields and leaving the farmer in a precarious situation. The persistent overuse of saline water disrupts the soil components, rendering it unsuitable for any form of agriculture in the future.

Excessive use of groundwater leads to depletion in the groundwater level. Because inland saline water primarily exists in arid and sub-arid zones, replenishment of groundwater through rain is ruled out.

Water scarcity because of mismanagement of available water sources is already a looming threat to agriculture, and the problem will only intensify in the future.

GLOBAL WARMING

Global warming – a global phenomenon and yet its effects are felt on the most basic levels of existence. Global warming refers to the long-term heating of the Earth's surface observed since the pre-industrial period (between 1850 and 1900) due to human activities, primarily fossil fuel burning, which increases heat-trapping greenhouse gas levels in the Earth's atmosphere.

The increase in Earth's temperature leads to climate change, which refers to long-term shifts in temperatures and weather patterns.

For a marginal farmer, the world revolves around cultivation. This limited expanse of land constitutes their entire livelihood. What does climate change mean to them? Why would they concern themselves with the Earth's temperature increase or climate fluctuations? They already grapple with the pressing issues of securing water for their crops and finding funds to purchase seeds.

The irony is, while the farmer does nothing to contribute toward climate change, they are the ones most affected by it. World leaders can comfortably sit in air-conditioned rooms, discussing the impacts of climate change and passing resolutions on how to address it; they don't come out and work in fields where temperatures have gone to record highs in 2024.

They will never experience its effects as profoundly as farmers in arid regions, whose crops failed because rains arrived late. While the farmer kept begging the skies to shower their mercy, another farmer was praying for the exact opposite. Rains had been flooding their district for days now; they had never seen the skies come down so viciously before.

The leaders do not face consequences of climate change like the fishermen who have witnessed the sea, their livelihood, turning on them, bringing cyclones and tsunamis, and destroying their homes in front of their eyes.

Or like the farmer in the Horn of Africa, who has experienced 5 failed rainy seasons in a row. Or the farmer who had to leave their ancestral land, their home and move away from their family in search of work because their land had become barren.

These farmers have done nothing to increase the earth's temperature; it is the big industries and affluent people who are burning fossil fuels and are responsible for the dramatic change in weather patterns. And yet, while the rich class barely feels the world changing, farmers at the most marginal level feel its effect tenfold.

It is necessary for the upcoming generation, Gen Z, to understand the implications of these issues. The emerging generation is presently quite detached from its roots. From the perspective of Generation Z, comprehending the severity of this situation is challenging because they are accustomed to constant and radical changes.

Planned obsolescence is the norm. Swift transformations are not natural but are perceived as a necessity. The world is filled with examples of such changes. A new smartphone model being launched every month, the concept of 'use and throw' items, buying and rapidly discarding clothes in the world of fast fashion, 30-second videos on social media, and instant foods, from noodles to whole meals; these are just a few examples.

All these point toward radical change and instant gratification of needs. Anything that takes time, is a slow process, even if it's beneficial, is seen as primitive and <u>outmoded</u>. They are so inclined to discard the 'old ways' that they even reject things beneficial for them.

We are not saying this to criticize the ideologies or practices of Generation Z. Many among them aspire to make a difference and are conscious of environmental threats. They possess the intent but lack direction; they need to realize that change is not an instantaneous process. We can't magically fix everything overnight; it takes time, and it's a gradual journey. The Earth is huge!

Radical solutions will not work. We have to apply solutions slowly and patiently and focus on long-term goals, not short-term benefits. Imagine the earth revolving around the sun in 200 days. Will you age differently?

The purpose of listing all these problems is not to paint a hopeless picture of the future and plunge into despair. The first step toward creating a solution to a problem is to understand its gravity and depth. Only when we grasp the seriousness and urgency of the issue can we work on creating a sustainable solution. Now that we have understood the gravity of the situation and the predicament of farmers at its most fundamental level, we must devise solutions to address all the difficulties one by one.

Conclusively, we have discussed major problems affecting farmers and crop production, an area of work which is essential to the existence of the entire human race. Now we will focus on the action plan to start solving these problems from grassroots levels, keeping in mind that the result has to be a sustainable future for both the producer and the consumer.

In this chapter, you learned,

Coming up…

Hunter gatherer societies
Dawn of agriculture
Domestication in ancient civilizations
Mythological reference
Historical connection
Dodo bird
The terror of Bengal
Colonialism
CO2 emissions
Rising pollution
Capitalism
Industries
Forests cleared
Industrial revolution
Environmental pollution
Destruction of animal habitats
Invention of plastic
Animal cruelty
Livestock rearing
Cash crops
Saps soil of nutrients
Degrades land
Less land to grow food crops
Less food production
Inflation
High production cost
Land reclamation
Terraforming
Desertified land
Mu Us desert, china
Mumbai and Palm islands
Veganism
Radical change
More land required for cultivation
Land obtained by clearing forests
Causes imbalance in the food web
Eg. camel
Eg - Choctaw hog

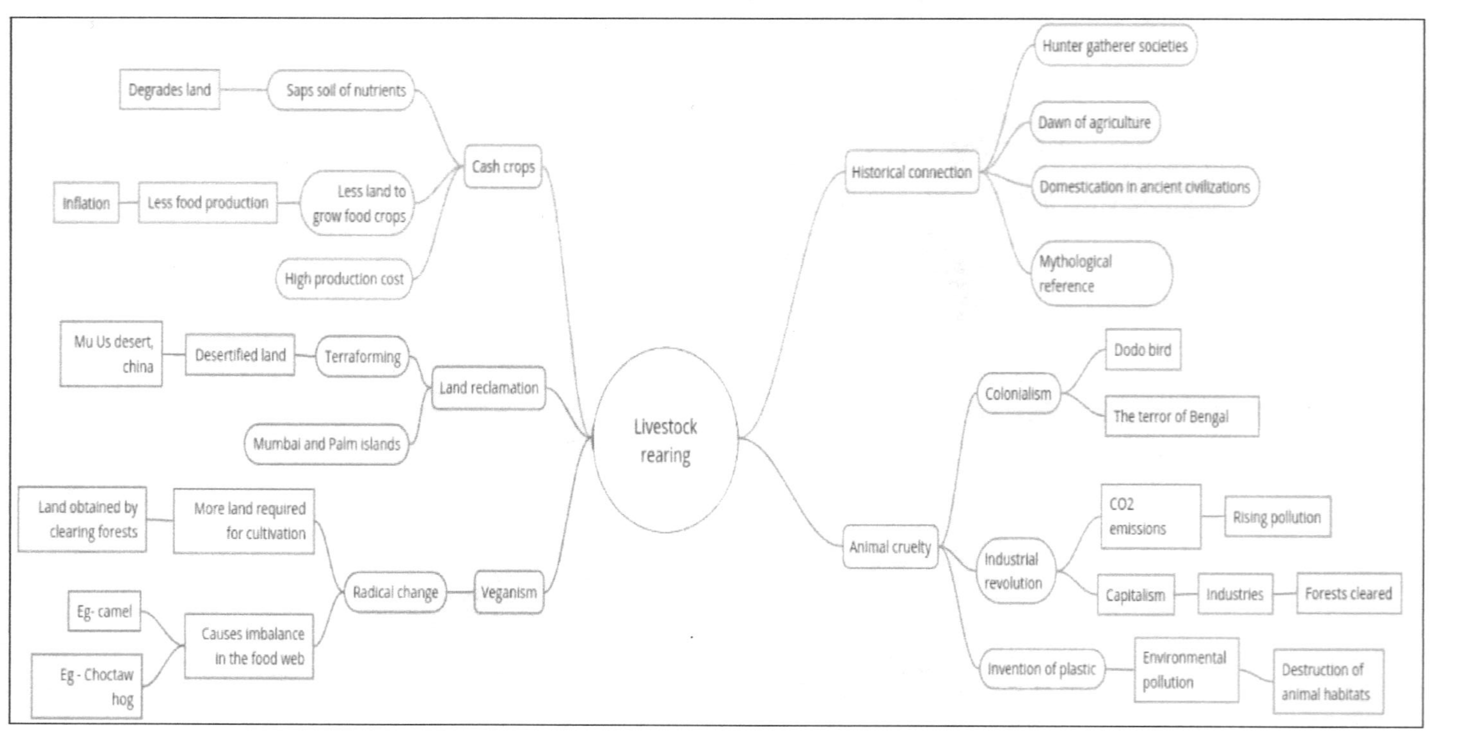

CHAPTER 2

Livestock Rearing

IN THE PREVIOUS chapter, we discussed the issues affecting cultivators worldwide (with emphasis on marginalized farmers). These issues require coordinated, large-scale efforts to bring about meaningful change, underscoring the critical role that global institutions play in tackling such challenges.

Global institutions serve as important platforms for international cooperation, leveraging their vast resources and collective expertise to implement solutions that go beyond national borders. By promoting partnerships across countries, they are uniquely positioned to address multifaceted problems, promoting sustainable development and economic stability worldwide.

There are many such institutions that are dedicated to the welfare and upliftment of mankind. One such institution is the *International Bank for Reconstruction and Development (IBRD)*. It is a global development cooperative owned by 189-member countries and is headquartered in Washington, D.C., United States. It assists countries by providing financial products and advice to help reduce poverty and support development.

IBRD was established in 1944 to assist in the rebuilding of Europe following the widespread destruction caused by World War II. It engages with middle-income countries (MICs) and creditworthy poorer countries. Middle-income countries are nations that aren't too rich or too poor. They fall into a middle category based on how much money the average person earns in a year. These countries are divided into 2 groups:

1. Lower middle-income countries like India, Kenya, Vietnam, etc.
2. Upper middle-income countries like China, Brazil, and Turkey, etc.

IBRD offers innovative financial solutions, including financial products (loans, guarantees, and risk management products) and knowledge and advisory services (including on a reimbursable basis) to governments at the national and subnational levels. Examples of projects undertaken by the IBRD are:

1. *The Maharashtra Project on Climate-Resilient Agriculture Project for India* –

The aim is to enhance climate resilience[41] and profitability of smallholder farming systems in selected districts of Maharashtra.

Approval date: February 27, 2018

Commitment amount – US$420.00 million, which is more than 3360 crore Rupees

We discussed the farmer suicide in India. Maharashtra has the highest number of farmer suicide rate in the country. In 2023, a staggering number of 2,851 farmers committed suicide under distress. In such a scenario, projects like these are of utmost importance, particularly due to the country's significant reliance on agriculture as a source of livelihood for millions of people and as a driver of economic growth. We do not wish to throw fatality numbers just to prove a point. The author feels deeply saddened while referring to such deaths by suicide.

2. *Philippine Rural Development Project Scale-up*

The aim is to improve farmers' and fisherfolk's access to markets and increase income from selected agri-fishery value chains.

Approval date – June 29, 2023

Commitment amount – US$ 600.00 million, which is more than 4800 crore rupees

3. *Nigeria for Women Program Scale-Up Project*

The aim is to institutionalize Women Affinity Groups (WAGs) and other platforms for women's economic empowerment and enhance the economic opportunities of unbanked women.

Approval date: June 22, 2023

Commitment amount – US$ 500.00 million, which is more than 4000 crore Rupees

The IBRD estimated 500 million (50 crore families) families around the world involved in small-scale farming. They comprise a large proportion of the world's poor, living on less than $2 a day (172 INR of family income per day).

Similarly, there is *The Food and Agriculture Organization of the United Nations (FAO)*. The organization's aim is to achieve food security[42] and make sure that people have regular access to enough high-quality food to lead active, healthy lives. Headquartered in Rome, Italy, FAO works in over 130 countries.

As per the *Food and Agriculture Organization of the United Nations*, about 83% of farms worldwide – that is, 5 out of every 6 farms in the world – are smaller than 2 hectares (4.94 acres), which is roughly the size of about 5 football fields.

Population and land area are currently at loggerheads.

'The more the population increases, the less land area per capita is available.'

This gives an idea of the complications of land fragmentation, its catastrophic effect on marginalised farmers; and since you are still reading, we know that we have your attention.

Let us discuss possible solutions to this growing problem.

The first solution that we will explore is livestock farming. In this chapter, we are going to describe –

1. The historical connection our species has with other animals
2. The past and future of livestock farming
3. How we can use livestock farming for the upliftment of marginalized farmers[43].

Before proceeding further on how livestock farming can be a sustainable alternative, we must first make a few things clear.

The content that will follow henceforth is human-centric. We are not ostriches who prefer to ignore the clear and present danger by sticking their heads in the sand, neither are we sheep that follow the leader into a ditch.

We are humans. For millennia, we have exploited the available resources for our betterment, and we will continue to do so. The question before us is to identify what is ethical.

This approach examines how our farming practices affect both society and the environment. We'll look at how managing these activities can benefit both humans and the ecosystems we rely on.

Presently, our species is the alpha of this world, which means that we sit at the top of the food web. We are the ultimate decision-makers on this globe.

Our species is not the physically strongest, but we are the ones with mental muscles and have used our brains beyond basic instincts. Thousands of years ago, humans were in the middle of the food chain.

We were consumers of plants and animals, and were consumed/ hunted by a higher-level predator. Over time, our species rose through the ranks and currently sit atop the pyramid. Even to this day, there are instances of hyenas/leopards/man-eating animals targeting humans, but those are rare occurrences, and we do ensure maneaters are hunted and killed.

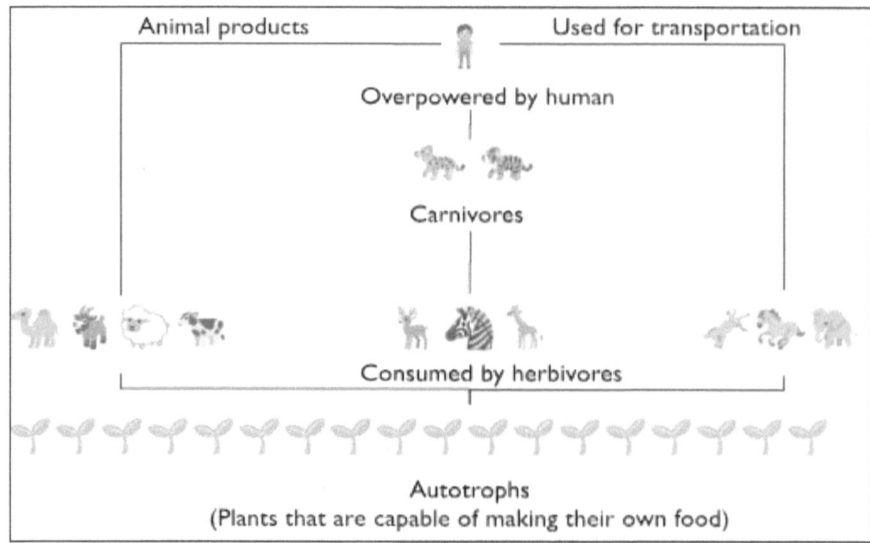

Figure 25: Diagram of a food chain depicting humans as alpha

Charles Darwin's theory of 'Survival of the Fittest' states that the organisms who best adapt to the environment are more likely to survive and reproduce, but this no longer applies to humans. We are no longer adapting to the environment; instead, we have forced the environment to adapt to our needs. We are living in Antarctica, deep in the Amazon, and on remote islands too.

Presently, humans are the alpha of the food web. From this perspective, other animals are seen merely as components or supplies in the food web. This, in no way, is degrading them; we are merely referring to them as constituents of an ecosystem. An ecosystem which has been in existence for thousands of years. But now the hierarchy has changed.

HUNTER-GATHERER SOCIETIES

Livestock farming is not a recent phenomenon, invented for the easement of our species. Consuming animal products as a part of our diet is a complex evolutionary event, and our ancestors, down to the first Homo sapiens, practiced it.

Humans have coexisted with other animals as parts of a natural cycle for thousands of years, and this bond of coexistence holds both our past and our future. We should not hesitate to claim that livestock farming is and will be even more essential for a sustainable existence of our species in the near and distant future.

Now that we have clarified that the ensuing content will be human-centric, let us shift the focus toward the sustenance of our species.

To understand the significance that the bond of coexistence between humans and animals in an ecosystem holds for our future, we must first understand how it has impacted our past. Humans and animals have shared a mutually coexistent bond for millennia, dating back to the time when our species was in the primary stages of evolution.

We are of course talking about Homo sapiens, our ancestors (we are now Homo sapiens sapiens). The existence of modern Homo sapiens dates back nearly 160,000 years (1 lakh 60 thousand years) ago.

They were primarily hunter-gatherers, and their diet consisted mainly of animal products and wild plants. To hunt and forage for food, Homo sapiens were constantly on the move; in fact, mobility was an essential survival strategy.

Settlements were therefore impractical and unnecessary for their lifestyle, unless to avoid extremities.

Hunter-gatherer societies still exist in the world, and their sources of nourishment are still like those of our ancestors[44].

1. **The Hadza tribe** are an indigenous ethnic group in Tanzania known for their unique hunter-gatherer lifestyle. They live in small, nomadic bands in the East African savannah, primarily around Lake Eyasi.
   The Hadza rely on hunting wild game with bows and arrows and foraging for roots, tubers, and berries. They have maintained their traditional way of life for thousands of years, offering valuable insights into human evolutionary history.

2. **The Tsimane tribe** resides deep within the Amazon rainforest of Bolivia, living in small, isolated communities along the Maniqui River and its tributaries.
   They subsist primarily through hunting, fishing, and horticulture, cultivating crops such as plantains, maize, and cassava.
   Their lifestyle is marked by a profound connection to nature and traditional wisdom, offering valuable lessons in sustainable living practices.

3. **The Inuit** are indigenous peoples inhabiting the Arctic regions of Canada, Greenland, and Alaska.
   They have a rich culture deeply intertwined with the harsh environment they call home.
   Traditionally, the Inuit are skilled hunters and gatherers, relying on hunting marine mammals like seals, whales, and fish, as well as foraging for berries and plants during the brief Arctic summer.
   Their communities are built on strong kinship ties and a deep respect for nature, allowing them to thrive in one of the world's most extreme climates.

Figure 26: Men of the Hadza tribe with their hunting dogs[45]

Figure 27: The Tsimane Tribe of Bolivia[46]

Figure 28: Inuit people on a traditional sled after a hunt, Cape Dorset, Nunavut, Canada[47]

Question: What does the present-day lifestyle of these communities tell us about our collective past?

Opinion –

1. Their relationship with the environment around them. Despite animal products being a large part of their diet, these communities are not over exploiting their resources.
    They have maintained a balanced position in the ecosystem they live in, by neither overusing nor overexploiting the resources that are available to them.

2. While hunting and gathering is their main source of sustenance, it is also highly unpredictable.

Our ancestors led a nomadic lifestyle and were constantly on the move. All their energy was focused on traveling in search of food, and they had no time or energy to do much else.

But necessity is the mother of invention. Somebody invented the wheel, tools, technology and we grew—after all mankind has always had to choose 'to be or not to be'.

HISTORY OF AGRICULTURE AND ANIMAL DOMESTICATION

The Neolithic period, also known as the New Stone Age, was marked by the initiation of a settled human way of life. During this era, humans acquired the skill of cultivating plants and domesticating animals as the primary source of sustenance, transitioning away from a reliance on hunting and gathering.

The age lasted from 10,000 BCE – 2,000 BCE[48] (this is 12,000 years ago to 4,000 years ago).

Agricultural practices were first developed during the Neolithic Revolution. Before we delve into the details of when, where, and how, let's take a moment to emphasize the significant role agriculture played in our evolution and how it proved to be a major turning point for the entire human race.

Agriculture changed our lifestyle drastically. One of the major changes was the start of permanent settlements. Humans could now stay in one place to grow crops, and settlements began to emerge alongside rivers to facilitate easy irrigation for crops.

Cave dwellers turned to small communities, which then turned into villages, which in time formed entire civilizations. Historians and archaeologists have reported that most of the ancient civilizations developed alongside rivers.

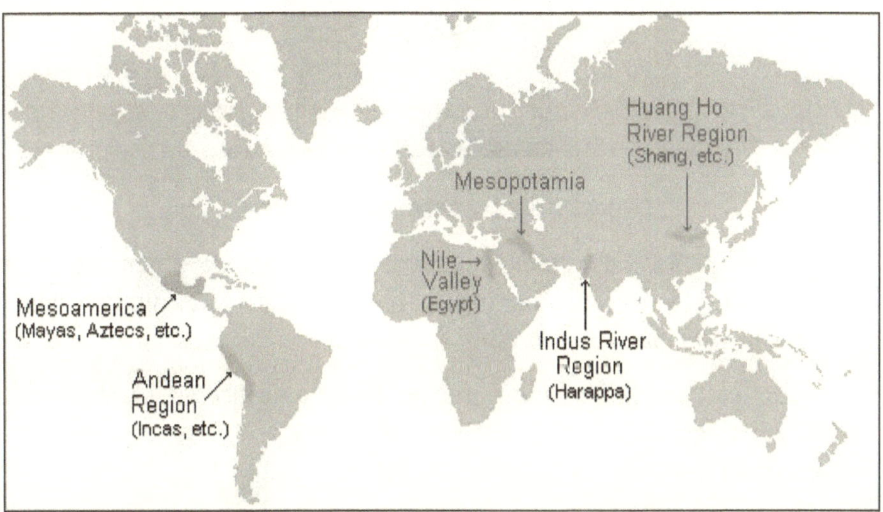

Figure 29: Ancient civilizations and the rivers they flourished on

1. The Indus Valley Civilization developed alongside the Indus River.
2. The Mesopotamian Civilization flourished on the banks of Tigris and Euphrates.
3. The Egyptian Civilization was sustained by the Nile River.
4. The Aztec Civilization had a system of interconnected lakes, fertile soil, and a temperate climate, all of which facilitated successful agriculture. The Aztecs created chinampas or artificial islands and used them for agriculture.
5. The Inca Civilization flourished along the Andes mountain range. The Inca developed an intricate system of agricultural terraces (through terrace farming) and irrigation channels to enhance crop yields.

Figure 30: Illustration of terrace farming

Agriculture ensured a stable supply of food, which gave humans more time and energy to invest in other things. One could say it was a major building block of advanced human civilization.

Based on historical records, people first domesticated plants about 10,000 years ago (8,000 BCE), between the Tigris and Euphrates rivers in Mesopotamia (present-day Iran, Iraq, Turkey, and Syria).

The first domesticated plants in Mesopotamia were wheat, barley, lentils, and certain types of peas. People in other parts of the world, including eastern Asia, parts of Africa, and parts of North and South America, also domesticated plants. Other plants that were cultivated by early civilizations included rice (Asia) and potatoes (South America).

Around the same time that plants were being cultivated as crops, people in Mesopotamia started domesticating animals for meat, milk, and hides. These animal hides, or skins, were utilized for clothing, storage, and constructing tent shelters.

It was not as if humans had not domesticated animals before. Evidence suggests that dogs and wolves were domesticated by hunter-gatherers to assist them in hunting.

However, the application of dogs in hunting was not very widespread, nor were they used for other domestic purposes such as plowing, removal of weeds, or clearance of land, etc.

Different parts of the world domesticated different animals native to their lands; however, one thing common among all domesticated species was that they were primarily herbivores (plant eaters).

This provides us with a direct link between agriculture and animal domestication. With crop cultivation, humans could now grow vegetation to feed these animals. Also, these animals helped clean up the land of all growth, making the land suitable for agriculture.

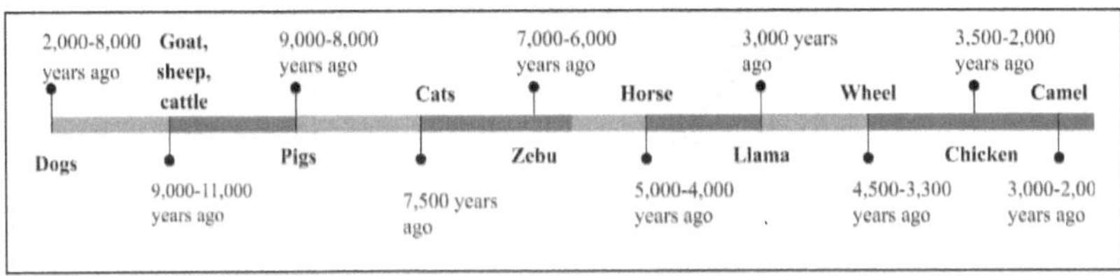

Figure 31: Timeline of the domestication of animals

Goats were probably the first animals to be domesticated, around 10,000 years ago, followed closely by sheep and cattle, and later pigs[49]. In Southeast Asia, chickens were also domesticated about 10,000 years ago.

Later, people began domesticating larger animals, such as oxen or horses for plowing and transportation. In the Indus Valley, bronze models of carts have been found at Harappa and 'Chanhu-daro'. These bullock carts had solid wheels. The bullock cart combined 2 critically important ideas – the use of animal power and the wheel.

Figure 32: Terracotta figurines indicate the yoking of zebu oxen pulling a cart and the presence of the chicken, a domesticated jungle fowl[50]

Figure 33: Bronze Late Harappan figures from a hoard at Daimabad, c. 2000 BCE[51]

The first conclusive evidence of horse riding was found in Kazakhstan and dates back to 3,500-3,000 BCE.

The Caral-Supe Civilization, the oldest in the Americas (modern-day Peru), was already cultivating the '3 sisters' of squash, beans, and corn, as well as other vegetables, and had domesticated the llama as a pack animal prior to 3000 BCE.

The Olmec civilization, the Maya, the Aztec Empire and others followed the same model.

The use of domesticated animals was not limited to agriculture. Before the discovery of plant fiber like cotton, animal hides were the norm for making clothes.

Figure 34: A domestic llama[52]

The Mesopotamians wore clothes made from the hides of the goat and sheep they domesticated. The wool from these animals provided the early Sumerians with the raw materials for their clothing.

Hanks of sheep or goat wool, probably still attached to a tanned hide, were stitched or knotted together in horizontal bands to fashion wrap skirts called 'Kaunakes'. Kaunakes continued to be worn for hundreds of years, even as the manufacture of woven materials became more prevalent.

In the Egyptian civilisation, Pharaohs also wore, as symbols of power, leopard skins over their shoulders and a lion's tail hanging from their belt. Before the development of linen, Egyptians wore clothes made of animal hide or woven papyrus reeds.

Even Gods across varied mythologies – Norse, Greek, Indian, Egyptian, et al. are known to adorn themselves with animal hides[53].

Figure 35: Statue of Iku-Shamagan, King of Mari, wearing the Kaunakes. c. 2500 BCE[54]

Figure 36: Indian Deity[55]

Figure 37: Hercules fighting the Nemean lion[56]

Figure 38: The Book of the Dead was a guide to the deceased's journey in the afterlife. The figures with animal heads are Egyptian Gods, guiding the dead person's soul[57].

Adorning skins to take on an animal's qualities is not an uncommon motif in stories, especially in traditional folklore. For example, the Soothsayer wore a wolf skin. Animals also played a very significant role in wars. While some animals

Facilitated communication, like the messenger pigeon. Others were used to transport ammunition and medical supplies, like donkeys, mules, and camels. Some animals were a direct part of the war, used for both transportation and mounted attack, like horses, elephants, and camels.

Horses were used in warfare from the earliest recorded history. With the development of the light, spoked wheel in the second millennium BCE, horses came to be used to draw military chariots, remains of which have been found in tombs across Eurasia. The use of horses as cavalry mounts probably spread eastward from Western Asia in the early part of the first millennium BCE.

One of the first depictions of equids (a mammal of the horse family) is the "war panel" of the Standard of Ur, in Sumer, dated c. 2500 BCE, showing horses (or possibly mules) pulling a four-wheeled wagon. While the standard does not show horses in actual combat, only pulling wagons, these equids clearly had a role to play in the victory depicted in the picture below.

Figure 39: The war panel of the Standard of Ur

**Figure 40: Chariot racing on a black-figure hydria from Attica,
c. 510 BCE (2534 years ago)[58]**

The chariot was the supreme military weapon in Eurasia roughly from 1700 BCE to 500 BCE but was also used for hunting purposes and in sporting contests such as the Olympic Games and in the Roman Circus Maximus.

Figure 41: Bas-relief of a quadriga race in the Circus Maximus (2nd–3rd century)

It wasn't until around 900 BCE that warriors themselves commonly fought on horseback. Among the first mounted archers and fighters were the Scythians, a group of nomadic Asian warriors who often raided the ancient Greeks.

Figure 42: Scythian mounted archer, Etruscan art, early 5th century BCE[59]

Across Europe, the Middle East, India, and China, rulers of varying ranks, from minor chiefs to esteemed pharaohs, embraced the chariot as their predominant weapon.

They portrayed themselves riding chariots, engaged in chariot-driven warfare, and incorporated depictions of chariots and horses into their tombs as symbols of authority.

Naturally, the aristocracy surrounding these rulers followed suit, leading to the emergence of charioteers as elite forces in every polity.

The horse transformed from a mere food source into a prized military asset. Horse breeding assumed a crucial role for these states, with influential kings aspiring to maintain well-equipped stables to meet the chariot needs of their armies.

Figure 43: Han dynasty, China bronze models of cavalry and chariots[60] (157-87 BCE)

Figure 44: Chariot detail at Airavatesvara Temple (India) built by Rajaraja Chola II of the Chola Empire in the 12th century CE (800 years ago)[61]

Figure 45: A golden chariot made during the Achaemenid Empire (Persian) 550–330 BCE[62]

The companionship between the horse and humans has been depicted in literary works and epics of ancient times as well. In the Greek epic, the Iliad, horses were like human companions: they shared the toil and danger of the heroes, who in turn cared for them, addressed them by name, and urged them on in battle. The tale of the 'Trojan Horse', a decoy used by the Greek soldiers to gain entrance to the city of Troy, is a well-known symbol of deceit even today.

Figure 46: Depiction of the Trojan Horse on a Corinthian aryballos (c. 560 BC) found in Cerveteri, Italy[63]

In Indian mythology, many gods have chariots pulled by horses, symbolizing energy and vigor. In the epic Ramayana, the Ashvamedha yagna is mentioned.

According to the ritual, a horse is selected and consecrated, ritual offerings are made, and the horse is allowed to wander freely for a specific period, usually one year, accompanied by a group of priests and warriors.

All those who accept the sovereignty of the king undertaking the Ashvamedha yajna honor the horse, pay tribute to the king, and become his vassals. A ruler who wishes not to accept suzerainty, however, captures the horse and confronts the army following the horse.

Following a year-long period, if the horse remained untouched by any adversaries and returned to the king's capital unharmed, it would be ceremoniously sacrificed.

Figure 47: Queen Kaushalya performing the Ashvamedha ritual; illustration to the Ramayana[64]

The noteworthy mentions of the horse in ancient artifacts and epics showcase its importance in ancient times.

The elephant was yet another majestic animal used in warfare. Because of its huge size and considerable power, it proved to be a deadly weapon in armies.

The first use of elephants by humans began about 4,000 years ago in India. In India, elephants were initially used for agricultural purposes. They could rip trees out of the ground, clearing wide areas for farming and construction.

Because they quickly demonstrated their trainability as well as their strength, it was only a matter of time before the giant animals were incorporated into military use. According to Sanskrit sources, this transition took place around 1100 BCE.

Virtually every ruler in India possessed elephants and used them to further his own ambitions. From the kings ruling Magadha as early as the 6th century BCE to the Mauryan dynasty (4th century BCE to 2nd century BCE), the Cholas (4th century BCE to 13th century CE[65]) and other powerful empires, elephants were a significant part of their armies. King Bimbi Sara (c. 543 BCE), who began the expansion of the Magadha kingdom, relied heavily on his war elephants.

The Nandas of Magadha (mid-4th century BCE – 321 BCE) had about 3,000 elephants. The Mauryan and Gupta empires also had elephant divisions; Chandragupta Maurya (321-297 BCE) had about 9,000 elephants.

The army of the Palas was noted for its huge elephant corps, with estimates ranging from 5,000 to 50,000 elephants.

Figure 48: Rajput painting depicting a war elephant in an army[66]

The Indian epic of Mahabharata, the tale of 'Ashwathama, the elephant and the warrior, is famous.

According to the legend, Bhimsen killed an elephant named Ashwathama. When Drona came to him and asked him, Yudhishthir announced that "Ashwathama is dead" – then said in a much lower tone of voice:

"Either the man or the elephant."

Drona did not hear those additional words and, thinking that his son was killed, was devastated and no longer had the heart to fight, losing his life. (Not to forget that the speaker of these words was known as a truth speaker).

Figure 49: Bhima kills an elephant named Ashwatthama. Folio from Razmnama (Persian translation of the Sanskrit epic Mahabharata)[67]

The use of horses and elephants has been minimized in the past few centuries. Up until the invention of the car in the 18th century, horse-drawn carriages were the norm. However, with technological advancement in the field of transportation, the use of horses saw a steady decline, as did their numbers. Nowadays, horses are seen mostly on farms or as a spectacle in Indian weddings.

Elephant numbers saw a dip in their population after the 18th century when they were no longer used in wars. The last appearance of elephants in battle was in the Afghan War of 1878-80. Presently, elephants are seen only on display in zoos or in their wildlife habitats.

However, it wasn't only war that the 'beasts of burden' facilitated, but they also contributed greatly to the shaping of trade routes.

The Silk Road, a network of Eurasian trade routes active from the first century BCE until the mid-15th century, contributed significantly to the exchange of goods and ideas among diverse cultures.

Animals were an essential part of the story of the Silk Road. While those such as sheep and goats provided many communities with the essentials of daily life, horses and camels both supplied local needs and were key to the development of international relations and trade.

Important as horses were, the camel was arguably of far greater significance in the history of the Silk Road. Domesticated as long ago as the fourth millennium BCE, by the first millennium BCE, camels were prominently depicted on Assyrian and Achaemenid Persian carved reliefs and figured in Biblical texts as indicators of wealth.

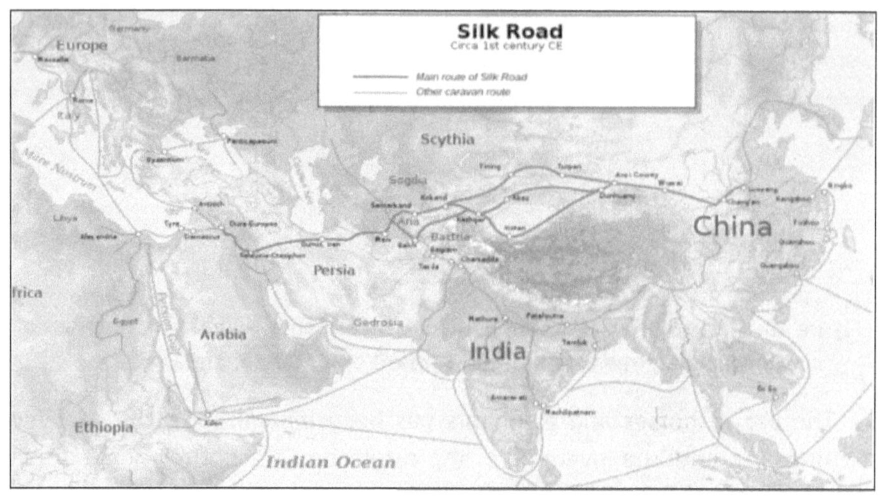

Figure 50: Map of the Silk Road in 1st century[68]

The camel's great virtues include the ability to carry substantial loads – 400-500 pounds (250kg) – and its well-known capacity for surviving in arid conditions. The secret to the camel's ability to go for days without drinking lies in its efficient conservation and processing of fluids (it does not store water in its humps, which are largely fat).

Camels can maintain their carrying capacity over long distances in dry conditions, eating scrub and thorn bushes. When they drink, though, they may consume 25 gallons at a time; so caravan routes do have to include rivers or wells at regular intervals.

The use of the camel as the dominant means of transporting goods over much of Inner Asia is, in part, a matter of economic efficiency – camels are cost-efficient compared to the use of carts requiring the maintenance of roads and the kind of support network that would be required for other transport animals.

When animals were domesticated, there was a substantial increase in their population.

Through domestication, a system of coexistence was formed where humans took care of feeding and providing shelter for domesticated animals, and the animals, in turn, provided humans with products. The key to this system was, of course, balance, one where animals were not exploited.

They were not milked for products beyond their capacity. Our ancestors were very much connected to the animals they domesticated, evident from Harappan seals imprinted with bulls, Sumerian tablets depicting milking of cattle, and Egyptians who are known for their fondness for their pet cats (mummies of cats were discovered in tombs).

It was because of this connection that people had with domesticated animals that prevented them from crossing the threshold where care turned into cruelty.

COLONIALISM AND ANIMAL CRUELTY

The people of ancient civilizations had a balanced relationship with animals; they were connected to them as domestication was a major source of sustenance. This historical relationship is now heavily tipped toward humans.

Animal cruelty exists on a large scale. Activities like animal-based product testing, game hunting (shikaar) for fun, poaching, and killing them for their body parts (like a rhino's horn or an elephant's tusk or a tiger's skin) are rampant. Destruction of their natural habitats and polluting them is a crux of our cruelty toward animals.

Talking about colonialism, in the past, it represented the practice of acquiring full or partial political control over another country, occupying it with settlers, and exploiting it economically[69].

India was a colony until 1947, and every resource was owned by the colonizers. In today's world, colonialism still exists in the form of overseas territories, for example, the Commonwealth countries. The Commonwealth is an organization consisting of the United Kingdom and most of the countries that were previously under its rule[70]. King Charles serves as the head of state in 14 Commonwealth countries in addition to the United Kingdom. These include the Falkland Islands, Tristan da Cunha, Montserrat, Bermuda, and others.

- Colonialism played a significant role in the destruction of natural habitats and the extinction of many native species.
- Invasive species were introduced in the colonies to make these foreign lands more 'suitable' to the palate of the colonizers.
- Examples include the water hyacinth or 'Kochuri Pana' in Bengali, which is native to South America but was brought to Bengal by the East India Company, specifically Warren Hastings (the first Governor-General).

The story goes as – Hastings brought this flower to please his wife around the end of the 18th century[71]. However, he was clueless that water hyacinths are among the fastest-growing plants, capable of doubling in size every 2 weeks.

A few more highlighting factors were:

- They clog waterways.
- Native vegetation cannot compete with its growth spurt.
- In its native land, South America, there were animals that consumed this plant as a food source, thus preventing it from growing unattended. But in Bengal, there was nothing to stunt the growth of the plant.

It came to be known as the 'Terror of Bengal' as it soon grew to cover entire water bodies, inhibiting the growth of fish and other aquatic organisms due to the cut down of light and lack of oxygen in the clogged water bodies.

It spread from Bengal to other parts of India primarily due to human activity, as it was introduced as an ornamental plant and subsequently transplanted to various water bodies. The connectivity of waterways allowed the plant to travel long distances, while seasonal flooding and monsoons further facilitated its dispersal.

Boats and ships also carried fragments of water hyacinth to new locations, enabling its spread. The plant's rapid reproduction through seeds and vegetative means contributed to its quick establishment in different regions. Additionally, the absence of natural predators in India allowed water hyacinth to proliferate unchecked.

The author has first-hand seen the destruction it can cause in a short time. Anasagar Lake, an artificial lake[72] in the author's hometown Ajmer, Rajasthan, was clogged by this plant recently.

Figure 51: Anasagar Lake, Ajmer, Rajasthan before and after

Game hunting was a favorite leisure-time activity of the colonizers, and many native species were hunted into extinction. For example-

- The Dodo birds were abundant on the island of Mauritius in the Indian Ocean.
- Devoid of natural predators, the birds remained unthreatened.
- Portuguese sailors first encountered them around 1507.
- They rapidly diminished the Dodo population, considering them an accessible source of fresh meat for their voyages.
- The later introduction of monkeys, pigs, and rats to the island had devastating consequences for the vulnerable birds, as these mammals preyed on their eggs.
- The last dodo met its demise in 1681. Regrettably, there are very few scientific descriptions or museum specimens available for these extinct birds[73]

Figure 52: Skeleton cast and model of dodo at the Oxford University Museum of Natural History, made in 1998[74]

Humans were initially dependent on hunting and gathering for survival for a millennium. We cannot consider hunting during those times as cruel, but now perhaps hunting for game could be such a consideration for many. The colonizers began a prolonged battle against our environment.

THE INDUSTRIAL REVOLUTION

(1700s – mid-19th century)

When the Industrial Revolution started, perhaps people had not imagined the scale and speed at which it was going to degrade the environment. The Industrial Revolution, spanning from the latter part of the 1700s to the early 1800s, marked a period of profound transformation in Europe and America.

The introduction of innovative technologies, ranging from mechanized looms for textile production to steam-powered locomotives, along with advancements in iron smelting, revolutionized predominantly rural societies of farmers and artisans who crafted goods by hand.

A significant migration occurred as many people relocated from rural areas to burgeoning cities, where they found employment in factories equipped with machinery.

Fueling the Industrial Revolution was the widespread use of coal, contributing to significant air pollution in burgeoning industrial cities.

Throughout the 1800s, escalating air pollution resulted in respiratory illnesses (like asthma, chronic bronchitis, allergic alveolitis,[75] and higher mortality rates[76], particularly in regions heavily reliant on coal. Additionally, the continuous combustion of fossil fuels releases carbon into the atmosphere.

The rapid industrialization of this era led to severe pollution and the exploitation of natural resources, causing enduring environmental damage.

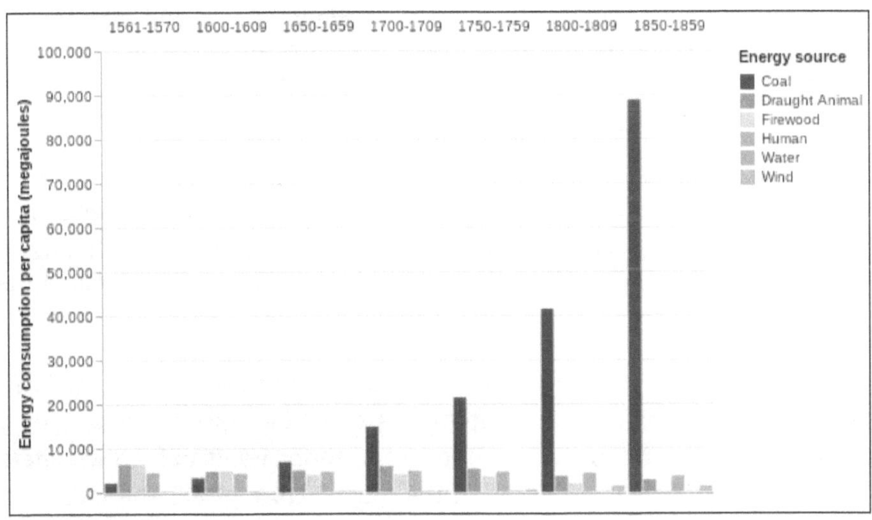

Figure 53: Annual energy consumption per head (megajoules) in England and Wales, 1561-1859

Following is a graph to showcase the sudden increase in the use of coal during the Industrial Revolution[77].

But worse was yet to come...

INTRODUCTION OF PLASTIC

The invention of plastic seemed to have cemented the destruction we were causing to the environment. In 1907, Leo Baekeland invented Bakelite, the first fully synthetic plastic, meaning it contained no molecules found in nature.

Did you know the original meaning of plastic is "pliable and easily shaped"? It is completely non-biodegradable. Because it wasn't made from nature, it could not be re-absorbed by it. Even a small bottle of plastic would take 450 years to degrade. Following below is a table of different kinds of plastics, their thickness in microns[78] and the time it would take them to degrade.

Table 7: Thickness (in microns) of plastic items and their degradation time

Plastic product	Thickness (in microns)	Degradation time
Polypropylene	50mu	200-450 years
HDPE – High-density polyethylene (trash bags)	18mu	450 years
LDPE – Low-density polyethylene (food bags)	25 mu	500-1000 years

Wonder what is more cruel: consuming animal products, which are part of a millennia-old natural process, or destroying their habitats, making them uninhabitable and driving down their numbers, to fulfill our greed.

For greed is the reason we shifted to using plastic in everything. After its invention, any biodegradable item that could be replaced by synthetic non-biodegradable trash was replaced. From storing items to food wrappers to even clothes, plastic was used in the manufacture of all. The Industrial Revolution brought along capitalism with it.

PLASTIC AND CAPITALISM

Capitalism refers to an economic system where private businesses can have ownership of capital goods[79]. A capitalist is the one providing capital. As with anything, capitalism has its own set of advantages and disadvantages.

Advantages

- It creates a competitive environment. In a competitive market, consumers have a wide array of choices.
- Cost of products is market-driven

Disadvantages

- It creates a monopoly environment; that is, if a few large companies dominate a specific industry or market, they can exert significant influence and control over prices and supply.
- There is a single-player advantage. For example, earlier, the only social media platform in existence was Facebook.

There are 2 kinds of assets – tangible assets and intangible assets. Tangible assets have a physical form and can be touched or seen, like machinery, factory buildings, etc. Intangible assets do not have a physical form but have an inherent value, like intellectual property.

Labor refers to the physical and mental effort exerted by individuals in the production of goods and services. A laborer is an individual engaged in physical work or manual labor as part of their occupation.

Capitalists hire laborers who are compensated with wages. In this arrangement, laborers do not possess ownership of the means of production; rather, they utilize these resources on behalf of the capital owners. Consequently, workers lack any entitlement to the means of production or the profits generated by their labor, as these go to the capitalists.

The profit motive, or the desire to earn profits from business activity, is the driving force of capitalism. This leads to competition, as companies try to be the most affordable producer of a product to sell more and increase their earnings.

Plastic satisfies the need for 'low cost production'.

On the surface, it seems like the ideal material: it's flexible, durable, and, most importantly, economical – very economical.

Depending on the specific type of plastic, a kilogram of new raw material is incredibly inexpensive, often costing only a few cents.

This affordability makes it much more cost-effective for manufacturers to produce new items rather than recycling old ones. This is why manufacturers persistently use it, and as consumers, we eagerly devour it – it's dirt cheap.

For example, it costs $0.26 (₹21) to produce a can of Coca-Cola, and it is sold to the consumer for about $1.00 (₹83) in the US[80].

The virgin spot market price for HDPE (High-density polyethylene), a commonly used petroleum thermoplastic[81] is about 50 cents per pound (₹92 per kg). Examples of products made from thermosetting plastic include everyday items like plastic chairs, garbage bins, pipes, shampoo bottles etc. Whereas the average market spot price of aluminum is an estimated $1.50 per pound (₹275 per kg).

There are 2 ways to see this:

1. The quantity of product that one can create with 1 pound of HDPE as compared to aluminum is exponentially higher. (e.g. containers, toys, pipes, bags, etc.)
2. The surface area that 1 pound of HDPE can cover is a lot more than what 1 pound of aluminum can if used for durable products such as chairs (294 sq. inch compared to 103 sq. inch for Aluminum per pound).

For the difference of a mere 1 dollar, manufacturers are destroying entire ecosystems and doing irreparable damage to the planet. Around the world, one million plastic bottles are purchased every minute, while up to 5 trillion plastic bags are used worldwide every year. In total, half of all plastic produced is designed for single-use purposes – used just once and then thrown away[82].

By just investing a little extra money, manufacturers could produce goods that are biodegradable. Instead, plastic bottles dominate the market when a much more sustainable alternative of aluminum or other metals (naturally occurring) is present.

Another example of this could be paper bags versus plastic bags. Paper bags are one hundred percent recyclable because they don't contain toxic and poisonous gas that plastic bags emit during recycling. However, paper bags cost 3 to 4 times as much to produce, and therefore, many have switched to single-use plastic.

Products were now redesigned to be used only once, from water bottles to polybags, cutlery to straws. Today, half of all plastics produced go into single-use applications.

Perhaps nothing highlights the illogical nature of capitalism quite like this – we use materials that can last forever to create products intended for disposal after a single-use. Planned obsolescence is what we would call this.

Of the 7 billion tons of plastic waste generated globally so far, less than 10% has been recycled[83]. Every year, millions of tons of plastic waste end up in the environment or are transported thousands of kilometers away to places where they are predominantly incinerated or discarded. Synthetic fabrics are in the same league as single-use plastic.

Since ancient times, we have worn clothes made from natural elements like cotton, wool, silk, animal hides, etc. These clothes are made of animal or plant-based fibers and are thus biodegradable. Synthetic fibers take a lot longer since they are predominantly made from plastics. Following below is a timeline of different materials and the time they take to decompose.

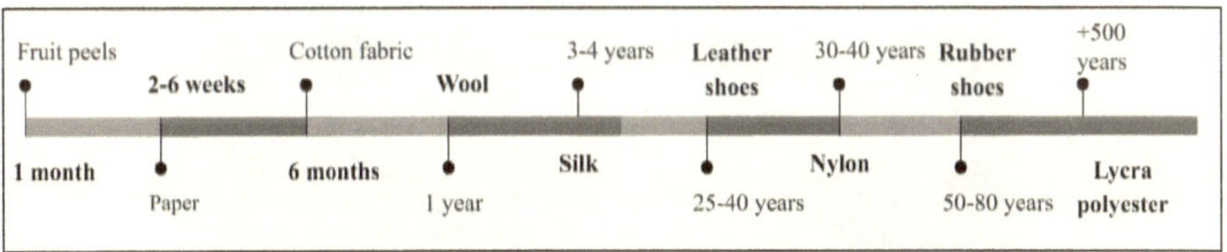

Figure 54: Timeline of decomposition of various materials

Chile's Atacama, the driest desert in the world, is increasingly suffering from pollution caused by fast fashion.

Figure 55: Mounds upon mounds of clothes in the Atacama Desert, Chile[84]

Fast fashion is the business model of replicating recent catwalk trends and high-fashion designs, mass-producing them at a low cost, and bringing them to retail stores quickly while demand is at its highest.

The blindingly fast pace at which clothes are now manufactured, worn, and discarded means that they've become more disposable. The social effect of rampant consumerism in the clothing industry – such as child labor in factories or derisory wages – is well-known, but the disastrous effect on the environment is less publicized.

Some 59,000 tons of clothing arrive each year at the Iquique port in the Alto Hospicio free zone in northern Chile[85]. The clothing, being non-biodegradable and containing chemical elements, is not allowed in municipal landfills. The fetid mountain in the Atacama Desert of discarded clothing can now be observed from space[86].

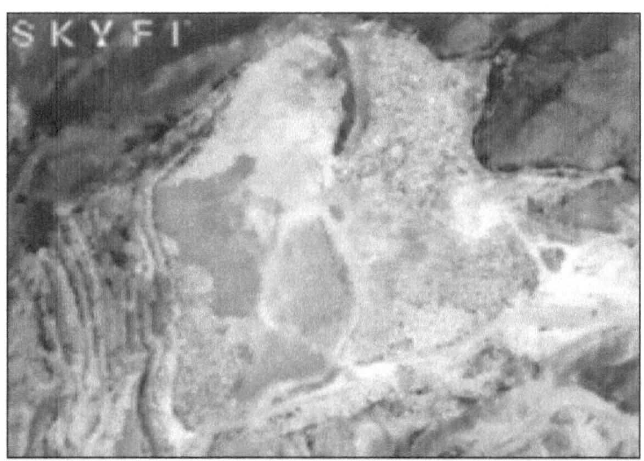

Figure 56: Pile of discarded clothes in the Atacama Desert, northern Chile, as seen by a satellite[87]

While capitalists enjoy the high profits by polluting the environment, workers are exploited for their labor, with wages always kept lower than the true value of the work being done. In fact, the author believes that labor is being made landless by capitalists.

This leads to enormous wealth disparities and social inequalities: Capitalism has created an immense gap between the wealthy and the poor, as well as social inequalities.

Now that we have discussed capitalism and the plastic industry, let us talk about cruelty toward animals. The dumping of non-biodegradable and toxic waste, as well as land reclamation, is cruelty toward non-human sentient beings.

This form of cruelty toward animals is most prevalent in the world as of today – pollution and the irreversible damage it is causing to their habitat. At present, there is not a single sphere of the earth not carrying pollutants. From the expanse of the sky above us, the land we live on, and the depth of the ocean below us, humans have extensively polluted all 3 spheres of life.

Plastic pollution has a severe impact on wildlife as it doesn't just vanish. It can persist for hundreds of years, breaking down into tiny pieces that can be easily consumed. Plastic is harmful, posing a threat to wildlife by causing fatalities or rendering them more vulnerable to diseases.

Animals may get entangled or harmed by plastic, disrupting habitats and creating challenges for certain species to thrive and reproduce naturally, resulting in population declines.

The influence of plastic extends across all forms of life, affecting organisms at the microscopic level, throughout the food chain to large predators, and even impacting humans.

Figure 57: Cows consuming plastic waste

Figure 58: The unaltered stomach contents of a dead albatross chick[88]

Figure 59: An American Robin dead after becoming tangled in discarded fishing line[89]

Every year, plastic kills 1 million seabirds and 100,000 sea mammals, turtles, and fish[90].

Figure 60: Turtle stuck in a fishnet[91]

Humans invented plastic, and animals are harmed by it. They eat it, get caught in it, or get sick because of it. Plastic pollution occurred so rapidly that animals were unable to adjust their behavior around this new material.

The effect of plastic in forests and wildlife is devastating. Microplastics are very small pieces of plastic that pollute the environment. A microplastic is defined as a plastic particle that is less than five millimeters. The surfaces of tiny fragments of plastic may carry bacteria, viruses, and protists that act as vectors for diseases. Microplastics can further interact with soil fauna, affecting their health and functions.

Based on their research, the UN Environment stated, "Earthworms, for example, make their burrows differently when microplastics are present in the soil, affecting the earthworm's fitness and the soil condition."[92] This can further damage the rest of the environment by reducing forest flora that is dependent on earthworms.

We talk about animal cruelty based on the consumption of animal products. But what about the cruelty we are perpetrating by destroying their homes, the resources they survive on, and even wiping out entire species?

While livestock farming has been in existence for thousands of years, concerning itself with only domesticated animals, environmental pollution is affecting almost all species of the planet, both flora and fauna.

VEGANISM

Many people have come up with veganism as the answer to stop the consumption of animal products. Veganism is the practice where people abstain from consuming any animal product. The vegan diet excludes animal-derived ingredients and is exclusively plant-based. However, the author believes veganism is not the solution to this problem and would like to answer the question of why in a 3-part argument.

To present the first and most basic argument, we would like to restate our statement, **'any change that is radical is not sustainable'**.

Veganism is a radical change in the sense that it completely disregards the existence of the natural food chain and our part in it. To suddenly stop consuming animal products, which have been a part of the human diet for thousands of years, is an extreme step and is not sustainable.

Let's, for a moment, assume that we do stop consuming animal products and go for a plant-based diet. Will that be sustainable? To understand this, we would ask the reader to imagine what would happen if all carnivore and omnivore animals in a jungle (lion, tiger, bear, hyena etc.) stopped consuming the herbivores and instead started consuming plants.

If all animals only ate plants, what do you think would happen to the flora of that jungle? It would disappear at an alarming rate simply because there are too many consumers.

From the world's largest animal, the blue whale, to small insects like the ladybird, carnivores and omnivores make up a large part of the food web. Some animals even practice cannibalism, where they consume members of their own species, often to eliminate competition for food or mates.

Chimpanzees and bears, for example, will hunt and consume the young of family members, sometimes their own offspring. Praying mantis females will kill and eat the bodies of their mates. Even the plant kingdom is not excluded from this. Though fewer in number, there are carnivorous plants too, like the Venus flytrap or the sundew, which consume insects.

Consuming other organisms is not exclusive to humans; in fact, it is a big part of the natural ecosystem. Animals from every habitat – air, water, and land – consume other organisms. Birds like eagles, vultures, and owls; land animals like the polar bear; all members of the Felidae family (cat family) from house cats to wild cheetahs; wolves; and marine animals including sharks, piranhas, and the killer whale are just a few examples.

And the food chain does not always follow the straight line of autotrophs consumed by herbivores who are then consumed by carnivores.

Nature is much more complex than that. To give an example, Killer whales, or orcas, hunt seals and sea lions. Seals and sea lions are carnivores that consume fish, squid, and octopuses. Octopuses feed on crabs, clams, snails, small fish, and even other octopuses.

But why are we going on about herbivores, carnivores, and omnivores and who's consuming whom?

The food web is a very complex natural phenomenon, where even the smallest being can affect the entire ecosystem. At the start of this chapter, we explained that the content following is human-centric. This is what it meant.

(Have you heard of the butterfly effect? The original Chinese proverb says-

"The flapping of the wings of a butterfly can be felt on the other side of the world."

They say that if a butterfly flaps its wings in the Amazonian rainforest, it can change the weather half a world away.

We are not glorifying the consumption of other animals or putting our species on a pedestal. It simply means that nature has a cycle, of which we are a part too, and currently we stand at the top of this food web. And as a component of it, we must play our part too, or it will disrupt the balance of this cycle.

Mark Twain believed that humans are the only evil creatures in existence because of our sense of right and wrong. Nothing a tiger does is immoral because it has no moral sense. Evil, as a trait, is unique to humanity because of our moral compass. I'm not saying that we should abandon this conscience; however, this moral compass should not interfere with the law of nature either.

Let us understand this through another example. What happens if we eliminate even one component from a food chain? Let us take carnivores, for example. The disappearance of large carnivores will lead to an overpopulation of herbivores, disrupting the ecosystem. For instance, wolves and cougars are traditional predators of white-tailed deer.

But hunting and development have eliminated these predators from the northeastern United States. Without natural predators, the population of white-tailed deer has skyrocketed. In some areas, there are so many deer that they cannot find enough food. They frequently stray into towns and suburbs in search of food. (The author met with an accident in Connecticut, USA when a deer jumped on the highway).

Now that we have explained the food chain, its complex workings, and our significant part in it, let me come back to the question we proposed at the beginning of this argument.

What if all humans stopped consuming animal products and had an exclusively plant-based diet? The same thing that happened with the white-tailed deer. There will be an overwhelming number of consumers of plants and not enough produce.

Our personal observation: In our farmhouse, we fenced the walls with barbed wire, preventing the entry of any large four-legged creature (predator) such as dogs.

The result: The nests of pigeons and other birds can no longer be found on the property.

The reason: Cats have become the apex predators inside the walls. They have no fear or worry and therefore hunt freely, causing chaos in the entire local biodiversity.

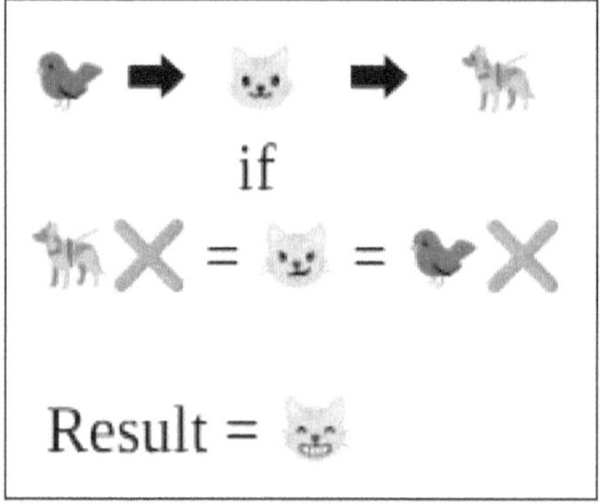

Figure 61: How cats became the apex predators in our farmhouse

The Rebuttal:

The purpose of this argument is not to degrade animals as mere food sources for humans but to understand our role as a component of the food chain.

Thousands of years ago, when humans started domesticating animals, we were somewhere in the middle of the food chain. We were predators, but we were also prey. However, our species has evolved to dominate Earth and its ecosystem, and we have to acknowledge and accept our position at the heart of the food web presently.

Our crucial role at the core of the food web means that many species and ecosystems are directly or indirectly impacted by our existence. Therefore, we cannot simply take extreme action that reverses the entire food chain and disrupts the ecosystem.

Up to now, we have discussed what would happen to the ecosystem and food chain if we stopped consuming animal products. In the second part of our argument, we would like to discuss what would happen to domesticated animals if we stopped the consumption of animal products. Would it benefit them? Would they be better off?

To answer this question, we would like to give an example again, this time of our home state Rajasthan, India. Rajasthan is known for its desert, the Thar Desert, and for the 'ship of the desert', its camels.

As early as the 2000s, camels were widely used all over the state, from villages to towns and even in cities. They were used for transportation of people and goods, for plowing the fields, for their products, and wool fiber made from their hair. Camel carts were a regular means of transportation, and they were used to commute frequently.

However, the camel population has nosedived in the state from 1992, when it was 746,000, to 2019 when it dropped down to 213,000. Overall, the camel population in India dipped by almost 37 per cent since 2011 and 75 per cent since 1992[93]. Camel carts are now more of a spectacle, a rare happening and not the everyday occurrence that they used to be.

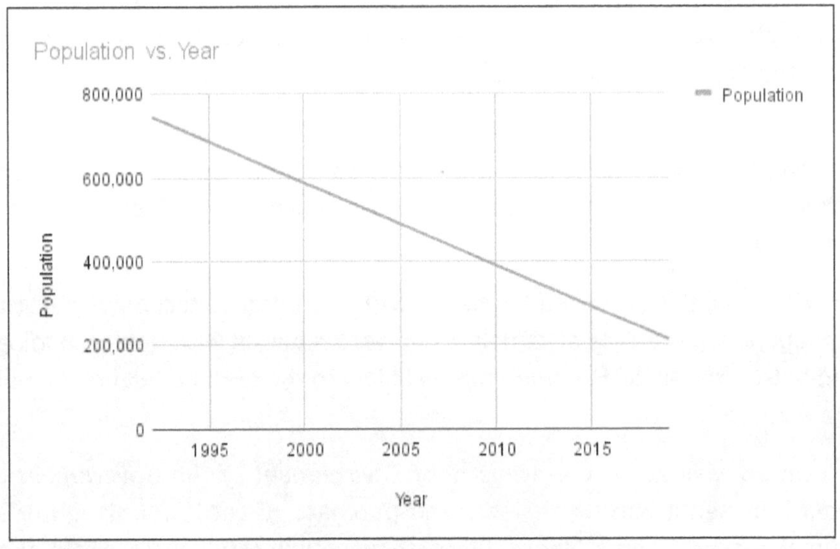

Figure 62: Graph depicting the decline in camel population in Rajasthan, India from 1992-2011

Why did this happen? What is the reason behind this drastic drop in the camel population? There are 3 reasons for this change.

1. **Mechanization** – The camel was an important draught animal (animals used in agriculture and for transportation purposes) in Rajasthan, but slowly, mechanization overtook it. Close to 217,000 km of roads have been added to Rajasthan since independence, which has resulted in automobiles taking over camels in transportation.
2. **Tractor sales** increased by over 400 per cent since 2000, supplanting it for plowing; and farmers now prefer synthetic fertilizers over camel manure. Another factor for the decline has been a lack of pastures and grazing land for these animals.
3. **Policy failure** – Rajasthan declared camels to be state animals in 2014 and enacted the **Rajasthan Camel (Prohibition of Slaughter and**

   Regulation of Temporary Migration or Export Act. This act banned the selling or transporting of these camels outside the state. This has left the animals without a market outside the state. Thus, the steep decline in numbers.

Another example is of the oxen. Oxen were a crucial part of agriculture in India. Because of their big bodies, they were quite strong and capable of carrying heavy things. They were used by farmers to clear land for cultivation, plow the fields, and bring in the harvest.

Oxen could also provide food for the table. Not only this, but their mechanical power was used in the extraction of mustard oil. This was done using an ox mill and a Kachi Ghani, a cold pressing machine. The oil extracted was known as 'Kachi Ghani ka Tel'.

However, things started to change with the onset of technology. Just as it happened in the case of camels, oxen were replaced with new technology and better machines. However, the real blow to the oxen population in India came in 2017.

On 26 May 2017, the *Ministry of Environment of the Government of India* imposed a ban on the sale and purchase of cattle for slaughter at animal markets across India. Since they couldn't slaughter cattle they didn't need, farmers started releasing male calves and unproductive older females.

Currently, India is home to over 5 million[94] stray cattle wandering the streets. These cattle frequently gather at garbage dumps in search of any available scraps of food. The majority are male and are often in distress, either starving or injured from collisions with vehicles.

Due to insufficient feeding, these cattle can become aggressive, and local news frequently reports incidents of people being attacked by bulls on the streets. In addition to the immediate dangers, stray cattle pose a health risk as they can carry diseases.

In some instances, farmers release diseased cattle, unable to cull them, leading to potential outbreaks.

This is likely what happened in 2022 when lumpy skin disease affected more than 2 million cattle[95].

Another example of animals decreasing in numbers because they were no longer consumed is the Choctaw hogs, a breed of domestic pig. This pig was prized by the Native American Choctaw tribe as a meat source.

But displacement of the tribe led to the breed's downfall. Today, Choctaw hogs live on just a few farms in a single county in Oklahoma. The animals are still extremely vulnerable to inbreeding, and only 100 or so remain.

The fate of the camel and Choctaw hogs is the fate of all farm animals if humans stopped consumption of animal products. If all humans were vegan, then there would be no need to raise animals for their products. That would mean we'd only ever see milk-producing animals like cows, goats, sheep or egg and feather-producing chickens and other animals like pigs or turkey at the zoo.

Yet another impact of lessened consumption of animal products is the consequent production of non-natural products. Raising livestock requires continuous investment and care. They must be fed regularly, require regular check-ups, etc. If the demand decreases, it means that the farmer would be spending more on raising the livestock than what he would earn by selling the products. This will lead to the entry of adulterated and non-natural animal products in the market.

Imagine a farmer has 5 cows, each of which produces 5 liters of milk daily.

5 l + 5 l + 5 l + 5 l + 5 l = 25l

If the cost of raising them is causing him more loss than profit, what will he do? He must earn money without loss. He would get rid of 2 cows and keep only 3. To make up for the 10 liters of milk from the 2 cows, he might add water to increase the volume and quantity of milk.

$$5l + 5l + 5l + 15l = 25l$$

To keep up with the same amount of production, he might start adulterating the milk. Milk is the most adulterated food in India during the festive season. It is commonly mixed with water, urea, caustic soda, soap, detergent, and even chalk to increase the quantity of milk.

The adulterants like detergents in milk, synthetic components, urea, caustic soda, and formalin lead to catastrophic effects on health if taken for a long time as they can cause severe health problems like food poisoning, gastrointestinal complications, impairments, heart problems, cancer, or even death.

Worse still, it could lead the farmer to altogether get rid of cows and instead establish a synthetic milk-producing machine. This will be a one-time investment instead of the continuous investment he had to make in cattle rearing. To create synthetic milk, key synthetic dairy proteins are produced to form a liquid-style product, which then has minerals, vitamins, fats, and lactoglobulin (dairy protein) added to replicate traditional cow's milk.

These non-natural products are very harmful to human health. Other examples of food adulteration include ghee (butter, clarified by boiling) made from vegetable oils and plastic rice. If any product selling for less than 2000 rupees (25$) claims to be pure ghee, the author can mathematically prove it is not possible to manufacture and package it profitably.

The definition of purity is altered to showcase it as pure. For example, pure ghee (mixed cow and buffalo milk).

The third part of our argument will focus on the plant-based diet required in veganism.

In the absence of consumption of animal products, nourishment will be based solely on plants, and it will drastically increase demand for vegetarian items. This step will put excessive strain on both the cultivable land and the cultivators.

Since the focus of our discussions is the upliftment of marginalised farmers, the prospect of a vegan diet becomes even more important to debate. Vegan diets will increase the demand for staple foods, and the farmer will be forced to cultivate them to fulfill the food demand. The hydroponics technology, if used for a vegan lifestyle, will lead to high costs.

We have already explained how cultivation is not sustainable on such a small area of land, as the amount the farmers earn after selling their produce is more or less the same amount they invested to grow that crop.

The difference between these 2 amounts is not much, and marginalised farmers remain in a perpetual state of poverty. If we are trying to bring them out of this cycle, additional demand for food crops is not the solution. It will only add to the problem.

We have discussed how it will affect the cultivator, but what about the land they cultivate on? As we already stated in the previous chapter, the area under cultivable land is being expanded at the expense of forests. Take the example of Brazil, home to the Amazon rainforest, also called the 'lungs of the earth'.

Figure 63: Deforestation in the Maranhao state, Brazil, in July 2016[96]

Large increments were reported in the cropland area of Brazil between 1990 and 2019, where the cropland area increased by 13%.

How do you think they are gaining new land to cultivate? By cutting down millions and millions of trees. By destroying the habitat of the planet's most varied flora and fauna.

Deforestation has greatly altered landscapes around the world. About 2,000 years ago, 80 percent of Western Europe was forested; today the figure is 34 percent. In North America, about half of the forests in the eastern part of the continent were cut down from the 1600s to the 1870s for timber and agriculture.

Figure 64: Amazon rainforest fire in Brazil's indigenous territory in 2017[97]

China has lost great expanses of its forests over the past 4,000 years, and now just over 20 percent of it is forested. Much of Earth's farmland was once forest.

Conversion to cropland dominates forest loss in Africa and Asia, with over 75 percent of the forest area lost being converted to cropland. In South America, almost three-quarters of deforestation is due to livestock grazing.

According to the Food and Agriculture Organization of the United Nations (FAO), agricultural expansion drives almost 90 per cent of global deforestation.

Worldwide, more than half of forest loss is due to the conversion of forests into cropland, whereas livestock grazing is responsible for almost 40 percent of forest loss.

This decrease in forest area is recorded when most humans still regularly consume animal products, and it constitutes a significant portion of their diet. Imagine if we all went vegan and opted for a plant-based diet instead.

There is already an extreme strain on available land for food production. What would happen if it became our only source of nourishment?

Sometimes people's response to this argument is that trees can just be replanted again. And it is true. Trees can be planted, but forests cannot. When we cut down trees in a forest, we are essentially destroying a whole ecosystem, and that includes every living and non-living thing in that forest.

Ecosystems like that take thousands, even millions of years to form. Replanting trees will not bring back the ecosystem we destroyed.

Today, the greatest amount of deforestation is occurring in tropical rainforests, aided by extensive road construction into regions that were once almost inaccessible. Building or upgrading roads in forests makes them more accessible for exploitation.

Slash-and-burn agriculture is a significant contributor to deforestation in the tropics. With this agricultural method, farmers burn large swathes of forest, allowing the ash to fertilise the land for crops. The land is only fertile for a few years; however, after which the farmers move on to repeat the process elsewhere. Tropical forests are also cleared to make way for logging, cattle ranching, and oil palm and rubber tree plantations.

After looking at this information, does it really seem fitting that veganism is environmentally friendly? All it will do is increase the rate at which forests are being cleared to turn into cultivable land. How can it be the solution when it is giving birth to a more serious problem?

Another aspect is the idea of superfoods such as spirulina or seaweed, which give all the required nutrition for very little effort. But it is not viable.

LAND RECLAMATION THROUGH TERRAFORMATION

However, this argument does raise another significant question. Expanding cropland is not the only reason for deforestation; livestock grazing also contributes significantly to the issue. If we are to focus on livestock farming as a sustainable course of action, we cannot do it at the expense of forests.

Then how do we build pastures for livestock while avoiding deforestation?

And the solution to this problem is land reclamation. *Land reclamation refers to improving land for use that was previously under the sea or in a very poor condition.* Take the example of the Palm Islands of Dubai.

The Palm is the world's most instantly recognizable land reclamation site, shaped like a giant palm tree stretching out into the Persian Gulf. The project cost $12bn (£8.5bn), and the area of land reclaimed was 5.6 km square.

With this amount spent on the author's district of 3 million people, everyone could enjoy a good lifestyle for at least one generation. Since each individual would get 3 lakh 30 thousand. A family of 4 would get 13 lakhs, which is good enough to buy 1-acre land.

Figure 65: Palm Islands, Dubai[98]

Yet another example of land reclamation on a mega scale is Mumbai, the 'City of Dreams'.

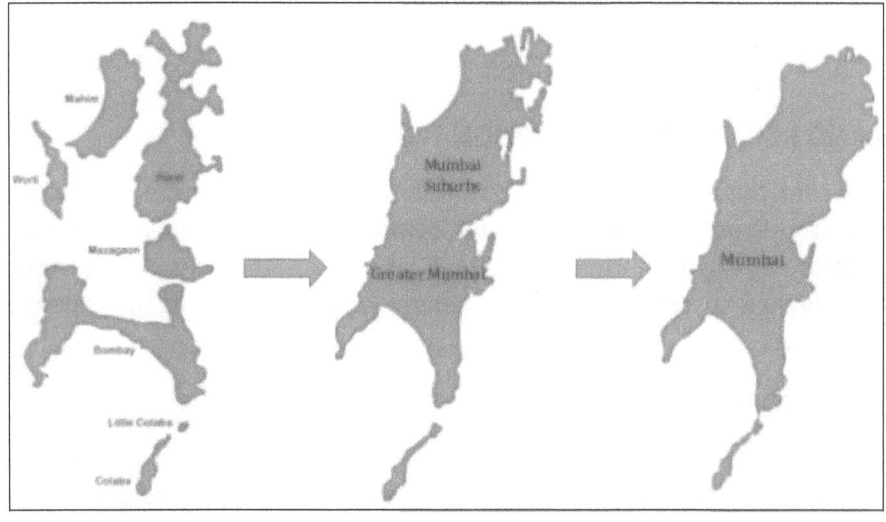

Figure 66: Seven separate islands converted into one city, Mumbai[99]

Mumbai was a scattered group of 7 islands just a few centuries ago and today is one of the biggest metropolitan cities in the world.

If we can reclaim land on such a large scale from the sea to build cities, we can surely do it to build pastures from land that has turned barren.

In the previous chapter, we talked at length about the increasing land degradation taking place due to intensive agricultural practices, which sap the soil and destroy its nutrients. It is this land, which is no longer fit for cultivation, that we must reclaim through terraforming.

Terraformation (literally earth formation as terra means earth) refers to the process of transforming an environment to make it habitable.

To explain this process, we would like to give the example of a woman named Yin Yuzhen who has actually transformed a desert from a barren unyielding land to a flourishing forest. This occurrence is in China, a country severely affected by desertification, with more than a quarter of its territory covered in desert.

Desertification is the degradation of fertile land, which changes it into a desert by losing its flora and fauna. This can be caused by drought, deforestation, climate change, human activities, or improper agriculture, and even by introducing foreign elements such as rabbits in Australia.

The size of the problem is enormous in China. Research shows that currently, 27.4% of the land in China has undergone desertification, affecting about 400 million people.[100]

The expanse of desertified land, amounting to 2,630,400 km², is equivalent to 710 times the area of the smallest state in India, Goa, and 836 times the area of the smallest state in the USA, Rhode Island.

The nation implemented the Great Green Wall of China project in 1978 to hold back the expansion of the Gobi Desert. Some causes and impacts of desertification include "aeolian desertification," caused by wind erosion after vegetation is destroyed, "water and soil loss," caused by water erosion mainly distributed in the Loess plateau, "salinization," caused by poor water management, and "rock desertification," mainly occurring in the Karst region of Southwestern China.

The Great Green Wall project is expected to continue until 2050 and aims to plant around 88 million acres of forests in a wall stretching about 3,000 miles and as wide as 900 miles in some places.

While the government is doing all it can to implement afforestation and reduce areas under desert, one woman has turned the Mu Us desert, one of the 4 major deserts of the country, into a green land, all on her own. Yin Yuzhen has devoted 30 years of her life to bring life to the desert around her.

Figure 67: Yin Yuzhen[101]

Figure 68: Before and after picture of the Mu Us Desert, China[102]

Through a process of trial and error, she learned which species of plants had a higher rate of survival. In the beginning, the survival rate of saplings was merely one percent.

Through constant dedication and hard work, Yin has brought the survival rate up to 70%. It was very difficult for her to grow trees in a land devoid of water and any kind of flora or fauna.

In the beginning, she planted the local willow tree saplings, but when they didn't survive, she devised a strategy of planting trees in concentric circles to avoid further desertification and decrease soil erosion. In the outermost circle, she planted saplings of tall, hardy trees such as poplars and Mongolian Scots pine to keep the desert at bay.

Then in the middle, she planted smaller trees and stabilizing bushes, and in the innermost circle, she planted fruit trees and crops.

Figure 69: An illustration of Yin Yuzhen's strategy. The outermost circle has tall, hardy trees like poplars and Mongolian Scots pine, the middle circle features smaller trees and stabilizing bushes, and the innermost circle contains fruit trees and crops.

Her intelligence, coupled with hard work and an unbending spirit, turned a man-made desert into a land flourishing with life. At present, there are over 300,000 native trees and plants with at least 100 different species. In fact, 80% of the Mu Us desert has now turned into a forest, and it can no longer be called a desert.

What do we learn from the example of Yin Yuzhen? Land, even the most barren, even desert land, can be turned green again. It takes patience and is a laborious process. It's a long-term project, but the end result will be a permanent solution (at least until human greed takes over).

Now there are 2 things that we would like to point out when talking about reclamation of desert land through terraforming. The first is the difference between 'desert' land and a desert.

Land desertification refers to a form of land degradation by which fertile land turns into a desert. This means that the desert land was once-fertile and had a thriving ecosystem. However, it was degraded over time because of human activities like intensive agriculture, consequently making it barren.

It is this land that we refer to when talking about land reclamation. Many people think that land reclamation through terraforming means turning the Sahara, the world's biggest desert, into a blossoming forest. And this is not logically possible for 2 reasons:

1. The Sahara is not desert land; it is a natural desert. It has been existing for millions of years and has a complex ecosystem of its own. Not to mention, the Sahara is intricately connected to other ecosystems on the planet and directly or indirectly affects thousands of species of flora and fauna.

Trying to launch a mega land reclamation project on this land would mean interfering with its nature and it could have catastrophic effects on humanity. There are studies that we can refer you to in order to understand the potential impact. Please see the end of this chapter for more reference to this context.

2. A project of this scale will require a lot of capital, not to mention international consensus. We simply cannot afford the capital, time, and resources required. But here comes the twist: we cannot invest in mega-projects, and we don't have to!

The solution that we are going to talk about operates at the micro level. The subject of our discussions, as we keep repeating again and again, is marginalized farmers. These farmers own small patches of land, and it is this small piece of land that the farmer has to reclaim through terraforming. The author invites every small landowner to try their hand at this approach.

CASH CROP

Cash crop can be defined as a crop produced for its commercial value rather than for use by the producer. For example, sugarcane and cotton.

Before we move forward, let's reflect on the initial problem we started addressing: the limitation of available land. This directly impacts the quantity of crops that can be cultivated. These crops play a dual role, serving as both a food source for humans and fodder for domestic animals such as cows and goats.

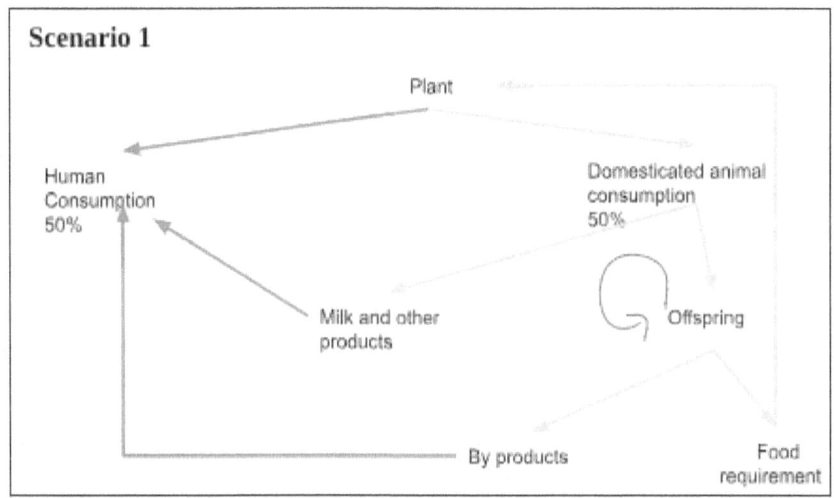

Figure 70: Scenario 1

Like land, fossil fuel (petrol, diesel) is also a limited resource. This scarcity has prompted significant exploration into alternative energy solutions, with particular attention given to ethanol. Ethanol is a renewable fuel made from various plant materials collectively known as "biomass." [103]

Ethanol comes from crops like sugarcane or corn, and it's seen as a renewable energy source that can be added to regular petrol. However, we don't have unlimited land to grow the crops needed for ethanol. This raises concerns about whether we can grow enough crops for both food and fuel.

Imagine if in diagram 43 a portion of the agricultural output of sugarcane is diverted for a third commercial purpose, that is, ethanol production.

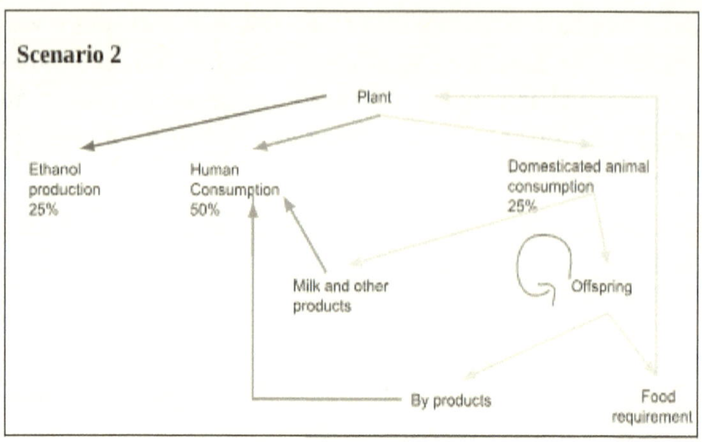

Figure 71: Scenario 2

This amount won't be deducted from the human's portion. As a result, where 50% of the produce was used as fodder for domestic animals earlier, now only 25% is available. The rest is diverted for ethanol production.

The cane part of the crop is used as fodder for livestock, but as a result of this scenario, the availability of fodder will be reduced.

Sugarcane is used to make a variety of products for human consumption like sugar, jaggery, syrup etc. Imagine if an amount were deducted from the human's portion too.

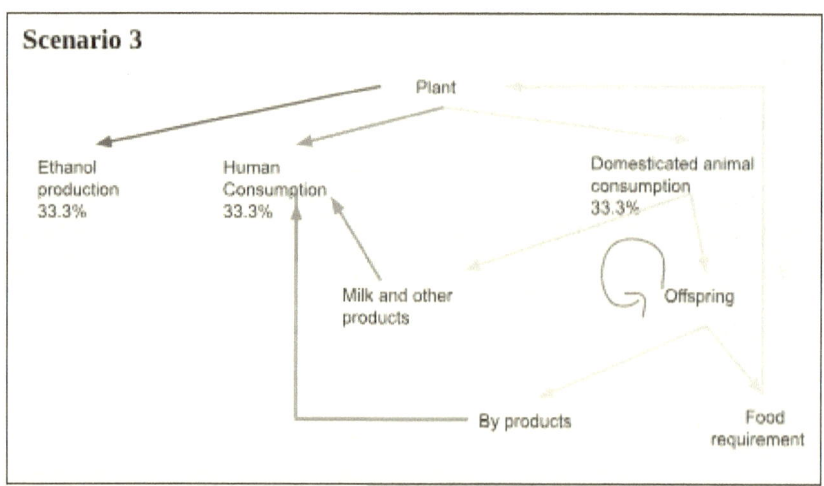

Figure 72: Scenario 3

Both of these scenarios will have the same result: an increased price of products. There are 2 reasons behind the increase in the price of a product:

1. The cost of raw materials increases. In Scenario 2, since the availability of fodder available for livestock decreases, its price will increase. If the basic raw material (fodder) becomes expensive then the price of the finished product (milk, cheese etc.) will automatically increase.
2. When a product is scarce and in low supply within the market, its price tends to rise. Rarity often translates to increased value, as seen in the case of gold, which is an expensive commodity due to its limited availability. Diamonds, being even scarcer, commands higher prices.

In Scenario 3, the end products of sugarcane like jaggery and sugar will be produced in lesser amounts since the amount of valuable raw material has decreased. The scarcity of a product directly influences its market price, with a decrease in availability leading to an increase in its value.

This, in turn, will be commercially exploited by artificial sweetener manufacturers, which, as of now, we know, is not a very healthy choice in the long run.

Conclusively, growing cash crops on a limited amount of land will result in a shortage of food crops, which will then lead to inflation. When the price of commodities increases, the common man often compromises on quality to get more quantity, hence consuming low-quality products that are available in greater quantity. Also, commercially, it will not make much sense.

Another such fuel is biodiesel. Biodiesel is a renewable fuel that is produced from natural vegetable oils, animal fats, and waste cooking oil. It can be made from oils which have been extracted from plants such as palm, soybean, oilseed, or sunflower. Two of these – palm and sunflower – are major cash crops and will have the same consequences as in the case of sugarcane.

Cash crops come with a lot of complications that a marginalised farmer just cannot afford. Let us take the example of cotton. Cotton is the most widespread profitable non-food crop in the world. Its production provides income for more than 250 million people worldwide and employs almost 7% of all labor in developing countries[104]. Approximately half of all textiles are made of cotton.

All parts of the cotton plant are useful.

- The most important element is the fibre or lint, which is used in making cotton cloth.
- The cottonseed is crushed to separate its three products – oil, meal, and hulls.
- Cottonseed oil is used primarily for shortening, cooking oil, and salad dressing.
- The meal and hulls that remain are used either separately or in combination as livestock, poultry, and fish feed and as fertilizer.
- The stalks and leaves of the cotton plant are ploughed under to enrich the soil.

Cotton has been used as a fabric in India from time immemorial. It has been cultivated in the Indus valley for more than 5000 years. India ranks first in the world in respect of acreage with about 8 million hectares under cotton and fourth in total seed cotton production (80 lakhs bales – 170 kg lint contains 1 bale).

However, one look at its cost of production and it will begin to become clear why it's not a sustainable alternative for a marginalised farmer. Production cost of cotton has been rapidly increasing in India. Before 2008-09, the total cost was less than ₹30,000/ha ($660.00/ha). It increased to ₹37,745/ha ($792.65/ha) during 2008-09 and continued to increase at the rate of 13.2% per annum to reach ₹73,179/ha ($1,170.86/ha) in 2014-15.

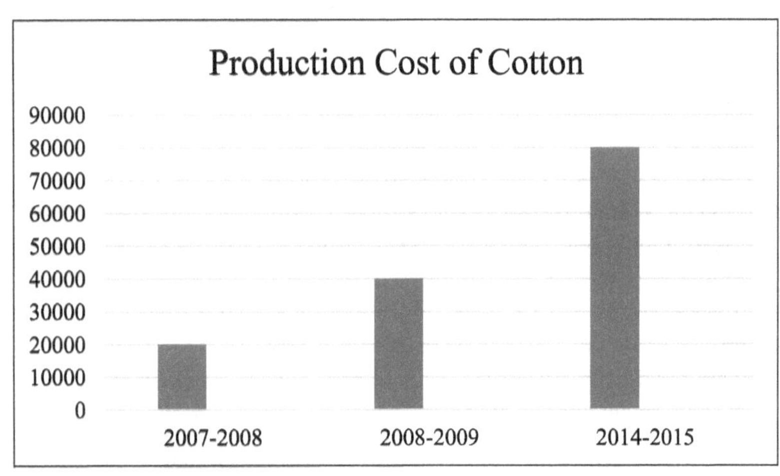

Figure 73: Increasing production cost of cotton (2007-15)

Table 8: Item-wise breakup of cost of cultivation (Rs per hectare) for the year 2014-15

	Cost Items	(₹/ha.)
	Operational Cost	92860
A	Human Labor	59437
B	Bullock Labor	33
C	Machine Labor	8897
D	Seed	3213
E	Fertilizer/Manure	8696+3738
F	Plant Protection Charges	2928
G	Irrigation charges	3632
H	Insurance	42
I	Miscellaneous	182
J	Interest on Working Capital	2060
	Fixed Cost	23274
A	Rental value of owned land	13328
B	Land revenue, cesses & taxes	9
C	Depreciation on Implements and Farm Buildings	1296
D	Interest on Fixed Capital	8642
	Total Cost	116134

Table source: Source: Directorate of Economics & Statistics, Ministry of Agriculture & Farmers' Welfare, Government of India[105].

Various components such as human labor, animal labor, machine labor, seed, fertilizer, manure, insecticides, irrigation charges and interest on working capital influence the cost of cultivation. Among the individual factors, human labor contributed the maximum to cost increase in cotton cultivation. Human labor contributed nearly 40% of the increase in total cost. Among the other components, the cost of fertilizers contributed 9.55% to an increase in the total cost. It is clear from the analysis that cultivating cotton is back-breaking work.

The cotton crop requires intensive care throughout its production, from the time of sowing seeds, regular irrigation, regular use of pesticides, and the most difficult work of handpicking the harvest.

And as if that was not enough, the cotton crop heavily drains the soil of nutrients. It requires large amounts of fertilizers to facilitate growth, and continuous cultivation of cotton leads to extreme soil degradation, making it infertile for future use.

The author would like to support this argument of not investing in cotton farming because now there are alternative fabrics purely made of plant-based cellulose which comes from husk and stems of cereal crops[106].

These fabrics need 99% less water and are by-products of the plant. Thus, they can satisfy the need for fabrics by simply using this stubble, which is currently burnt.

Conclusively, cash crops like cotton are not a sustainable alternative for marginalised farmers because they are extremely capital-intensive, time-intensive, require more human labor than regular crops, and lead to rapid soil degradation.

In this chapter, you learned:

Yes, 1 Acre is Enough!

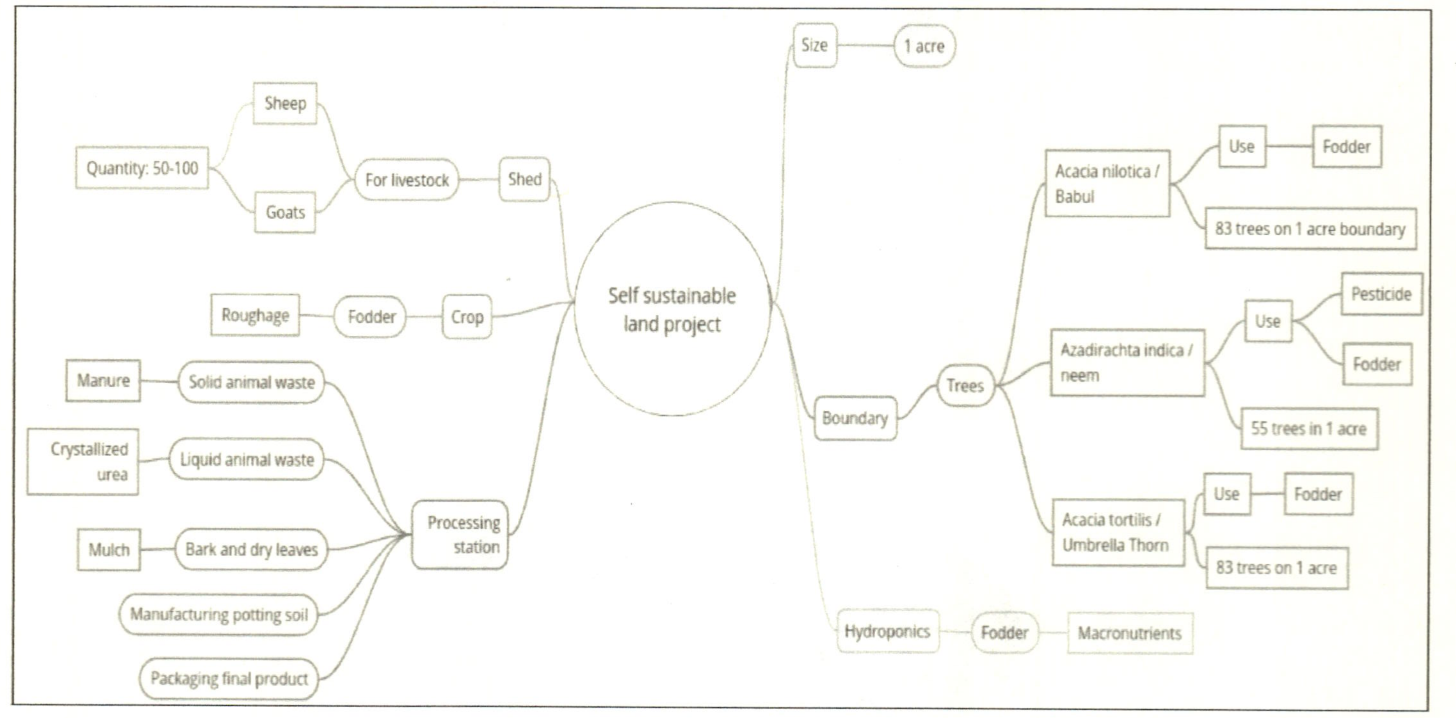

CHAPTER 3

1 Acre of Self-Sustained Land

WE STARTED THIS book with the following goals:

1. To find a sustainable alternative source of livelihood for marginalized farmers
2. A source of livelihood which is eco-friendly
3. Most importantly, it serves as a permanent solution to the problem.

Our proposed solution is livestock farming, modifying the land using organic methods for optimal use, and sustainability at grassroots levels – these 3 elements will create an end-to-end solution that will sustain generations to come.

As you read in Chapter 1, Image 4, you were Suresh's great-great-grandchild and left with only 1 acre of land (because of land fragmentation). Our solution is about how you work out a good future with 1-acre land for you and your family.

Imagine you have 1 acre of land (4046.86 sq. meters), with each side measuring 63.6 m.

Your main occupation will be livestock farming. Livestock farming refers to the activity of raising and breeding animals, commonly for obtaining certain products like milk, meat, or hide.

Different animals are raised for different purposes. For example, while oxen are raised for strength and consequent use in the fields[107], cows are raised for milk, goats for meat, and sheep for their hide.

ADVANTAGES OF REARING SMALL ANIMALS

In this particular case, for our land project, we are going to avoid raising big animals like cows and instead raise small animals like goats and sheep. There are several reasons for preferring to raise small animals over large animals:

1. Smaller animals are lightweight and thus easier to manage and raise, even in large numbers.

2. Smaller animals are more economical. In India, a single dairy cow will cost you anywhere from *₹40,000 – ₹80,000 ($479 – $959) whereas 1 female goat will cost you ₹10,000 – ₹12,000 ($119 – $144). Therefore, a goat will cost you almost 6 times cheaper than a cow. Even if we add another 5 thousand to the cost, we still have enough bandwidth to have multiple counts.*

3. Smaller animals occupy less space per animal. Following is a visual representation of the space taken up by a cow, a sheep, and a goat (in square feet).

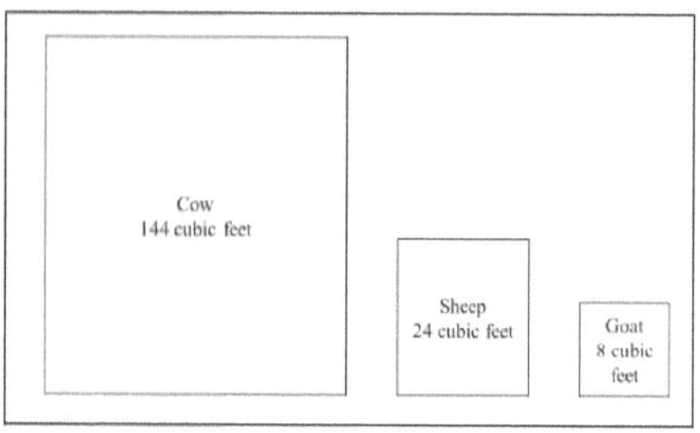

Figure 74: Visual representation of space taken by different animals

4. The bigger the animal, the more food it needs to sustain itself. Due to this fact, smaller animals once again stand at an advantage. A cow consumes approximately 25-36 kg, while a sheep consumes 2-3.5 kg, and a goat consumes 3-4 kg of fresh forage daily.

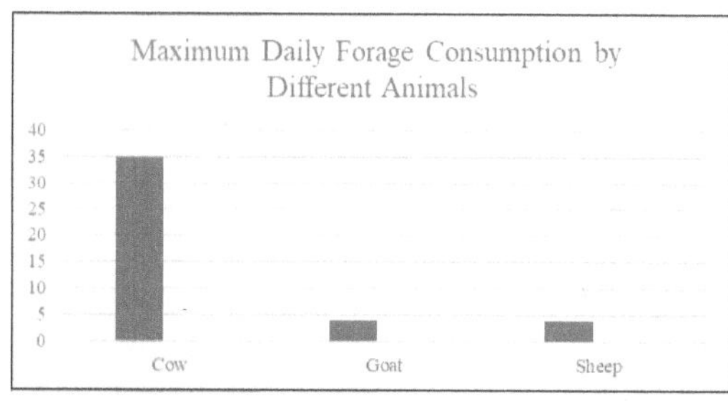

Figure 75: Food consumed by different animals on a daily basis

However, one must remember, every coin has 2 sides. Smaller animals do come with a lot of advantages, but they also come with their own risks. Risks that can be related to external factors such as an unhygienic environment, predators, seasonal changes, and internal factors such as diseases and herd management.

The good news is that you don't have to sit and understand the risks and how to manage them. We have already analyzed the risks involved in raising goats and prepared an all-round solution for risk management of the highest level, which decreases the potential harm that can be done. The author has spent 6 years studying the same and has practically implemented it.

The details of our proposed solution for risk management will come up later in Chapters 9 and 10.

Now that we have understood what kind of animals to raise for our main occupation, i.e. livestock farming, let us proceed to understand the structure of the 1-acre land.

STRUCTURE OF THE 1 ACRE LAND

This land must be divided into 4 parts, with each part measuring 1,011 sq. meters, as shown in the following diagram.

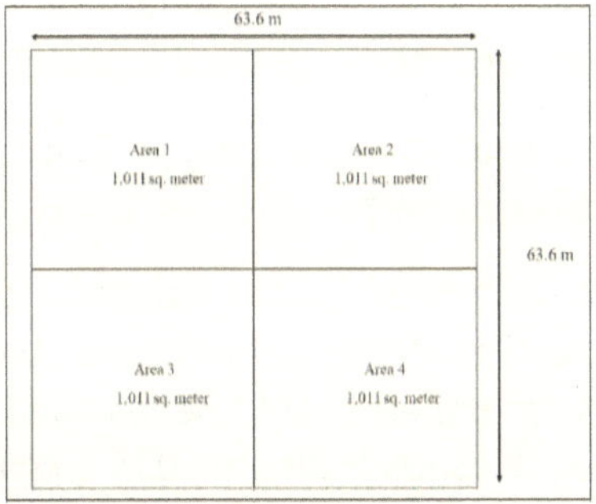

Figure 76: Diagrammatic representation of 1 acre with 4 divided areas

Along the perimeter of this plot, we are going to cultivate fodder trees such as Khejri (Prosopis cineraria), Mahua (Madhuca longifolia), Babul (Acacia nilotica), and others, whatever suits the climatic condition of that region. (For more information regarding fodder trees and their nutrition, see Chapter 4).

These trees will not only provide fodder and shade for the animals but will also prevent soil erosion as their roots will keep the soil in place. The trees will also absorb large volumes of carbon from the atmosphere, accumulating biomass.

Over time, the canopy of trees will cover the soil surface with fallen leaves. The annual leaf fall will deposit large volumes of carbon back down to the soil surface, building soil. Gradually, the top one-inch layer of soil will become rich in organic matter from the build-up of decayed plants and animals, also known as humus.

Humus contains important nutrients needed for plant growth, including nitrogen. It also gives soil the necessary structure and a crumbly, loose texture so oxygen can get in and reach the plant roots. Thus, we will have a continuous supply of fertile soil.

In area 1 we will cultivate **perennial fodder crops** or **multi-cut fodder crops.** These crops have the ability to regenerate after each cut, providing multiple harvests throughout the growing season. As the leaves regrow, this ensures a stable supply of fodder. (Detailed information on fodder crops is discussed in Chapter 6)

However, fodder crops require at least 4 months to mature, and once cut, they will take at least 5 days to regrow. Meanwhile, the livestock must be fed regularly.

Thus, in area 2, we are going to set up a hydroponics station to cultivate leafy vegetation. This will generate an additional food source for the livestock. (Detailed information on hydroponics is discussed in Chapter 8)

This area will also be used as a gathering point for the biomass produced by livestock manure and farm waste.

In area 3 we will build a shed for the livestock to live in. Livestock will produce a variety of animal products that will sustain you and your family. On the roof of the shed, solar panels should be installed to provide electricity. (Detailed information on the shed is discussed in Chapter 9)

Area 4 will be used as a processing station to process the excreta and urine of the livestock to make manure and fertilizers. (Detailed information on the processing station is discussed in Chapter 11)

For example, goat and sheep urine can be used as a basic ingredient for making liquid organic fertilizer. Organic fertilizer is the result of the decomposition of organic materials, either dry plants or waste, that is broken down by microbes, which are very important to increase the efficiency of liquid organic fertilizer derived from livestock urine.

Urine has a good nutrient content and is needed by plants. This is derived from goat and sheep and the fertilizer are produced through a fermentation process. This involves adding helpful bacteria and fungi. These indigenous microorganisms (IMO) can be found in places like animal digestive systems or on plants, and they help break down the urine and other organic materials to create a nutrient-rich fertilizer[108].

Goat urine contains approximately 1.13% nitrogen, 0.05% phosphorus, and 7.3% potassium. This nutrient composition is significantly beneficial for plant growth and soil health. Sheep urine, while less commonly detailed, generally contains high levels of nitrogen and potassium similar to goat urine.

These nutrients are crucial for plant growth and soil health. The higher potassium content in goat urine, in particular, is beneficial for plant metabolism and overall health. Manure obtained from these livestock is rich in organic matter and can be used as excellent soil fertilizer.

Our end goal is to transform this 1-acre piece of land into a self-sustaining source of livelihood, an end-to-end solution, where all our needs are met without external help. This will be a sustainable and permanent solution to the problem of land fragmentation and poverty of marginal farmers.

The livestock will provide animal products for the family's consumption, the trees will hold the soil in place and enrich it, at the same time also providing food for the livestock. The first and second areas will ensure that the livestock can have a stable food source without external investment.

You see the simple brilliance of this arrangement. It's like building a mini ecosystem on this small patch of land. This will ensure a stable income.

So, the 1-acre of land will look something like this:

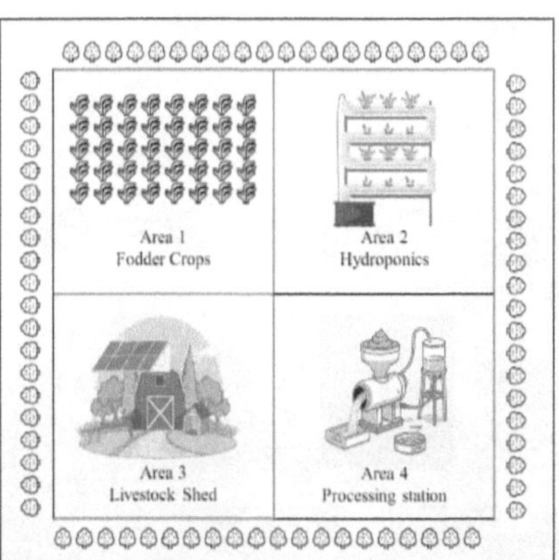

Figure 77: Diagrammatic representation of activities carried out in each of the 4 sections

In the next few chapters, we will extensively explain the workings of every individual area of land and further details regarding its implementation, revenue generation, employment generation, among other things.

In this chapter, you learned:

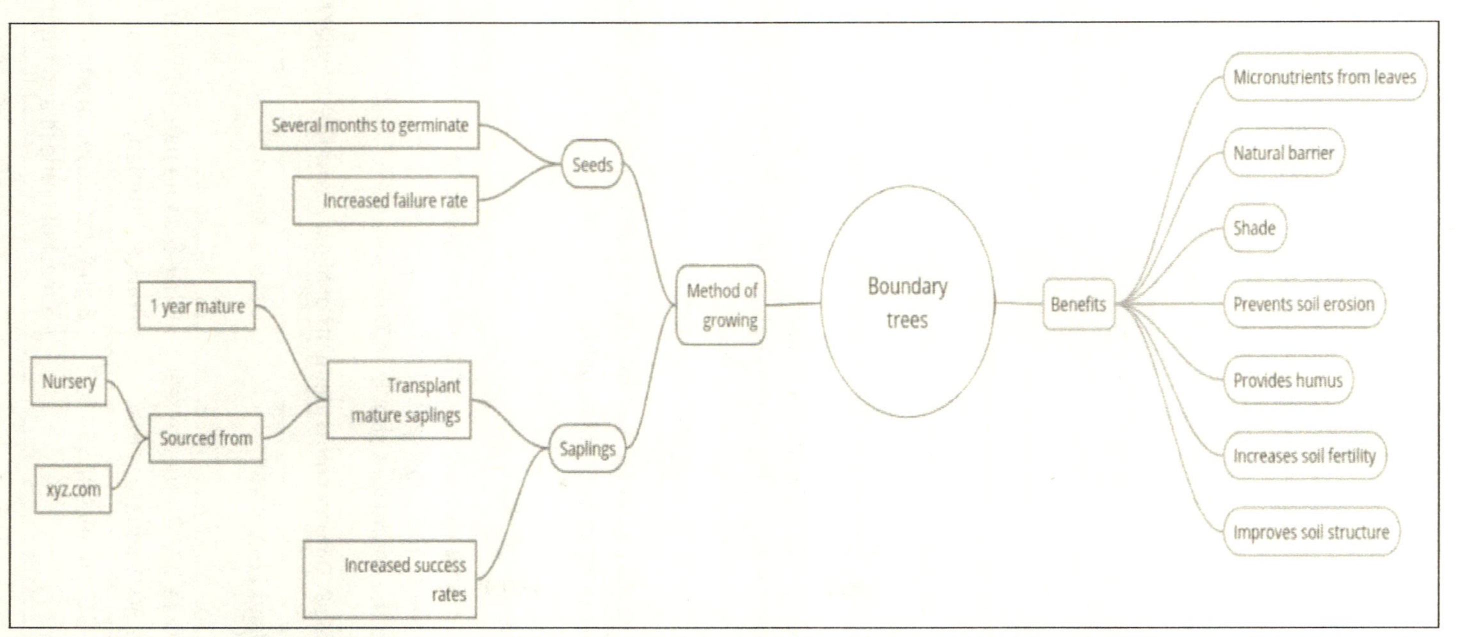

Several months to germinate
Increased failure rate
Seeds
1 year mature
Nursery
xyz.com
Sourced from
Transplant mature saplings
Saplings
Increased success rates
Method of growing
Boundary trees
Benefits
Micronutrients from leaves
Natural barrier
Shade
Prevents soil erosion
Provides humus
Increases soil fertility
Improves soil structure

CHAPTER 4

The Boundary

THE PRIMARY ISSUE is 'The ever-growing scarcity of land', hence our solution must be efficient and forward-looking. Based on our resolution of achieving the highest possible productivity without disturbing any natural process, we came up with a sustainable solution (discussed in Chapter 3).

Here is a recap of the components –

1. The perimeter of the land to be turned into a boundary made of trees.
2. The land itself is to be divided into 4 equal parts:

    a. Area 1 – To grow fodder crops
    b. Area 2 – To install a hydroponics machine for fodder
    c. Area 3 – Shed for rear animals
    d. Area 4 – Processing Station to process products for revenue generation

In this chapter, we focus on the natural barrier made with trees around the perimeter or boundary of the land.

PERIMETER OF LAND

We will take 1 acre as the proposed area required to carry out this project. Although bigha is the most popular unit of measurement in India, its size varies across the country, as shown in Table 9

Table 9: Different measurements of bigha across North India[109]

Term of Unit	Used Conversion	Used in States
1 Bigha	Pucca 27,225 square feet or 3025 square yards	Bihar & some parts of Uttar Pradesh, Punjab, Haryana
1 Bigha	8,712 sq. feet or 968 sq. yd	Bigha size is used in some parts of Himachal Pradesh and Uttarakhand.

1 Bigha	8100 sq. feet or 900 sq. yd	Bigha size is used in some parts of Himachal Pradesh and Uttarakhand.
1 Bigha	Kachha 9072 square feet or 1008.33 square yards	Some parts of Punjab, Haryana, and UP. Kachha Bigha is one-third of Pucca Bigha.

Bigha cannot be taken as a standard unit of measurement, so we use acres instead.

The total area of a 1-acre land is 43,560 square feet[110] or 4,046.86 square meters. While the area remains the same measures of the perimeter depend on the shape of the land.

If it's a square, each side will measure 208.7 feet or 63.6 m, then the total perimeter of the land will be 4 × 208.7 = 834.8 feet or 254.4 meters.

We can consider 254 or 255 meters, but if it's a rectangle, the measure of length and width could vary. For example, a rectangular piece of land of 1 acre could measure 660 ft x 66 ft (Perimeter = 1452 feet or 442 meters) or 544.5 ft x 80 ft (Perimeter = 1249 feet or 381 meters) or it could be an irregular shape.

We will proceed with 1 acre of square land which has a total perimeter of 834.84 feet or 254.4 meters (with each side measuring 208.7 feet or 63.6 meters). This is the measurement of the boundary on which trees are to be grown[111].

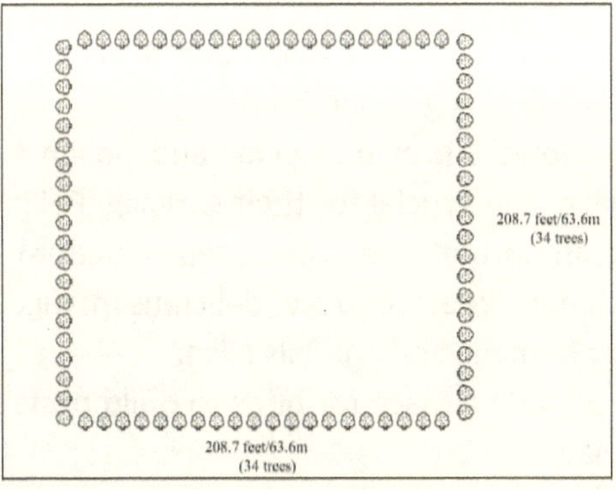

Figure 78: Diagrammatic representation showing an acre of land with a line of trees on its perimeter

WHY TREES?

In our opinion, trees are nature's nurturers. They breathe life into every element around them.

Starting from the bottom, their roots hold the soil in place, which in turn creates a habitable environment for soil microorganisms. Their stem throbs with life and provides a habitat for various kinds of flora and fauna.

For example, small animals make their home inside the trunk, and the stem acts as support for various kinds of vines and creepers.

The canopy, perhaps the most prominent feature of a tree, not only provides shade and shelter but also purifies the air around it and regulates the climate.

Let us take a mango tree. Every part of the mango tree holds importance and plays a significant role.

1. The Canopy – The large, spreading canopy of a tree provides ample shade and shelter.
2. Leaf – They perform photosynthesis, absorbing carbon dioxide from the atmosphere and releasing oxygen. This has 2 advantages:

    a. Earth's atmosphere is made up of 21% oxygen, and it's a life-giving gas for most organisms (aerobes) on this planet today. It is no surprise that forests are called the lungs of Earth.
    b. Trees absorb carbon from the environment and help to maintain the atmospheric composition.

3. Roots – Roots help bind the soil, reducing erosion and promoting soil health by maintaining its structure.
4. Flowers – Flowers provide nectar and pollen for bees and other insects, which are crucial for their survival. Pollinators such as bees play a very important role in plant reproduction[112].
5. Fruit – Mango trees produce delicious mango fruits, which are enjoyed by humans and animals alike.
6. Branches provide a place for birds to build nests and for animals to rest and play.

Figure 79: Illustration of a mango tree and its various parts

We have listed a very small portion of the many wonders that trees provide impartially. It is not to be taken for granted that they are actually life-givers. Every single tree holds a mini ecosystem within it from top to bottom.

A system that is visible to the naked eye, like providing shelter for animals, and ways that are so minuscule that we cannot even see them, yet they are of equal importance, like improving soil structure over years.

However, over decades and centuries, we humans have forgotten to appreciate these selfless beings. We have taken and taken without giving anything back to the earth. With each passing generation, the gap between us and our roots, our origin, keeps widening.

In fact, ask a random kid about the king of fruits and you will be surprised at how few know the answer.

The present generation, Gen Z, is the most impacted generation since they seem to be very much unattached from the natural environment around them. There seems to be apathy toward nature as a living being made up of micro-ecosystems. We could even claim that we, the previous generations collectively have left no means to understand and feel the connection with nature. How can they become attached to something which they never felt or saw?

With big industries and apartment buildings dotting the landscape of urban areas, while our rivers, oceans, and even mountains are dying – we have done irreparable damage to our planet, and we are nowhere near stopping and amending our mistakes.

The Gen Z can be called an 'instant noodle' generation. They are so removed from nature, from the slow processes that have built everything – from forests to fossil fuels to entire continents – around them, they no longer have patience and appreciation for gradual and incremental processes.

It takes years for a sapling to become a mature adult tree with strong roots, decades to form a new thin layer of soil, centuries to form a forest with a completely stable, diverse ecosystem and millions of years to form fossil fuels. Although this might be called slow-paced, but in the large scheme of things, this timeframe is pennies to the dollar.

Humans have disrupted this pace of nature. Take the current generation of our species, the generation which holds the future of this planet. Widespread practices of massive consumerism have become the plague of our times.

Anything and everything, from clothes to food to mobile phones, is built for short-term use. Clothes have become a symbol of status and an affluent lifestyle, and it is a race to fill one's wardrobe with more and more clothes and discard them after wearing them a couple or 3 times. The result? Mountains upon mountains of discarded non-degradable clothes polluting our deserts (like the Atacama Desert, Chile) and destroying habitats. Forget that, where does the garbage we dispose of daily go? How many of us care?

In such times, it has become an absolute necessity to educate our children in terms of sustainability. To connect them back to their roots and to encourage them to form a bond with the environment around them.

To summarize in the words of Sir David Attenborough, a renowned British broadcaster, natural historian, and author:

"If children don't grow up knowing about nature and appreciating it, they will not understand it. And if they don't understand it, they won't protect it. And if they don't protect it, who will?"

Remember our parents telling us not to eat the seeds of fruits, and us being scared of an orange tree growing out of our belly button?

How many modern parents do that? In fact, now they are interested in seedless fruits. Is that not a straightforward example of running away from nature? We just do not want to put in effort.

Now coming back to the boundary. Planting trees at the boundary is not only a sustainable solution, it is a way of rebuilding the bond with nature that our children have lost. After all, they will be the ones protecting and nurturing this land in the future. The author remembers the feeling of nurturing his trees and smiles, remembering talking to them.

There are many other benefits too of planting a wall of trees around your land. From the perspective of rearing animals on this piece of land and growing fodder crops to feed them, trees planted at the boundary play multiple roles in this little ecosystem, such as:

1. Browsing material
    a. Goats are 'browsers', which means that they like to browse through various parts of a plant and selectively eat what they like. The boundary of trees will provide them with enough material to browse through.
    b. Planting different kinds of fodder trees at the boundary will bring diversity of nutrients in the goats' diet. Different trees have different nutritional values and different parts that are consumed. For example, goats nibble on only the leaves of the Neem tree (Azadirachta indica) but they eat both leaves and pods (both fresh and dry) of the Babul tree (Acacia nilotica).
    c. Natural instinct – Browsing comes naturally to goats; we can say it is ingrained in their system. Thus, browsing not only promotes their natural behavior but also reduces stress and has a positive impact on their mental well-being. On the other hand, keeping them constrained in small enclosed spaces negatively impacts their health and increases stress levels.
    d. Physical health – Roaming around to browse through trees promotes exercise in goats and has a positive effect on their physical health. It makes them less prone to diseases, helps to maintain their muscle tone, and improves overall health.

2. Improves soil health

    a. Trees absorb nutrition from the soil for growth and development, but it's not like they deplete the nutrition levels. They give back the nutrition they take in the form of organic matter produced by decaying leaf litter. Over the period of a year, the topmost layer of soil is covered in nutrient-rich organic matter, and the nutrition goes back to the soil.

b. Tree roots retain moisture in the soil. This not only helps in preventing waterlogging on the surface but also helps in replenishing groundwater.

c. As the trees mature, their roots go deep and wide in the soil, creating channels and pores as they spread. These small spaces improve soil aeration. In simpler words, it helps the soil breathe.

d. Trees provide a habitable environment for all kinds of microorganisms in the soil. These microorganisms improve soil health by breaking down complex organic matter. Take earthworms, for example. Earthworms break down organic matter and excrete it. Their excreta is also called 'black gold' because it is so rich in nutrients.

e. Trees absorb carbon dioxide from the atmosphere through their leaves and give carbon back to the soil through their roots. Carbon as an element is known for bonding. In soil, carbon binds the grains together which leads to improved soil structure.

f. f. Roots of leguminous trees can convert atmospheric nitrogen into nitrogen compounds, which can be easily absorbed by other plants and increase soil fertility.

g. Tree canopy and roots prevent soil erosion by standing as a barrier between soil and eroding elements. The canopy reduces the impact of heavy rains and prevents water from eroding the rich top layer down to the topmost rich layer. While the roots bind the soil together and prevent erosion by strong winds.

We have covered the what and why of growing on the perimeter.

1. What to do?
   Ans. Plant trees at the boundary of our land.

2. Why do? That is, why plant trees?
   Ans. Trees have multiple benefits that we have already discussed.

It is now time to discuss the how and when. Let us go through them one by one.

Firstly, how should we do it? We are raising this question to find out the most optimal way of planting trees, which reduces the risk of failure and increases the chances of success. We have 2 options here-

1. Grow trees from seeds, that is from scratch.
2. Plant a year-old sapling which has already developed a root and shoot system and has a better chance of survival.

We would recommend going with the second approach. The reasons are:

- Germinating a sapling from a seed requires intensive care and attention as any minor external force can easily kill the sapling since it's just a baby.
- Germinating seeds do not have a 100 percent success rate. Even after weeks of care and nurturing, the seed might not germinate. If a farmer plants 50 seeds, there is no guarantee that all 50 will turn into saplings. The author conservatively estimates a 60% success rate depending on the process used.
- The activity is time-consuming and requires a lot of patience. For example, look at the following table which lists different germination periods of different species of fodder trees:

Table 10: Seed germination time

Local Name (English)	Hindi Name	Scientific Name	Seed Germination Time
Subabool	सुबहबूल	Leucaena leucocephala	1 to 3 weeks
Siris	सिरीस	Albizia lebbeck	2 to 6 weeks
Vilayati Kikar	विलायती की कर	Prosopis juliflora	2 to 8 weeks
Agasti	अगस्ति	Sesbania grandiflora	1 to 3 weeks, up to a month
Babul	बबूल	Acacia tortilis	2 to 6 weeks, but it can take longer for some species
Kumat	कुमत	Acacia senegal	2 to 6 weeks, but it can take longer for some species
Karanj	करंज	Pongamia pinnata	2 to 4 weeks

- Even after the seed has germinated, it's a long way until it turns into a sturdy plant. The chances of it dying, due to any reason, before it reaches the milestone of one year, increase the risk of failure. Imagine the acidity or alkalinity of the soil causing the sapling trauma or unfavorable conditions to thrive.

Instead of planting seeds on the boundary, we recommend planting one – or two-year-old saplings. Since they have already established a root system, they have a much higher rate of survival and require significantly less care than seedlings.

There are 2 ways of doing this:

1. Buy mature saplings (one to two-year-old) from our nearest government nursery[113]. This method saves time but costs more.
2. Create a nursery on a small area of your land where you can grow your own saplings from seeds, but in a very protected environment. The author has done the latter and recommends it for its therapeutic benefits.

The difference is, instead of directly planting seeds on the boundary, you grow them in your nursery and replant the mature saplings.

HDPE grow bags of 280 gsm, 24 inches by 24 inches, are available which could be used to plant and grow trees collectively at a different place and later transplanted.

This method is economically feasible (seeds cost less than grown saplings) but time-consuming.

Seeds and saplings of fodder can be bought on this site – sangamstrees. com or other aggregators sites.

Now comes the question of when. When should we plant trees on the boundary? The first thing to do before planting the trees is to create an artificial fencing around the land. After doing so, there are 2 approaches regarding when to plant trees.

1. Trees take years to develop. Unlike other activities to be done in area 1-4, the process of growing trees cannot be hastened. The first approach is to plant trees before starting any process of construction or installation.
2. The second approach is to carry on with the process of building the shed and installing a hydroponics machine first. Once all the other areas are completed, we can plant trees at the end.

Different varieties of fodder trees can be planted based on the climate and soil of the region.

Below are the different forms in which nutrition exists in animal feed:

1. Dry matter – Dry matter refers to feedstuff remaining after removal of water. It is calculated by determining the percentage of water and subtracting it from 100%.
    Dry matter = 100 percent minus water percentage

2. Crude protein – It is a chemical analysis of food that uses the nitrogen content to estimate the amount of protein.
3. Crude fiber – It indicates the portion of animal feed that cannot be digested and undergoes fermentation in the gut through microbial activity. It is significant in the diets of ruminant animals as it stimulates microbial activity in the gut and improves gut health.
4. Neutral detergent fiber (NDF) – It is the most commonly used measure for assessing fiber content in animal feed analysis. Forages low in NDF are usually of high quality and have high levels of intake.
5. Acid detergent fiber (ADF) – It is the least digestible plant component (including cellulose and lignin). Forages with low ADF concentrations are usually higher in energy.
6. Ether extract – It is the total fat (or crude fat) content of a feed. It may include fats, fatty acid esters, and fat-soluble vitamins.
7. Ash – It is a crude measurement of the total amounts of minerals in a diet (for example – calcium, phosphorus, iron, copper, zinc, etc).
8. Gross Energy – it represents the amount of energy in the feed.

The amount of dry matter to be fed to goats is calculated on the basis of their body weight. Following is a table with reference for feeding Sirohi goats (a goat breed from Rajasthan) based on their age, gender, and weight. The dry feed amount is calculated as 3% of their body weight for maintenance purposes.

Table 11: Dry feed requirements of goats

Age/Gender	Goat Weight (kg)	Dry Feed (kg/day)
Kid (3 months)	10	0.3
Kid (6 months)	20	0.6
Kid (9 months)	25	0.75

Adult Doe (Female)	35	1.05
Adult Doe (Female)	40	1.2
Adult Doe (Female)	45	1.35
Adult Buck (Male)	50	1.5
Adult Buck (Male)	55	1.65
Adult Buck (Male)	60	1.8

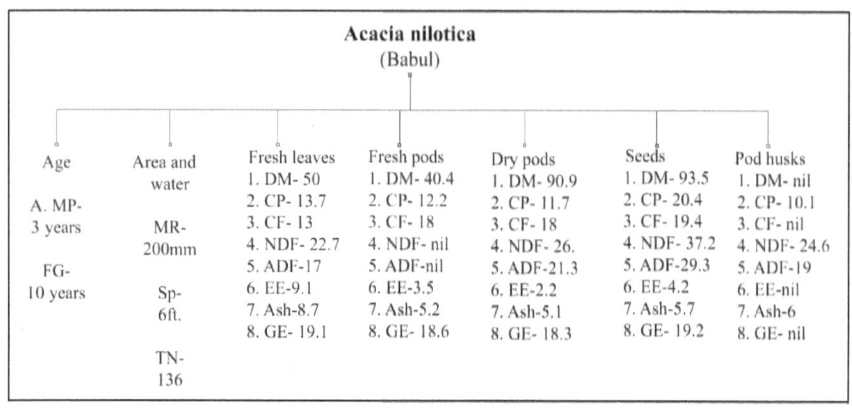

Figure 80: Nutrition in various parts of Acacia nilotica/Babul

Abbreviations used (with units of measurement):

1. A. MP – Average maturity period (in years)
2. FG – Full growth reached (in years)
3. MR – Minimum amount of rain required (in mm)
4. Sp – Space required between 2 trees (1 foot = 0.3048m)
5. TN – Number of trees that can be planted on the boundary of a 1-acre square
6. DM – Dry matter (% as fed)
7. CP – Crude protein (% DM)
8. CF – Crude fiber (% DM)
9. NDF – Neutral detergent fiber (% DM)
10. ADF – Acid detergent fiber (% DM)
11. EE – Ether extract (% DM)
12. GE – gross energy (**megajoules per kilog**ram or MJ/kg

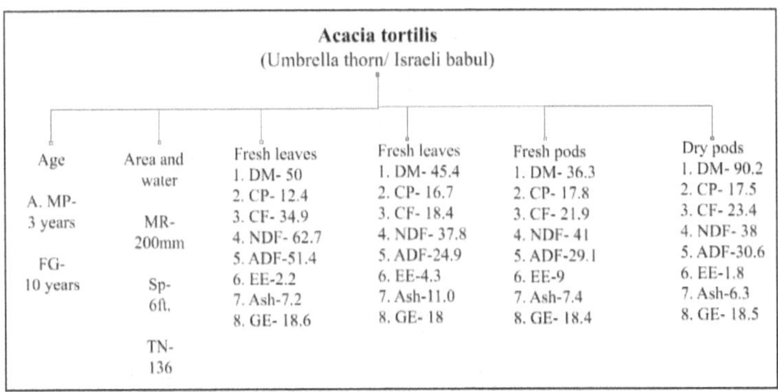

Figure 81: Nutrition in various parts of Acacia tortilis / Umbrella thorn

Abbreviations used (with units of measurement):

1. MP – Average maturity period (in years)
2. FG – Full growth reached (in years)
3. MR – Minimum amount of rain required (in mm)
4. Sp – Space required between two trees (1 foot = 0.3048m)
5. TN – Number of trees that can be planted on the boundary of a 1-acre square.
6. DM – Dry Matter (% as fed)
7. CP – Crude Protein (% DM)
8. CF – Crude Fibre (% DM)
9. NDF – Neutral Detergent Fibre (% DM)
10. ADF – Acid Detergent Fibre (% DM)
11. EE – Ether Extract (% DM)
12. GE – Gross energy (kilocalories per kg or kcal/kg)

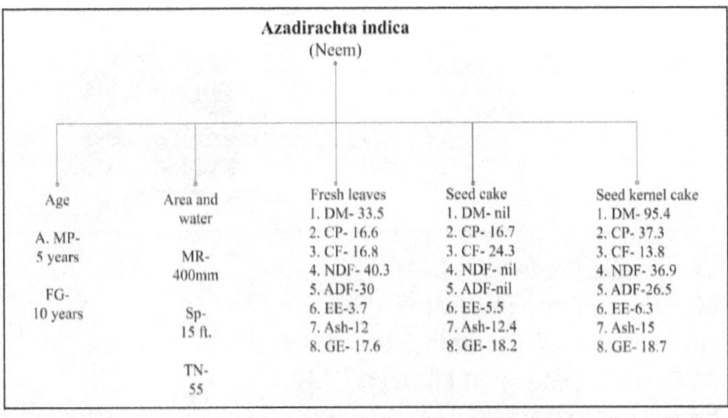

Figure 82: Nutrition in various parts of Azadirachta indica/ Neem

Abbreviations used (with units of measurement):

1. P – Average maturity period (in years)
2. FG – Full growth reached (in years)
3. MR – Minimum amount of rain required (in mm)
4. Sp – Space required between two trees (1 foot = 0.3048m)
5. TN – Number of trees that can be planted on the boundary of a 1-acre square.
6. DM – Dry Matter (% as fed)

Table 12: Acacia nilotica/Babul Picture for reference

Tree part name	Image
Fresh leaves	
Fresh pods	
Dry pods	
Seeds	

7. CP – Crude Protein (% DM)
8. CF – Crude Fibre (% DM)
9. NDF – Neutral Detergent Fibre (% DM)
10. ADF – Acid Detergent Fibre (% DM)
11. EE – Ether Extract (% DM)
12. GE – gross energy (kilocalories per kg or kcal/kg)

DRIP IRRIGATION

The main motive of creating this project is to create an ecosystem which is complete in itself. And every aspect of this project should reflect this motive by minimizing waste and using a well-thought-out approach in each scenario.

Following this aim, we propose to use drip irrigation for watering the trees instead of manual irrigation. This does not mean manual irrigation will not be required at all. You will have to manually water the trees once a week. From then on, drip irrigation pipes will ensure the soil remains moist at all times throughout the week.

Drip irrigation is a system of watering which involves 3 basic components-

1. A tank for storing water (capacity of tank varies according to irrigation needs).
2. A network of pipes connected to the tank, that reaches every nook and cranny of the area to be irrigated.
3. Emitters or in simple language, openings. The emitters are openings in the pipe and are placed near the roots of plant to be irrigated.

The process of setting up a drip irrigation system requires calculated decisions. Even a small error like not taking the elevation of the tank into consideration can drastically reduce the efficiency of the whole system.

To avoid such errors, let us understand, in depth, the role of each component and the most optimal way to use it.

Water Tank

When installing a water tank for drip irrigation, there are some things to take into consideration-

1. Tank size – The size of the tank you buy depends on the water needs of your trees or crop. For example, look at the following table showcasing water requirements of different fodder trees of arid and semi-arid regions.

Table 13: Water Requirement of Different Trees

Local Name	Scientific Name	Young (Years)	Water Requirement (Young)	Mature (Years)	Water Requirement (Mature)
सुबाबूल (Subabool)	Leucaena leucocephala	0-3	2-4 liters/day	3+	1-2 liters/day
सिरस (Siris)	Albizia lebbeck	0-3	3-5 liters/day	3+	1.5-3 liters/day
विलायती कीकर (Vilayati Kikar)	Prosopis juliflora	0-3	1-2 liters/day	3+	0.5-1 liter/day
अगस्ति (Agasti)	Sesbania grandiflora	0-2	4-6 liters/day	2+	2-3 liters/day
बबूल (Babul)	Vachellia nilotica	0-3	2-4 liters/day	3+	1-2 liters/day
कुमात (Kumat)	Acacia senegal	0-3	2-4 liters/day	3+	1-2 liters/day
करंज (Karanj)	Pongamia pinnata	0-3	3-5 liters/day	3+	1.5-3 liters/day

2. Location: Setting up the tank at a good location is important for optimal use. The tank should be close to the area that needs to be irrigated so that we don't have to spend a lot on installing pipes.

We recommend placing 2 tanks at both ends of your land.

3. Foundation: The foundation on which the tank is to be placed should be solid. You have to understand that this project is going to stand for a long time, and your approach has to be such that you do not have to perform frequent maintenance.

4.   Elevation: The height at which the tank should be placed.

There are 2 ways to ensure water pressure in the pipes connected to the tank. They are:

I. Gravity-fed

This method depends on the elevation of the tank. This system operates by harnessing the natural force of gravity. Gravitational force facilitates the downward flow of water through the pipes. To ensure uniform water distribution to all plants, it is crucial to appropriately leverage the gravitational force. We have to apply laws of physics pertaining to the volume of water, the pressure expected, the distance the water has to travel and also the friction that will impact the water flow. However, we will not bother you with the calculations and give you the recommended height.

We recommend that the tank should be kept at a height of 2m/8 feet above the ground to ensure equal pressure of water throughout the length of the pipe.

II. Pump

This method uses a submersible pump, the kind you see in desert coolers, to send water with slight force, generating pressure throughout the pipe.

From Table 5, we can infer the average amount of water required by fodder trees in arid and semi-arid regions.

Average Water Requirement per Day

For young trees: Average water needed per tree = 3 liters/day

Total for 136 young trees: 3 liters /day × 136 = 408 liters /day

For mature trees: Average water needed per tree = 2 liters/day

Total for 136 mature trees: 2 liters/day × 136 = 272 liters/day

This requirement can be easily fulfilled by a 500 – or 1000-liter tank. This is just an example to explain what to consider when determining the capacity of the water tank.

The numbers may vary based on tree species, number of trees planted, soil type, and climate.

The drip irrigation system is a one-time investment. Once it is placed, it will ensure-

1. Water is not overused
2. Each plant gets the required amount of water
3. It minimizes the risk of overwatering
4. It minimizes the risk of underwatering and
5. Delivers water directly to the roots of the plant preventing evaporation or runoff.
6. As the drip system waters, the roots directly, there is minimum wild growth below the tree canopy.
7. We can control the amount of water to be delivered, increasing precision and efficiency based on seasonal demands. To facilitate this, the water tank is strategically positioned at an elevated level.

The length of the pipe required for drip irrigation depends on the perimeter of the land in question. In the case of boundary plantation, more often than not, the length of the pipe required is equal to the perimeter of the land. So, for a 1-acre square land, the total length of the pipe required for boundary plantation would be 254.4 meters.

After taking care of the boundary, we must choose how to proceed further regarding the preparation of the 4 areas. We can either follow a consecutive or a concurrent approach. Our proposal is to work in 2 phases.

Phase 1 is to work on area 1 and area 3 concurrently, and Phase 2 is to work on area 2 and area 4 concurrently.

Phase 1 is followed by Phase 2. In the author's opinion, it is advisable to work in parallel on areas that require the same type of labor.

The course of action in this scenario is essentially labor-specific. Parallel preparation of the areas will ensure optimal utilization of resources and time and is also cost-effective.

In this chapter, you learned:

Coming up...

Carbohydrates
Proteins
Fats
Nutrition in goats
Vitamins
Minerals
Micronutrients
Macronutrients

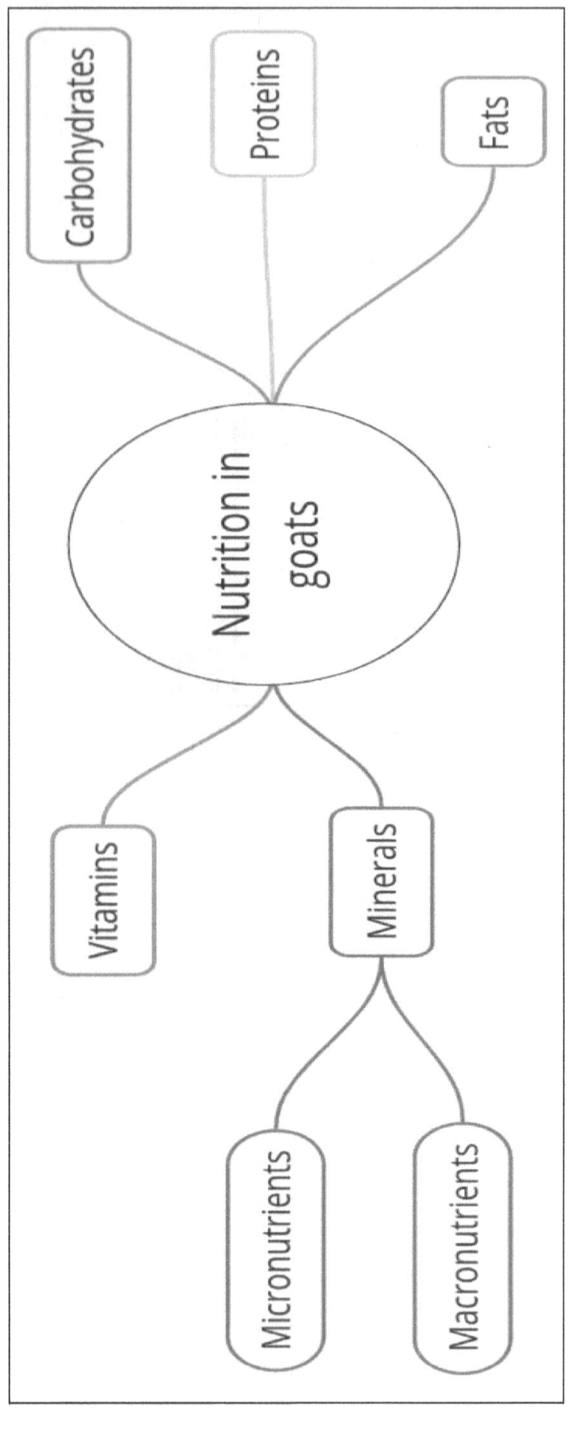

CHAPTER 5

Nutrition in Goats

THE FIRST AREA we will focus on after the boundary of trees is area 1, where fodder crops will be cultivated.

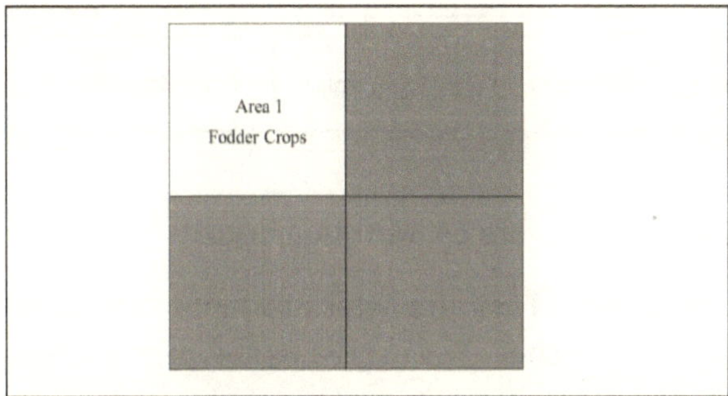

Figure 83: Area 1 where fodder crops will be cultivated

Before we get into the details of growing fodder crops, let us first understand the purpose of cultivating. The primary objective is to feed our livestock, but we also have to understand the different kinds of nutrients our livestock needs and what kind of crops provide each kind of nutrient[114].

The purpose of growing fodder is to provide the following nutrients to the livestock.

1. Roughage
2. Carbohydrates
3. Protein
4. Minerals
5. Vitamins
6. Fats

WHAT IS NUTRITION?

Nutrition is the process of providing or obtaining the food necessary for health and growth[115].

Food is defined as any substance that an organism consumes for nutritional support. It plays a crucial role within the organism's body by supporting growth, aiding in repairs, sustaining vital processes (breathing, reproducing, excreting, etc.), and providing energy.

Below is a list of nutrition requirements in goats.

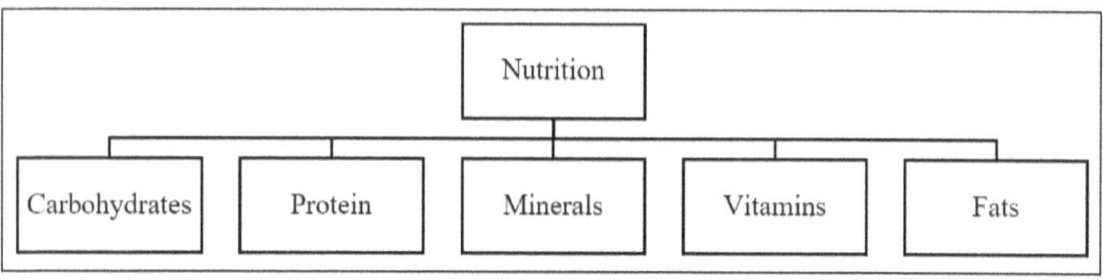

Figure 84: Nutrition in goats

1. **Carbohydrates**: They are vital nutrients that consist of sugars, fibers, and starches. They serve as the primary source of energy for goats.
2. **Fibers (carbohydrate)**: It contains cellulose which acts as roughage. Roughage is food with high fiber content, typically containing 18% crude fiber or more. They tend to be low in energy. Fiber adds volume (consumed in bulk) to a goat's diet and helps maintain a healthy digestive system.
3. **Proteins**: These are made up of building blocks known as amino acids. The body utilizes them for growth, production, and maintenance. In the diet, protein serves the purpose of accumulating new body mass and replacing proteins lost through regular wear and tear.
4. **Minerals**: They are inorganic nutrients[116]. They are crucial for proper functioning of the body and are needed in small quantities. They are further subdivided into-

   a. Macro minerals
   b. Micro minerals

5. **Vitamins**: They are organic compounds, needed in small quantities. They are crucial components in the body's metabolic machinery and aid in various metabolic processes. If there's not enough of a specific

vitamin, it can slow down or stop the particular process it's supposed to help with. Vitamins are classified into 2 types:

    a. Fat-soluble: Vitamins that dissolve in fat and are absorbed more efficiently by the body.

    b. Water-soluble: Water-soluble vitamins dissolve in water and cannot be stored in the body.

6. **Fats, or lipids**: They are rich in energy. In goat (and other ruminants) diets, the fat content is generally low, because of the low-fat content in plants. Fats can be stored and act as an energy source, particularly during periods of high energy demand, such as lactation[117].

NUTRITIONAL REQUIREMENT IN GOATS (per day)

Table 14: Nutritional requirement in goats (per day)

Age Group	Gender	Protein (g)	Carbo hydrates (g)	Roughage (g)	Minerals (g)	Vitamins	Fats (g)
Kid	Male/ Female	100-200	200-300	500-1000	50-100	As Required	30-60
Mature	Male	150-250	300-400	1000-2000	100-150	As Required	40-80
Mature	Female	150-250	300-400	1000-2000	100-150	As Required	40-80
Mature	Pregnant	200-300	400-500	1200-2200	150-200	As Required	50-100
Old	Male/ Female	100-150	200-300	800-1600	50-100	As Required	30-60

OPTIONS AVAILABLE TO SUPPLY THE NUTRIENTS

Table 15: Options available to supply the nutrients

Nutrient	Option 1	Option 2	Option 3
Protein (g)	200 g of Lucerne hay (लुसर्न घास)	200 g of Soybean meal (सोयाबीन खली)	200 g of Cottonseed cake (रुई के बीज की खली)
Carbohydrates (g)	350 g from Maize (मक्का)	350 g from Barley (जौ)	350 g from Oats (जई)

Nutrient	Option 1	Option 2	Option 3
Roughage (g)	1500 g from Berseem (बरसीम)	1500 g from Local grasses (स्थानीय घास)	1500 g from Sorghum stover (ज्वार का भूसा)
Minerals (g)	125 g of Mineral mix (खनिज मिश्रण)	125g from Salt Lick (नमक चाट)	125g of Limestone (चूना पत्थर)
Fats (g)	60 g of Linseed cake (अलसी का खाली)	60 g of Mustard cake (सरसों का खली)	60 g of Groundnut cake (मूंगफली का खली)
Vitamins	Provided through green leafy vegetables (हरी पत्तेदार सब्जियाँ)	Provided through vitamin supplements (विटामिन की खुराक)	Provided through Fresh Forage (ताजा चारा)

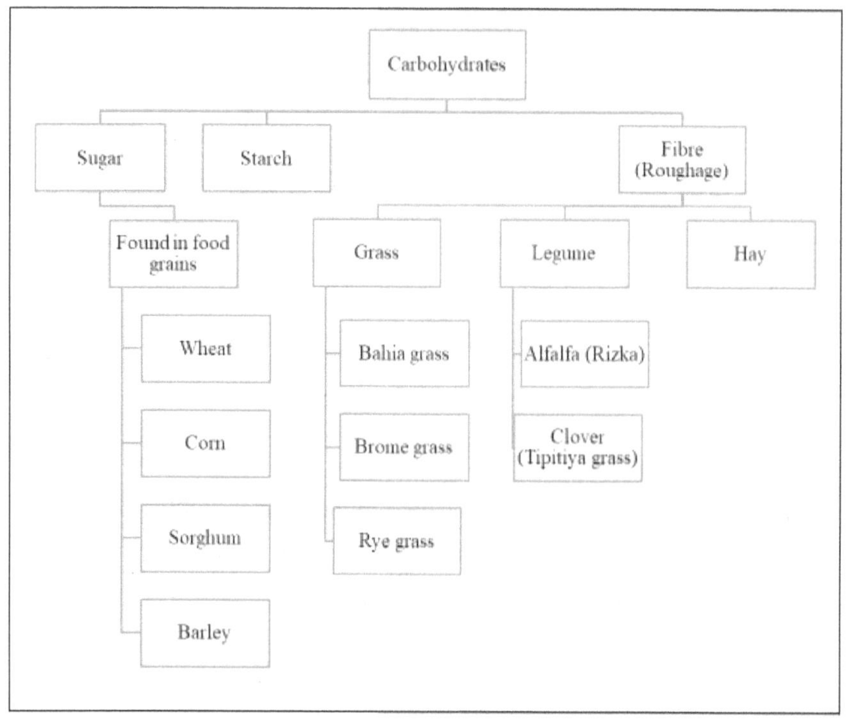

Figure 85: Different sources of carbohydrates in a goat's diet

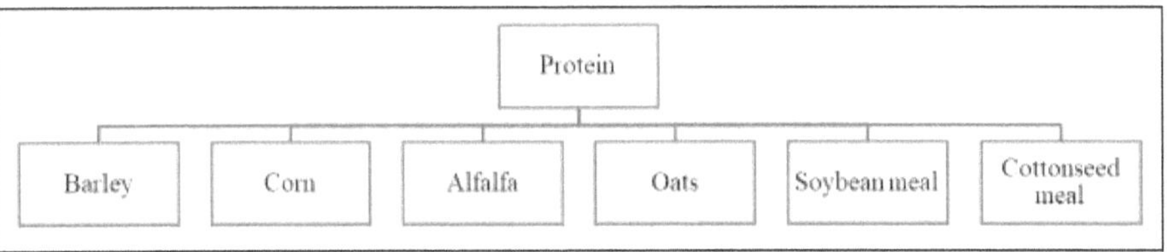

Figure 86: Different sources of protein in a goat's diet

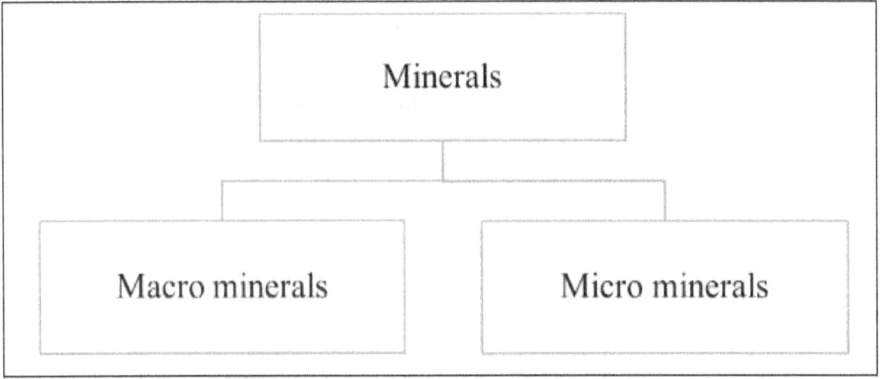

Figure 87: Different types of minerals in a goat's diet

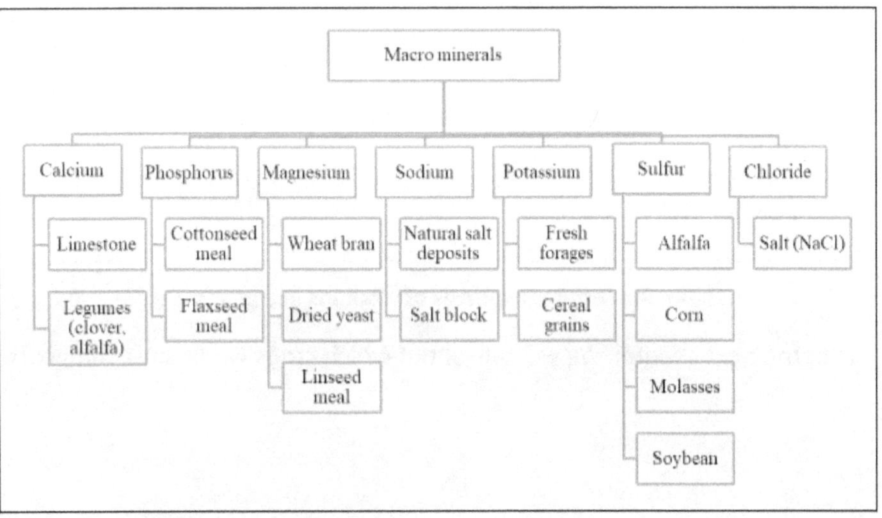

Figure 88: Different sources of macrominerals in a goat's diet

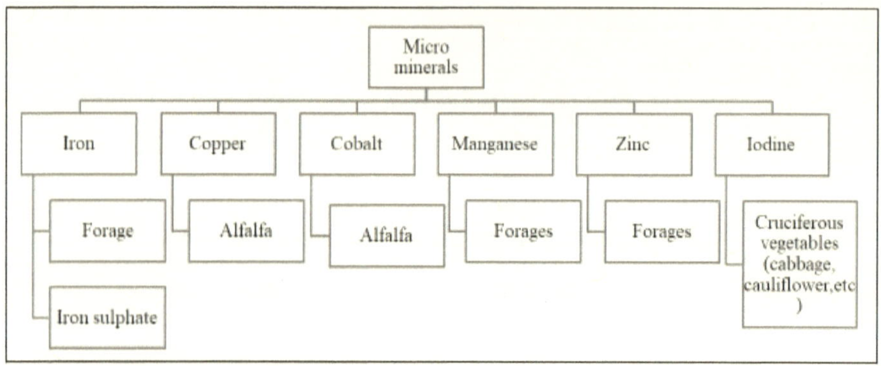

Figure 89: Different sources of microminerals in a goat's diet

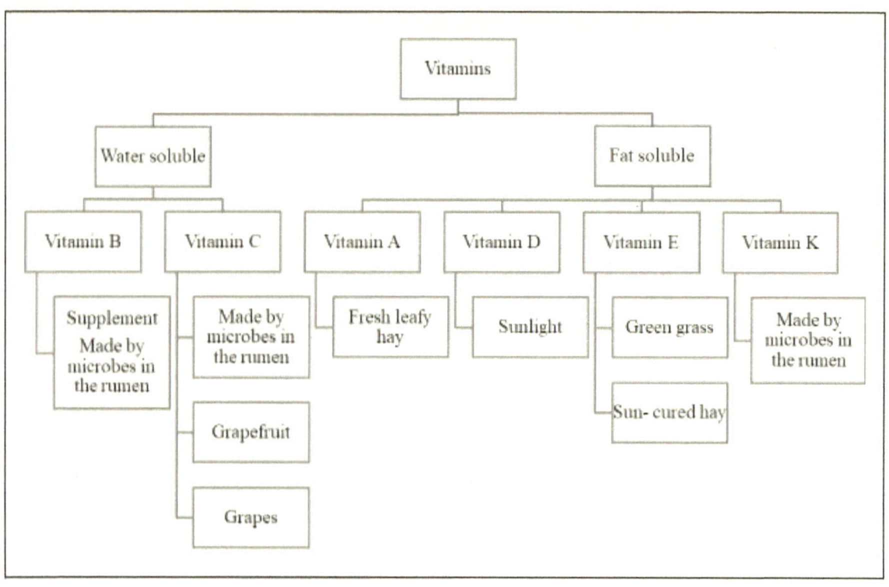

Figure 90: Different sources of vitamins in a goat's diet

In the next chapter, we will talk about which crops would best suit goats.

In this chapter, you learned:

Coming up...

pH
NPK ratio
Soil testing
Soil
Seed
Fertilizer
Irrigation
Disease prevention
Harvest time
Yield
Nutrition
Roughage
Input
Output
Purpose
Crops
Fodder
Crops of arid, semi arid regions
Diseases
Cowpea
Alfalfa
Pearl millet
Napier grass
Organic cure
Organic prevention

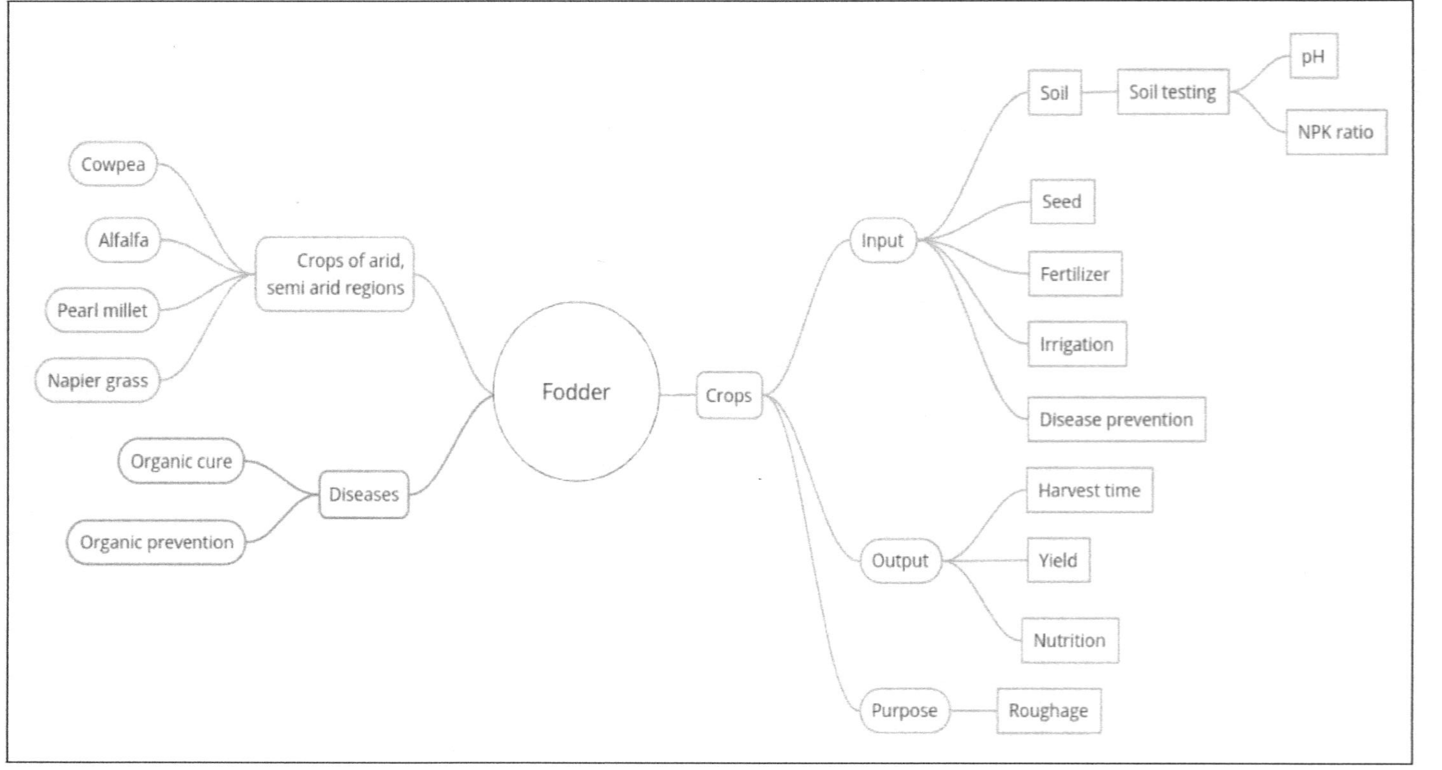

CHAPTER 6

Fodder Crops

GOATS REQUIRE ROUGHAGE, protein concentrates, mineral supplements, and vitamins in their diet.

Figure 91: Nutrients required in a goat's diet

Fodder crops will be a source of roughage; therefore, we should aim to grow bulk crops with multi-cut varieties (i.e. can be cut numerous times without uprooting).

In this chapter, we will be focusing on area 1 where we will grow fodder crops for the livestock.

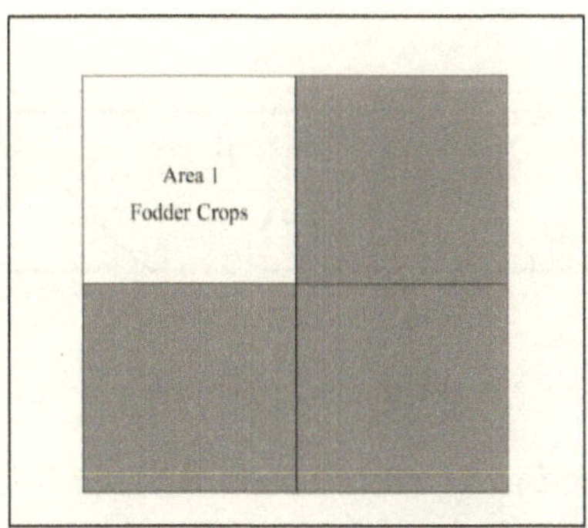

Figure 92: Area to grow fodder crops

Before commencing cultivation, we have to prepare the land. The process of preparing the land for cultivation has 3 steps:

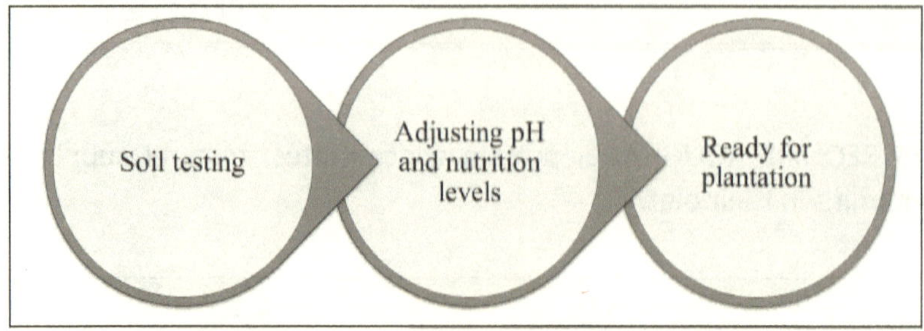

Figure 93: Steps of preparing land for cultivation

SOIL TESTING

Soil testing refers to the process of collecting soil from your land before planting and getting it tested to check the soil pH and nutrition levels. Let us understand this from the basic level.

- **pH Level**

Technically, pH stands for potential of hydrogen. It is effectively a measure of the concentration of hydrogen ions in a substance. But we do not need to get into the technicality of the term.

For our benefit, we only need to understand that pH informs how acidic, alkaline, or neutral the soil is. The pH scale ranges from 0 to 14, with 0-6 being acidic (0 is the most acidic), 7 being neutral, and 8-14 being alkaline (14 being the most alkaline).

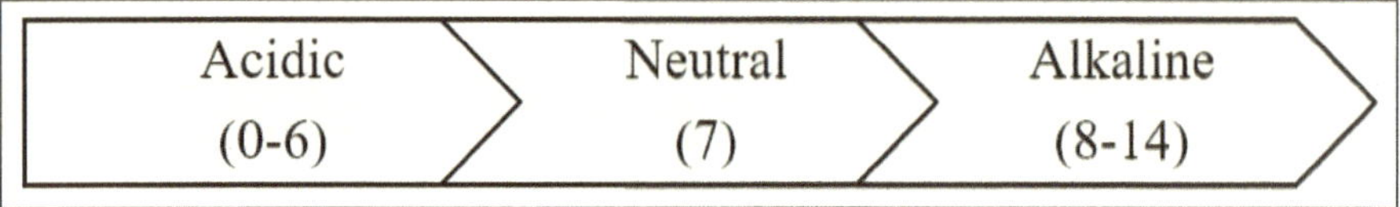

Figure 94: pH scale

But why do we need to know the soil pH? That is because it plays a very important role in plant growth.

Different plants need different kinds of soil pH for healthy growth. For example, plants like onions, potatoes, and tomatoes grow well in acidic soil, while others like peas and cabbage prefer alkaline soils, and others like pomegranate and celery prefer neutral soil.

If we plant tomatoes in alkaline soil, it will be a hindrance to their development. Knowing your soil is the best way to ensure you are providing the best possible environment for your crops.

- **Nutrition Level**

Nutrition level refers to the presence of the 3 primary nutrients that plants require: Nitrogen, Phosphorus, and Potassium, or NPK. These 3 are the primary nutrients.

Secondary nutrients include Calcium (Ca), Magnesium (Mg), and Sulfur (S).

Micronutrients include Iron (Fe), Manganese (Mn), Zinc (Zn), Copper (Cu), Boron (B), Molybdenum (Mo), Chlorine (Cl), and Nickel (Ni).

Why do we need to know the nutritional level of soil? So that we can have a balanced ratio of all nutrients. This will ensure that our crop has all the nutrients it needs, nothing less, nothing more.

WHAT IS NPK RATIO?

The NPK ratio tells you the percentage of each of these 3 nutrients. For example, an NPK ratio of **5:2:1** means that the crop requires-

- 5 parts Nitrogen
- 2 parts Phosphorus
- 1-part Potassium

To understand it better, look at the following table with NPK ratios of different crops.

Table 16: Nutrition requirement of crops

Crop	NPK Ratio
High Nitrogen Crops	
Corn (Maize)	5:2:1
Wheat	4:2:1
Rice	4:2:1
Barley	4:2:1
High Phosphorus Crops	
Beans (Legumes)	1:2:2
Root Vegetables	2:3:2
Tomatoes	2:3:1
Garlic	1:2:2
High-Potassium Crops	
Bananas	3:1:6
Potatoes	3:1:5
Tomatoes	3:1:4
Carrots	3:1:4

By knowing the nutritional level of your soil and the nutrition requirements of your crop, you can ensure that the soil has all the required nutrients for the healthy growth of the crop.

Now that we have understood what to test for, let us get to the 'how' part of our question. First of all, how do we collect a soil sample for testing?

As simple as it sounds, it is not just collecting soil from your field. To get an accurate measure of soil health on your land, you must follow a logical process to collect the soil. We have listed the simplified steps and provided a visual illustration to help you understand.

You will need:

1. A clean spade or trowel
2. A bucket.

3. A clean cloth/plastic sheet
4. Sample bags or containers (preferably clean bags).
5. A marker or pen for labelling.

Step 1: Divide Land Based on Visual Observation

- Walk around your field and observe any visible differences in soil color, texture (sandy, clayey, loamy), or plant growth. You can feel the soil with your hands. Some areas may feel grittier (sandy) or sticky (clay).
- Use these differences to divide your land into different sections. Let us assume you divide the area into 3 sections based on your observations.

Step 2: Collect Soil Samples

- In each section, collect soil from 5 to 10 different spots to get a representative sample.
- Process of collecting samples:

    i.   Remove any surface litter such as leaves, stones, or debris.
    ii. Dig a V-shaped hole up to a depth of about 15-20 cm (for field crops) or 30 cm (for deep-rooted crops).
    iii. Slice a 1-2 cm thick vertical section of soil from the side of the hole and place it in the bucket.
    iv. Repeat this at various spots within the section.

Table 17: Examples of field and deep-rooted fodder crops

Field Fodder Crops	Local Hindi Names (Script)	Deep-Rooted Fodder Crops	Local Hindi Names (Script)
Maize (Corn)	मक्का	Lucerne (Alfalfa)	राजका
Sorghum	ज्वार	Pigeon Pea	अरहर/तूर
Pearl Millet (Bajra)	बाजरा	Napier Grass	नेपियर घास
Barley	जौ	Sesbania	ढैंचा
Oats	जई	Cenchrus (Buffel Grass)	सेवन

Field Fodder Crops	Local Hindi Names (Script)	Deep-Rooted Fodder Crops	Local Hindi Names (Script)
Ryegrass	राईग्रास	Guar (Cluster Bean)	ग्वार
Berseem (Egyptian Clover)	बरसीम	Hybrid Napier	हाइब्रिड नेपियर

Step 3: Prepare Sample and Take for Testing

- Mix all the soil samples from one section thoroughly in the bucket.
- Spread the soil on a clean cloth or plastic sheet and let it dry in the shade (avoid direct sunlight).
- Once dried, mix the soil again and remove any pebbles, roots, or other debris.
- Take about 500 grams of the mixed soil and place it in a clean, labeled plastic bag or container.
- Label the bag with details like:

    i. Your name
    ii. Field section
    iii. Date of sampling
    iv. The crop you intend to grow

- Take your soil samples to the nearest soil testing lab or agricultural extension center.

    i. Contact local agricultural extension offices or Krishi Vigyan Kendra (KVKs) [118]in India. They often provide soil testing services at subsidized rates.
    ii. Many state governments and agricultural universities have soil testing labs. Farmers can send their samples to these labs for analysis. For example, here are some from the state of Rajasthan:

1. Rajasthan Agricultural Research Institute (RARI)
   Location: Durgapura, Jaipur

2. Rajasthan State Seed and Organic Production Certification Agency
   Location: Jaipur

3. Swami Keshwanand Rajasthan Agricultural University (SKRAU)
    Location: Bikaner

4. Maharana Pratap University of Agriculture and Technology (MPUAT)
    Location: Udaipur

    iii. Purchase affordable soil testing kits available in the market. These kits are also available online on aggregator sites.

Once you have done soil testing, you will know what nutrients your soil lacks and what its pH is. The next step after this is to adjust these levels to the requirements of your crop.

In this chapter, we have covered the first and last steps of preparing land and cultivating, that is how to test the soil and how to harvest the crop.

The process of adjusting the nutrition level in the soil by adding fertilizers is covered in Chapter 7.

Let us now move on to the details of crops to grow. Crops grown for roughage can be grown in combination with other crops. However, annual bulk crops that grow all year round can suffice the need for roughage in the goats' diet.

The growth of crops can be sped up artificially through genetic modification, but in order to have an organic, non-genetically modified/ altered food chain, we should prefer to use non-GMO[119] fodder[120].

Below is a list of 4 types of crops suitable to grow in arid[121] and semi-arid regions[122].

Table 18: Fodder crops of Arid and Semi-arid regions

Crop	Common Hindi name	Picture
Cowpea	लोबिया	
Alfalfa	राजका	
Pearl millet/	बाजरा	
Anjan grass	अंजन घास	

In India, arid regions comprise largely of the desert of Rajasthan, the Rann of Kutch, and the rain shadow area of the Western Ghats covering the states of Maharashtra, Karnataka, and Tamil Nadu. The semi-arid regions comprise the states of Punjab and Gujarat.

We recommend the reader to refer to the report on 'Nutritive Value of Commonly Available Feeds and Fodder in India'[123] (by Animal Nutrition Group, National Dairy Development Board) for more information on fodder crops grown in other types of climates and soil types.

To identify the climate of your region, you can consult government websites, which offer diverse information such as temperature, precipitation, wind speed, and more. By analyzing these factors, one can readily determine the prevailing climate in a specific area.

INPUT AND OUTPUT IN FODDER CROPS

Following is a detailed explanation of the input and output that goes into cultivating the fodder crops listed above.

Input – By input, we are referring to the raw materials required. It is a combination of the following –

1. Soil
2. Seed
3. Nutrient requirement
4. Irrigation
5. Diseases

Output – By output, we are referring to the outcome produced. It is a combination of the following –

6. Harvest time
7. Yield
8. Nutrition

Vigna unguiculata / Cowpea / Lobia[124] (Summer crop)

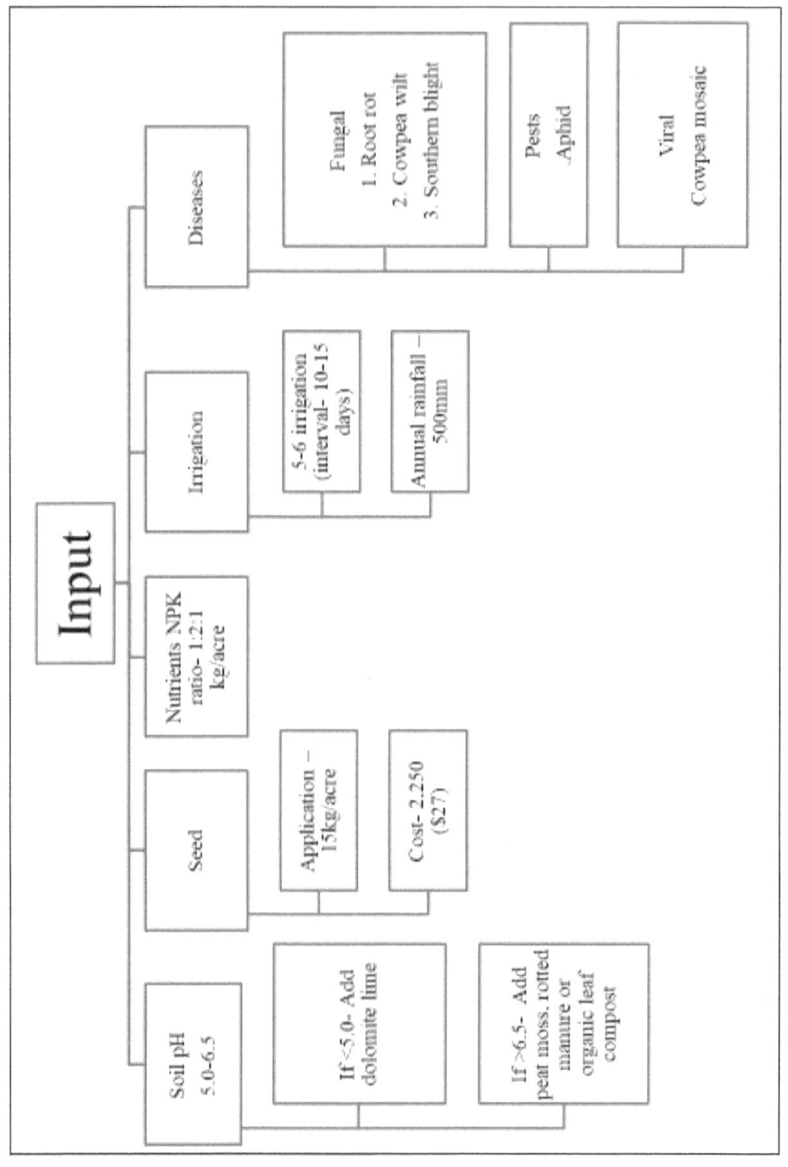

Figure 95: Input required in Cowpea/Lobia crop

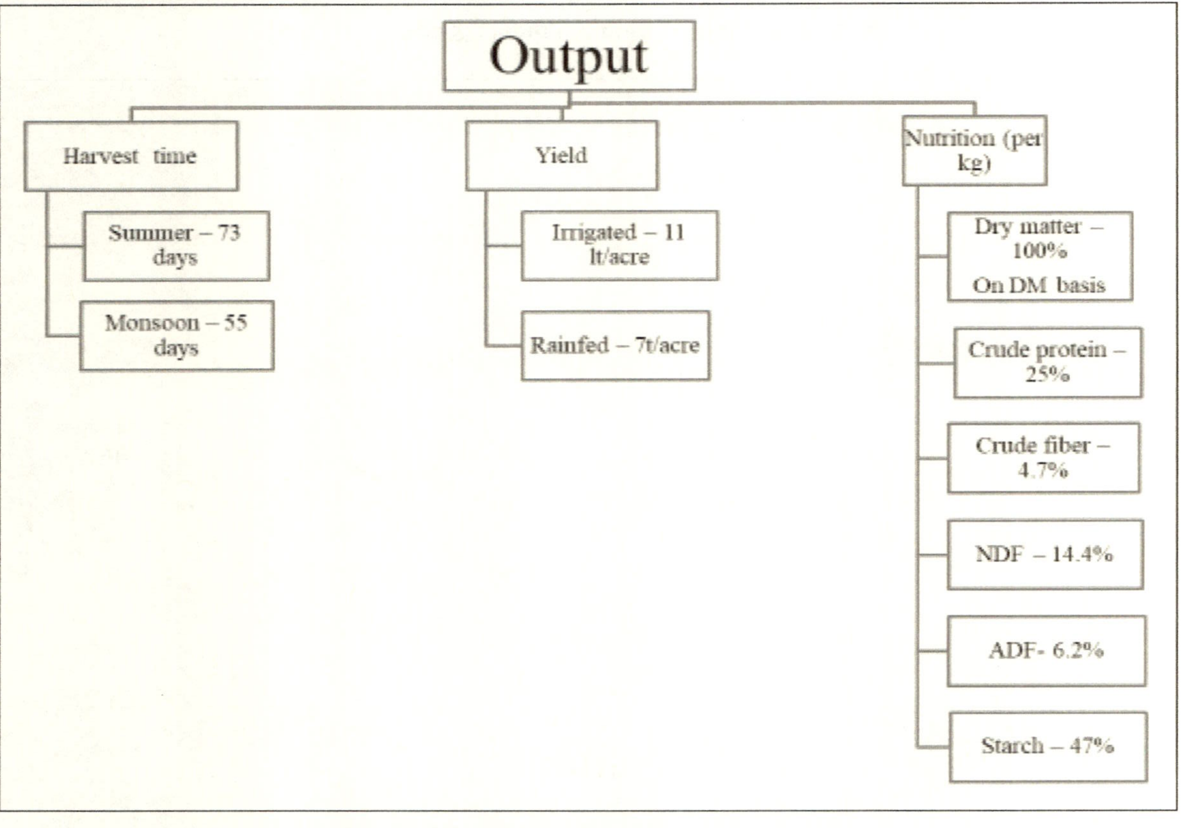

Figure 96: Output received in Cowpea/Lobia crop

Medicago sativa/ Lucerne/ Alfalfa/ Rizka (Winter crop)[125]

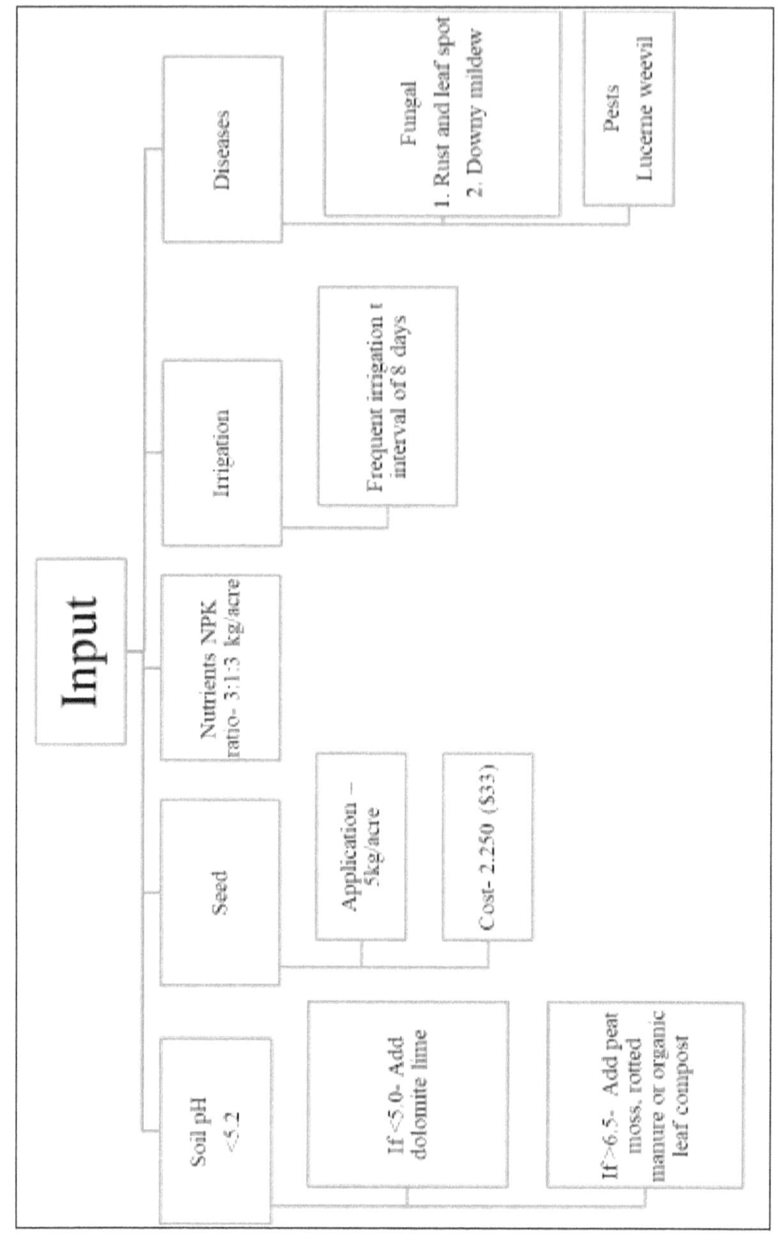

Figure 97: Input required in Alfalfa/Rizka crop

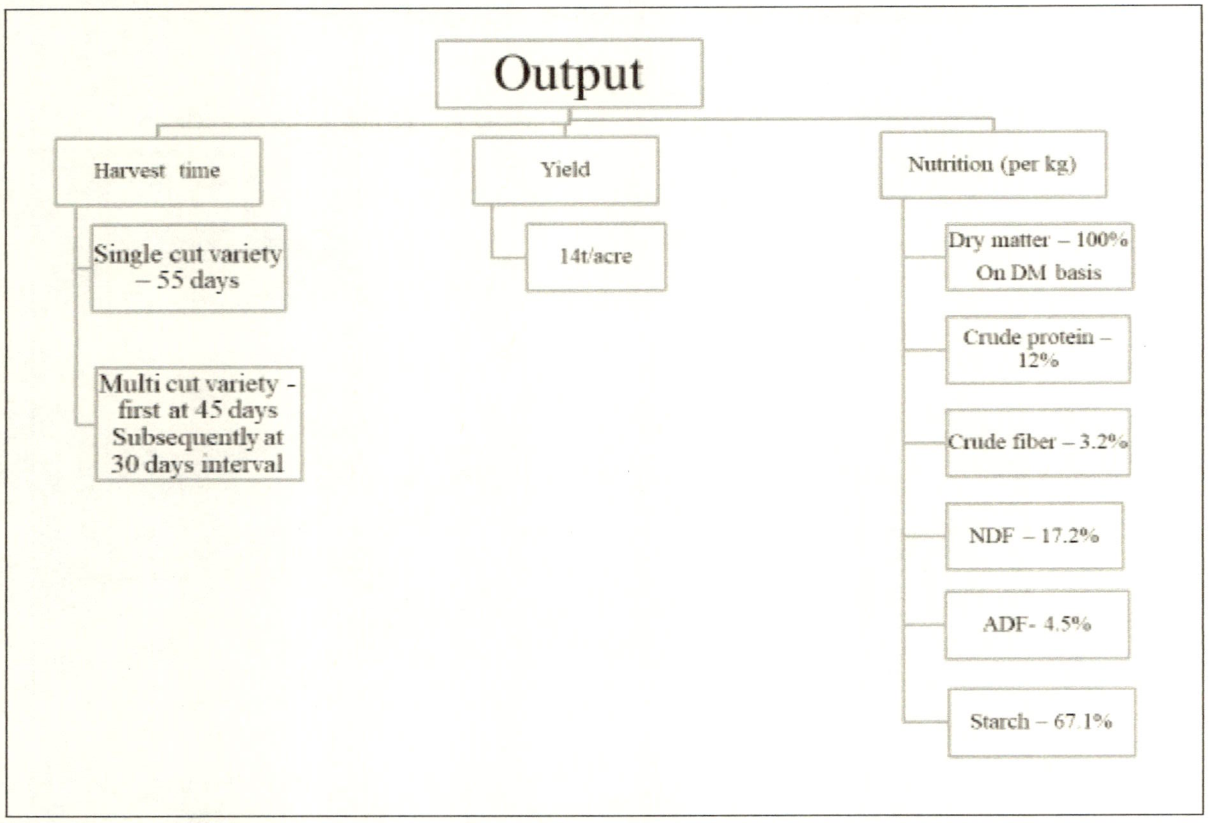

Figure 98: Output received in Alfalfa/Rizka crop

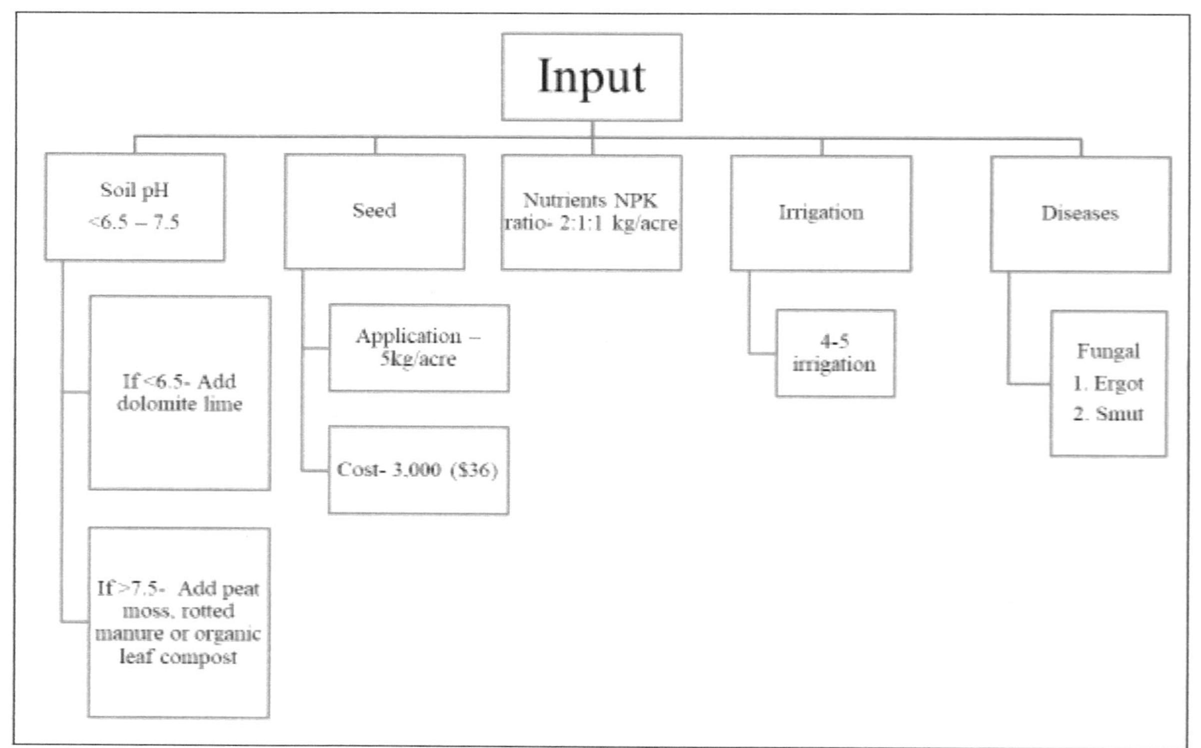

Figure 99: Input required in Pearl millet/Bajra crop

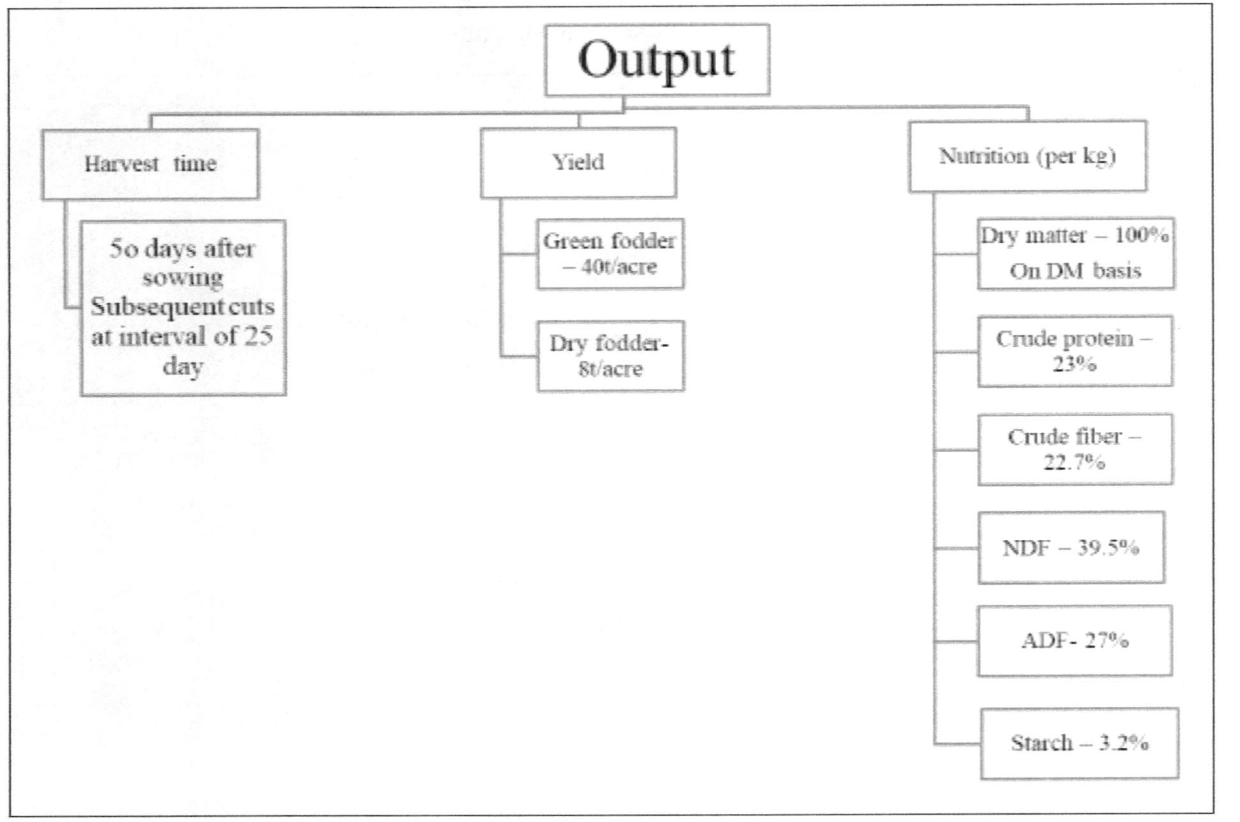

Figure 100: Output received in Pearl millet/Bajra crop

Pennisetum purpureum/Napier grass/Hathi ghas[127]

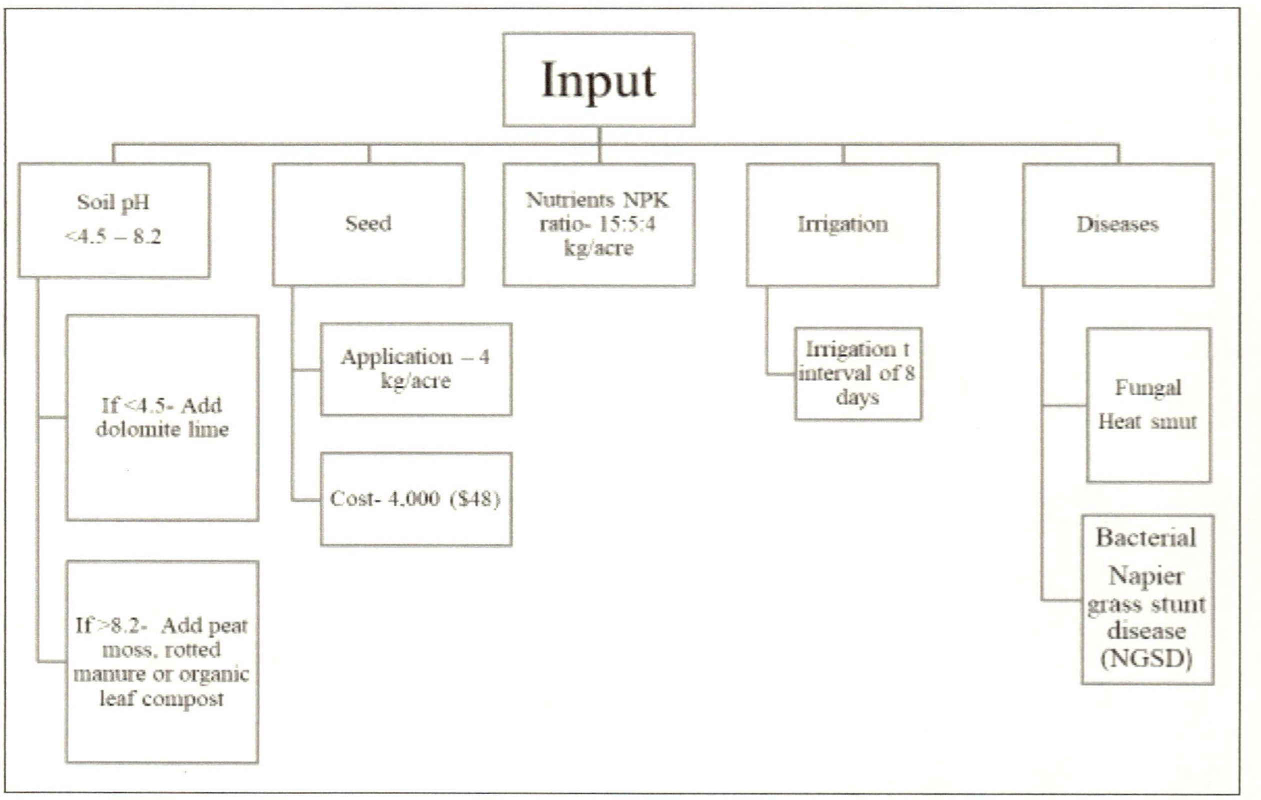

Figure 101: Input required in Napier grass/ Hathi ghas crop

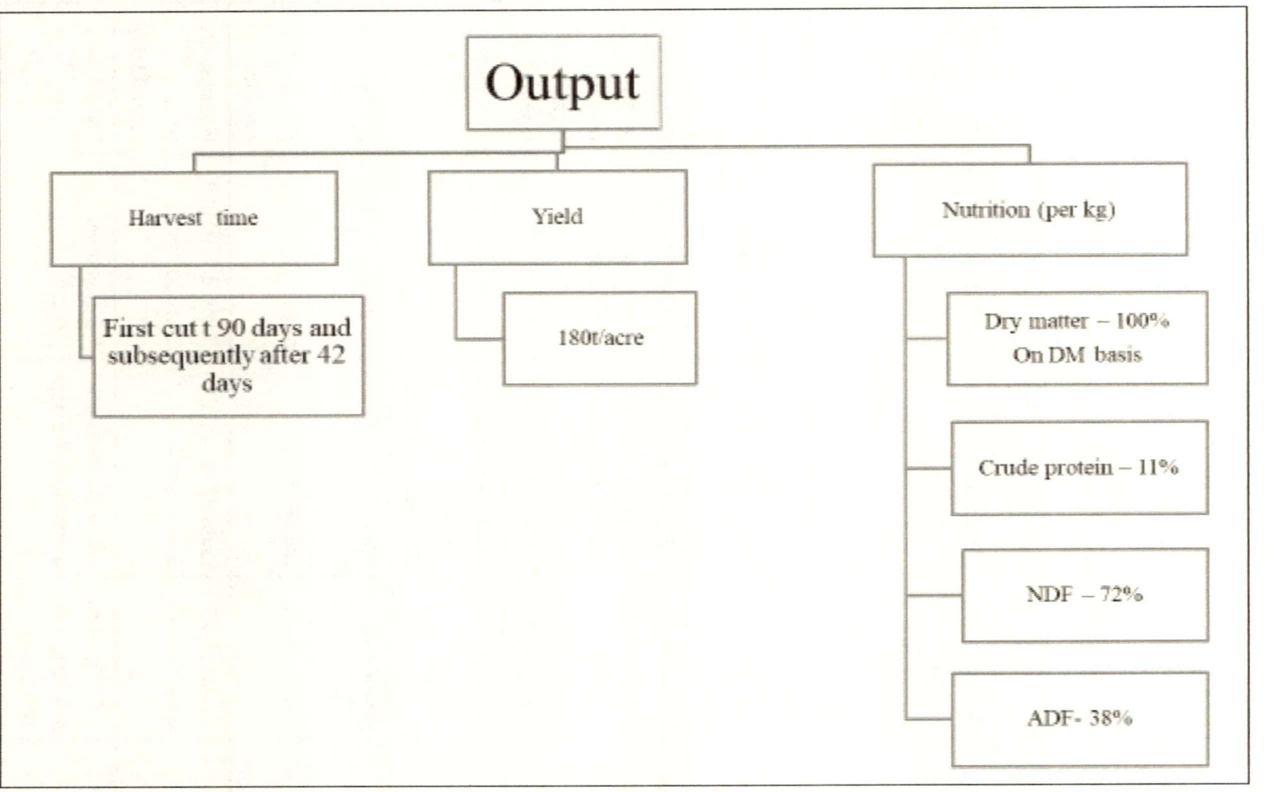

Figure 102: Output received in Napier grass/Hathi ghas crop

Table 19: Properties of fodder crops

Crop name	Cowpea/Lobia	Alfalfa/ Rizka	Pearl millet / Bajra	Napier grass / Hathi ghas
Seed application	15kg/acre	5kg/acre	5kg/acre	4kg/acre
Seed cost	$2,250 ($150/kg)	$2,750 ($550/kg)	$3,000 ($600/kg)	$4000 ($1000/kg)
	$27 ($1.80/kg)	$33 ($6.62/kg)	$36 ($7.22/kg)	$48 ($12/kg)
Soil type	All types of well-drained soils (sandy loams to heavy loams)	Well-drained fertile soils	Well-drained sandy loams to loam soil	Deep, fertile, well-draining soils
Soil pH	5.0-6.5	≥ 5.2	6.5-7.5	4.5-8.2
To increase pH (<5.0)	Add dolomite lime.	Add dolomite lime.	Add dolomite lime.	Add dolomite lime.
To decrease pH (>6.5)	Add peat moss, rotted manure, or organic leaf manure	Add peat moss, rotted manure, or organic leaf manure	Add peat moss, rotted manure, or organic leaf manure	Add peat moss, rotted manure, or organic leaf manure
Yield	11 t/ acre	(Green fodder) 40 t/acre (Dry fodder) 8 t/acre	14t/ acre	180t/acre
Harvest period	(Monsoon) 55 days	50 days	45 days	90 days
Crop name	Cowpea/Lobia	Alfalfa/ Rizka	Pearl millet / Bajra	Napier grass / Hathi ghas
Harvest period	(Summer) 73 days	(Subsequent cuts) Every 25 days	(Subsequent cuts) Every 30 days	(Subsequent cuts) Every 42 days
Irrigation	5-6 irrigations at intervals of 10-15 days	Frequent irrigation at intervals of 8 days	4-5 irrigations	Every 8 days
NPK Ratio	1:02:01	3:01:03	2:01:01	15:05:04

Table 20: Fodder crops nutrition table

Crop name	Cowpea/Lobia (vines and leaves)	Alfalfa/ Rizka (leaf)	Pearl millet / Bajra (leaf and stem)	Napier grass / Hathi ghas (leaf)
Dry matter	100%	100%	100%	100%
Crude protein	25%	23.1%	12.5%	10.2%
Crude fiber	4.7%	22.7%	3.2%	34%
Crude fat	1.5%	3.3%	4.8%	3.6%
Ash	4.3%	13%	2.8%	-
NDF	14.4%	39.5%	17.2%	64.3%
ADF	6.2%	27%	4.5%	40.9%
Lignin	0.5%	7.4%	1%	-
Starch	47%	3.2%	67.1%	-
Total sugars	4.6%	4.4%	2.2%	-
Gross energy	18.2%	18.8%	19.1%	-

LIME APPLICATION

Under the input heading, in the soil section, we recommended using lime to increase soil pH. Here are the instructions for lime application –

Formula: Lime requirement (t/hectare) = (target pH – current pH) x soil texture factor.

Soil texture factor = Loam to clay loam: 4, Sandy loam: 3, Sand: 2

Raising the soil pH by up to 1 unit is recommended.

For example, to raise a sandy loam soil of pH 4.8 ($CaCl_2$) to pH 5.5 ($CaCl_2$).

(5.5 – 4.8) x 3 = 2.1 tonnes of lime per hectare are required.

For example, to raise a sandy loam soil of pH 4.8 (CaCl2) to pH 5.5 (CaCl2).

(5.5 – 4.8) x 3×0.247105 = 0.52 tonnes or 520 kg of lime per acre is required.

ORGANIC CURE FOR CROP DISEASE

Managing any plant disease organically involves a combination of preventive and control measures. Here are some strategies to consider:

PREVENTION

(for fungal, bacterial, and pest-related diseases)

1. **Companion Planting**
   Some plants have natural repellent properties against certain pests and diseases. For example, marigold, garlic, basil, etc. These plants also provide a habitat for beneficial insects like ladybugs that keep the crop – destroying insects like aphids in check.

2. **Biofumigation**
   Certain plants, like mustard or marigold, can be grown and then incorporated into the soil as green manure to release compounds that suppress soil-borne pathogens.

3. Plants with a strong smell like peppermint or garlic can be sown in between the crops to repel ants and other pests. Solutions like peppermint, lemon juice, black pepper, or cinnamon solution can be sprayed over the soil in case of an ant invasion.

CURE FOR PEST INFECTIONS

1. **Neem oil**
   Neem oil is an excellent insecticide and pesticide. Mix a gallon of warm water with a teaspoon of liquid soap or insecticidal soap, which acts as an emulsifier for your mixture. Add a small amount of neem oil. Add one to 2 tablespoons of pure neem oil to your mixture[128].

2. **Garlic Spray**
   Garlic has natural insect-repelling properties. To make garlic spray, blend garlic cloves with water, strain the mixture, and spray it on affected plants[129].

3. Soil Solarization

Solarization involves covering the soil with transparent plastic to trap heat and raise soil temperatures. This method can help kill the pathogen and reduce its population in the soil. This is usually done during the hottest months of the year.

PRE-SEED TREATMENT

Many seed diseases can be eradicated through pre-seed treatment. Some examples of organic pre-seed treatment include:

1. Smearing the seeds with a paste of ash and water and sun drying before sowing. This controls seed borne disease and increases seed health.
2. Treating the seeds with buttermilk is advisable to prevent fungal infections (125ml/kg of seeds).
3. Seeds of cereals and legumes can be protected against pests by mixing them with a solution of cactus milk (100 ml in 1 liter of water) and drying for 8 hours in darkness before sowing. This protects them from stem borer larvae, termites and other pests.

In this chapter, you learned:

Coming up...

Organic fertilizers
DIY
Anaerobic
Fertifish
Farm yard manure
Bio enzyme solution
Aerobic
Compost
Vermicompost
Store bought
Blood meal
Bone meal
Kelp meal
Benefits
Sustainable in the long run
Locally sourced
Slow release of nutrients
Increase organic matter
Long term benefits
Process of making
Materials required
Steps
Application
Precaution

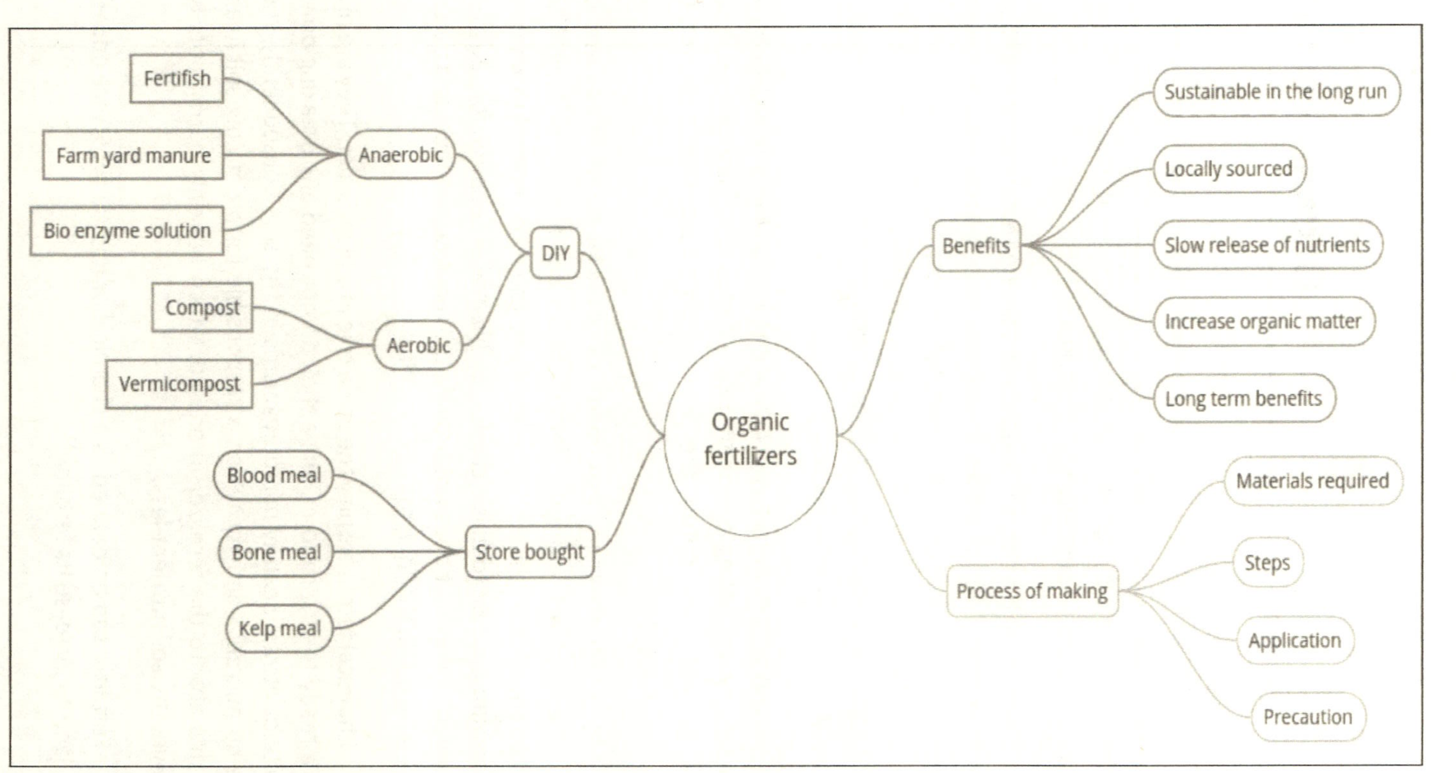

CHAPTER 7

Organic Fertilizers

ALL ECOSYSTEMS[130] AROUND you have one element which is omnipresent – 'diversity'. For example, you will never find a specific tree or plant growing naturally as the only species in a forest. Of course, don't count 'Pando' from Utah or Posidonia australis from Australia in this.

There must be diversity because while one tree or plant might consume more nitrogen (N), in return it will give back phosphorus and potassium. Similarly, another tree might consume more potassium and give nitrogen. So, in order to maintain balance, nature ensures a diverse group of flora and fauna grows in one place. Thereby, maintaining fertility and stability in the ecosystem. To conclude, nature is diverse.

However, commercial cultivation, also known as[131] monoculture, because it requires cultivating the same type of crop and harvesting it frequently, thereby not giving nature the required time to revitalize the soil through natural processes.

As a consequence, man-made or artificial supplements are used to provide nutrients and boost fertility in a small amount of time. These are called chemical fertilizers. These fertilizers can be compared to what fast food is to humans. Fast food is a cheap, readily available option for satisfying your hunger. However, it does not provide the required nutrients and deteriorates one's health in the long run.

Chemical fertilizers play the same role in a plant's diet. They are produced in a ready-to-absorb form. Since they do not need any breaking down, they will not attract healthy microorganisms in the soil. Consequently, there will be no microbial activity, which is responsible for promoting soil health. The plants absorb the fertilizer in one go, which not only burns roots but also leaves the soil nutrient-less.

Fertilizer can be defined as a chemical or natural substance added to soil or land to increase its fertility[132].

It can be mainly identified as either inorganic (factory-made) or organic (naturally sourced).

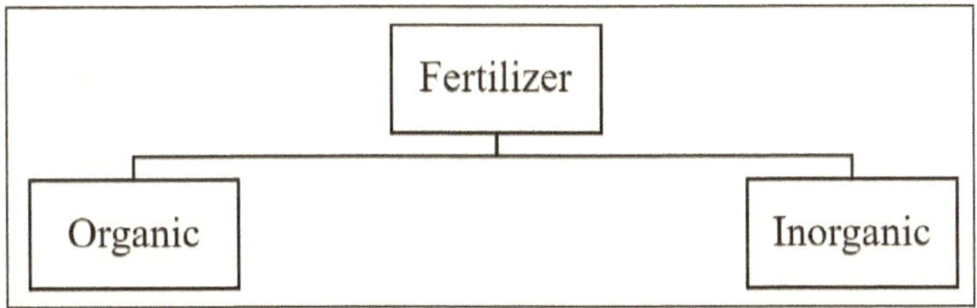

Figure 103: Types of fertilizer

Organic fertilizers are made from natural materials such as animal waste and plant remains.

Inorganic fertilizers are manufactured products with a specific potency of nutrients which are pre-determined.

In Chapter 1, we discussed the impacts of using inorganic fertilizers. They replenish nutrients much faster than organic fertilizers, but their benefit is short-term. As this book discusses the goal of building a self-sustainable patch of land, we have to opt for solutions (which may be time-consuming) that will sustain our future generations. From here onwards, we will discuss organic fertilizers.

ADVANTAGES OF ORGANIC FERTILIZER

Organic fertilizers are advantageous because:

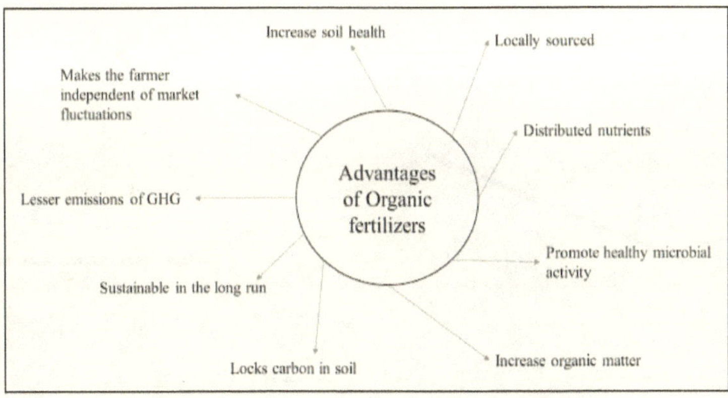

Figure 104: Advantages of organic fertilizers

4. They are usually made from locally sourced materials. Therefore, do not cause any lasting damage to the soil such as introduction of diseases foreign to the local ecosystem or fostering the growth of invasive weed species.

5. Nutrients are not concentrated in exceeding amounts but are distributed. Concentrated nutrients can burn the roots of plants and cause damage to the soil.

For example, Fertilizer A (inorganic) provides 100% nutrition immediately after its application. The plant roots cannot handle the concentrated amount and will burn, or they will absorb 100% at once, and the soil will have 0% nutrients for the next few months.

There are chemical fertilizers specifically designed to slow-release nutrients. These fertilizers are known as slow-release or controlled-release fertilizers.

Fertilizer B (organic) does not contain nutrition in ready-to-absorb form. It has to be broken down by soil microbes to provide nutrition. Thus, it will provide nutrition in small percentages like 10%, 20%, and ensure nutrients are available to the plant for months after application. Look at the following graph to better understand this concept:

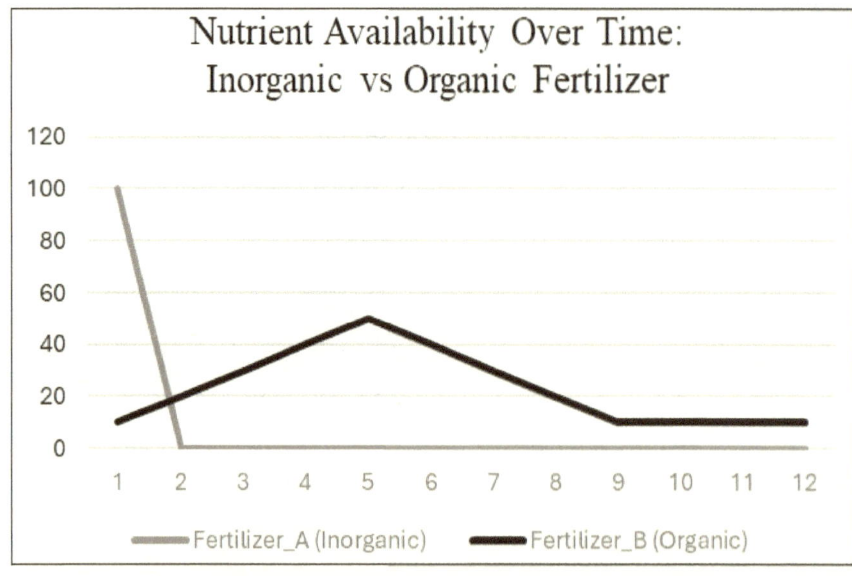

Figure 105: Graph showing nutrient availability over time

- **Fertilizer A (Inorganic)**: The blue line shows a sharp decline from 100% nutrient availability in the first month to 0% in the subsequent months.
- **Fertilizer B (Organic)**: The green line shows a gradual increase in nutrient availability over the first 5 months, followed by a sustained release in the subsequent months.

* There are chemical fertilizers specifically designed to slow-release nutrients. These fertilizers are known as slow-release or controlled-release fertilizers. There are different types of controlled-release fertilizers like coated fertilizers (Sulfur-Coated Urea, Polymer-Coated Fertilizers, Resin-Coated Fertilizers etc.), Urea-Formaldehyde Compounds, Isobutylidene Diurea (IBDU) etc.

They are generally more expensive than conventional fertilizers due to the additional processing required to create the coating or compound that regulates nutrient release.

Figure 105 clearly illustrates the immediate but short-lived nutrient release of inorganic fertilizer compared to the gradual and sustained release of organic fertilizer.

1. As stated above, the nutrients in organic fertilizers need breaking down first which stimulates the function of microbes in soil and also ensures a longer supply period as the nutrients are slowly absorbed by the plants.
2. Organic fertilizer increases the organic matter of the soil. Organic matter is the material in soil that contains carbon and is derived from living or dead plants and animals[133]. Carbon in soil increases its water and nutrient-holding capacity, and maintains soil texture.
3. The practice of tilling the soil releases trapped carbon into the atmosphere in the form of carbon dioxide. Organic fertilizers ensure that the carbon is locked in the soil instead of being released in the atmosphere.
4. Inorganic fertilizers are often available at subsidized prices and cost less to the farmer than organic fertilizers. For example, the table below shows the Subsidized rates of fertilizers in India (2022) (Per bag weight 50kg):

Table 21: Subsidized rates of fertilizers in India (2022)[134]

Fertilizer	Cost price to the exchequer (50 kg bag)	Sell price to the farmer (50 kg bag)	Burden on the exchequer (loss)
Urea (Imported)	₹ 2,450/- ($29)	₹ 266/- ($3)	₹ 2,183/- ($26)
DAP (Diammonium phosphate)	₹ 4,073/- ($49)	₹ 1,350/- ($16)	₹ 2,501/- ($30)
NPK (Nitrogen, Phosphorus and Potassium)	₹ 3,291/- ($40)	₹ 1,470/- ($18)	₹ 1,918/- ($23)
MOP (Muriate of Potash)	₹ 2,654/- ($32)	₹ 1,700/- ($20)	₹ 759/- ($9)

5. Cost price to the exchequer (Government) – The cost price (of the fertilizer) upfront which the government (exchequer) bears. It means that the burden of cost is on the exchequer[135].
    (It's the money collected by the government as taxes from common people as income / Goods and Services Tax).
6. Sell price to the farmer – The price at which the government sells the fertilizer to farmers.
7. Burden on the exchequer (loss) – The total difference between cost price and sell price that the government has to bear. The loss amount directly impacts the fiscal deficit.

Fiscal deficit is a shortfall in the income of a government compared to its spending. It is the difference between the total income of the government and the total expenditure incurred by it[136]. In simple terms, if the government is spending more than its income, a situation of fiscal deficit arises. To continue functioning, the state and union governments take loans from the Reserve Bank or international bodies. Since the government is buying the fertilizer at the original cost but selling it at a reduced price, it loses money during this transaction. This is directly added to the fiscal deficit, thereby becoming a burden on the taxpayer.

Note: It means that someone has to bear the cost, in this case, it is the government (indirectly – citizens). In 2022, the government of India spent Rs. 60,939 Crores ($7329 million) on fertilizer subsidy[137].

The other aspect is the short-term benefits versus long-term impact of these fertilizers on soil. Following below is a table depicting the amount of fertilizer one needs to cultivate an acre of rice (paddy) crop (a staple in India):

Table 22: Fertilizer required for rice (paddy) crop

Fertilizer	Applicationrate[138]	Government cost price per acre	Government sell price per acre
Urea	100 kg/acre	₹4,900 ($59)	₹532 ($6)
DAP	27 kg/acre	₹2,201 ($26)	₹729 ($9)
MOP	20 kg/acre	₹1,061 ($13)	₹680 ($8)
Total	147 kg/acre	₹8,162 ($98)	₹1,941 ($23)

According to Table 22, it costs a total of ₹8,162 worth of fertilizers to cultivate 1 acre of rice (paddy) crop, but the farmer gets the same fertilizer for ₹1,941 because it's a subsidized price, which is way cheaper than organic fertilizers (almost 50% cheaper).

The immediate result is increased yield, but if we look 10 years down the line, the results would be: increasing amounts of fertilizers required, decreased yield, and infertile soil.

The reason?

Inorganic fertilizers lower the carbon content of the soil, and they require regular tilling of the soil. Carbon atoms in the soil increase its water and nutrient-holding capacity and give it texture.

In its absence, the soil loses its retention capacity and can no longer hold water or nutrients. Over time, it loses all its fertility, requiring more input of inorganic fertilizers until it becomes completely barren. At the end stage, no amount of chemical fertilizers can bring back its fertility or restore its texture.

On the other hand, organic fertilizers have a rich carbon content and increase the organic matter of the soil. The raw materials required for organic fertilizers are sourced from the farm itself. In the circle of life, the nutrients of the soil return to the soil.

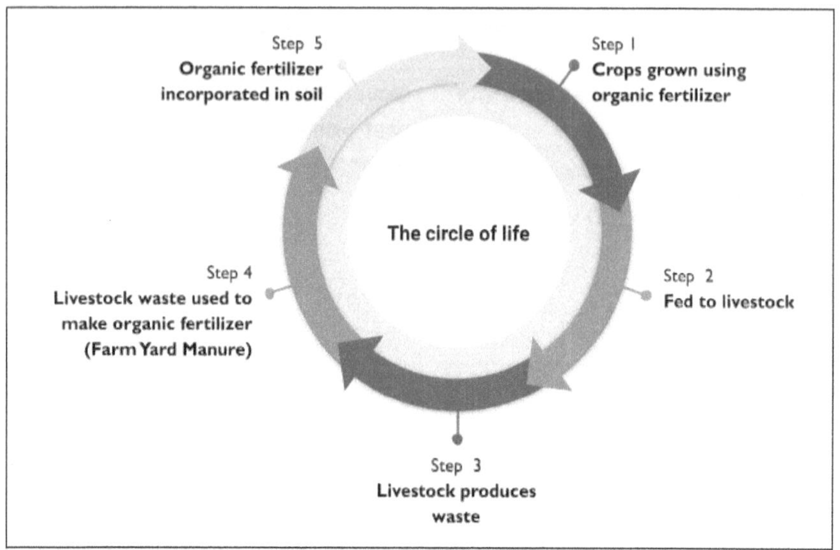

Figure 106: Circle of life of organic fertilizer

In the long run, it enhances soil health, increases water-holding capacity, and maintains soil texture.

Now think. Which of these fertilizers, inorganic or organic, will cost us more?

(Cost encompasses more than just financial expenditure)

8. Some organic fertilizers (like Farm Yard Manure) release small amounts of greenhouse gas (methane and carbon dioxide) during manufacture and application. However, this is nothing compared to the amount of emissions produced by factories that manufacture inorganic fertilizers. Today, fertilizer production consumes

approximately 1.2% of the world's energy and is responsible for approximately 1.2% of the total emission of the greenhouse gases in the world, consisting of 0.3% of pure CO2, 0.3% as N2O and 0.6% as flue gas CO2[139].

9. Although the process of organic fertilizer is slow and requires patience, it is a sustainable option.

10. The farmer can make their own organic fertilizer, thereby becoming self-dependent. They will not have to depend on outside sources and will be completely unaffected by price fluctuations.

DIY or Do It Yourself can be defined as the activity of building at home by oneself rather than employing a professional[140]. Farmers can create certain organic fertilizers on their own, which will give them a guarantee of quality. As the producer, you participate or oversee the entire process, leaving no aspect unattended. This hands-on approach ensures the quality of the final product. The only potential factors that remain beyond our control are force majeure or acts of nature (thunder, rain, sandstorm, etc.).

Organic fertilizers can be further subdivided into Aerobic and Anaerobic based on the presence of oxygen during production.

Aerobic can be defined as processes occurring in the presence of oxygen (requiring or utilizing oxygen). [141]

In this process, organisms use oxygen to break down organic matter and release carbon dioxide, water, and energy.

For example, fertilizers such as compost and vermicompost are produced in an open environment that allows a free flow of oxygen at variable rates.

Anaerobic can be defined as processes occurring in the absence of oxygen (lacking oxygen).

In such conditions, organisms break down organic matter without oxygen and produce lactic acid[142] and methane gas[143].

For example, fertilisers such as Farm Yard Manure (FYM), bio enzyme solution, and fertifish are produced in anaerobic conditions, in the absence of oxygen.

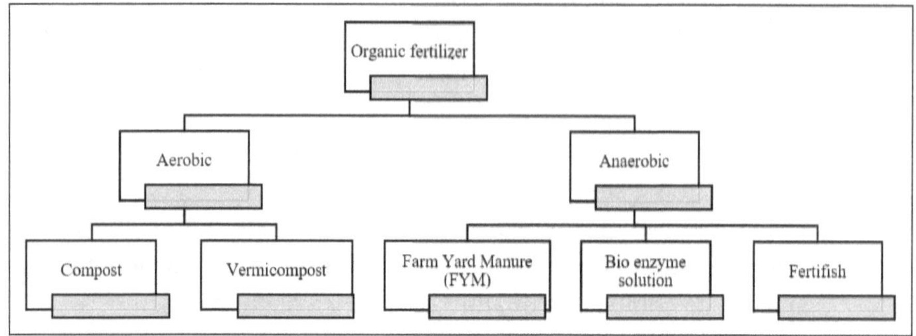

Figure 107: Types of Organic fertilizers that can be made at home (DIY)

Although it is possible to make the above fertilizers on your own, there are certain precautions to keep in mind. Diving into the manufacturing process without complete information can yield negative results and may harm the soil instead of revitalizing it. It is advisable to thoroughly understand the process first and then make the fertilizer.

AEROBIC ORGANIC FERTILIZER

1. COMPOST

Composting can be defined as the process of making vegetable matter or manure into compost[144]. It is a controlled decomposition of organic matter by microorganisms, such as bacteria, fungi, and other decomposing organisms, under aerobic (oxygen-rich) conditions. It transforms organic materials into nutrient-rich fertilizer.

Ingredients required:

1. Organic waste (includes all kinds of wastes that can be decomposed, from kitchen waste to dry leaves, animal waste etc.)
2. Water (pH 5.5-8: mildly acidic)
3. Surgical gloves

Steps:

1. Locate an area which is protected from direct sunlight and rain as these conditions will slow down the composting process.

2. Make a compost heap size 1m length, 1 m width and 1.5 m height. (total volume =1.5 m^3). Make sure to wear surgical gloves when handling the organic waste, to avoid contamination.
3. Start with a base layer of dry material like dry leaves and twigs or mulch for air circulation and drainage.
4. Stack with layers of organic waste. In a compost pile the Carbon: Nitrogen (C: N) ratio is very important as it provides the basic nutrition for microorganisms that will decompose the waste.
5. The ideal carbon-to-nitrogen (C: N) ratio for raw materials falls within the range of 25:1 to 30:1[145] which means 25kg:1kg.
6. Materials rich in carbon are dry and can be classified as 'Browns' whereas materials rich in nitrogen are moist and classified as 'Greens'. To maintain a healthy balance, for every 1 bucket of green (nitrogen) waste, add 25 buckets of dry (carbon) waste.
7. Following is a list of organic waste rich in nitrogen and carbon that you can add to the compost pile:

Table 23: Nitrogen and Carbon-rich organic waste

Browns (Carbon-Rich Materials)	Greens (Nitrogen-Rich Materials)
Dry Leaves	Grass Clippings
Straw or Hay	Vegetable Scraps
Cardboard and Paper	Coffee Grounds
Wood Chips	Manure
Cornstalks	Green Leaves
Pine Needles	Tea Bags
Tree Bark	Weeds

8. After constructing the compost pile, water it adequately, so that it is drenched till the bottom. Let it sit for 4 days.

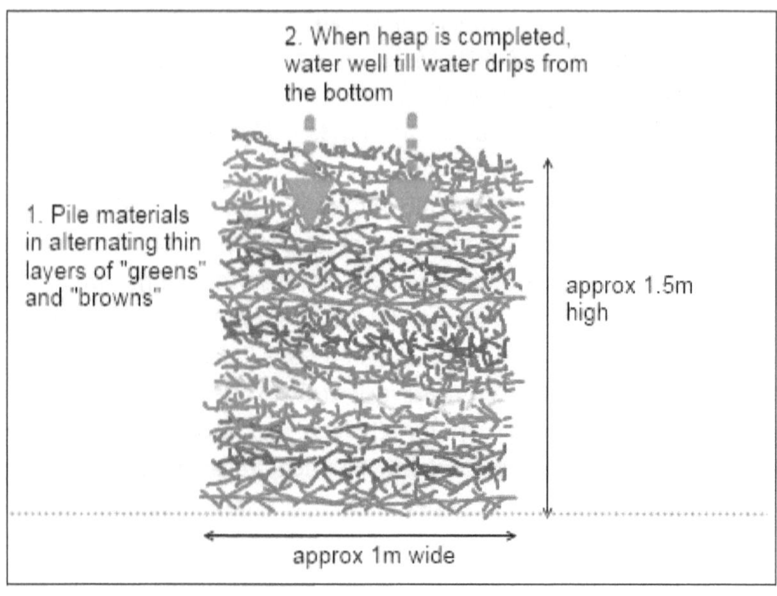

Figure 108: Diagrammatic representation of a compost pile[146]

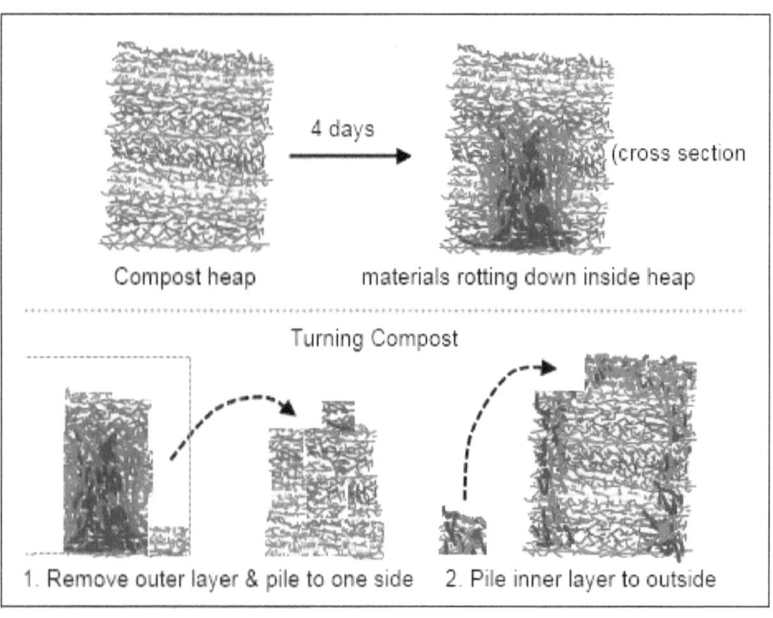

Figure 109: Diagrammatic representation of the process of turning a compost pile

9. After 4 days, turn it every second day for 14 days. This is called the Berkeley hot composting method.[147]

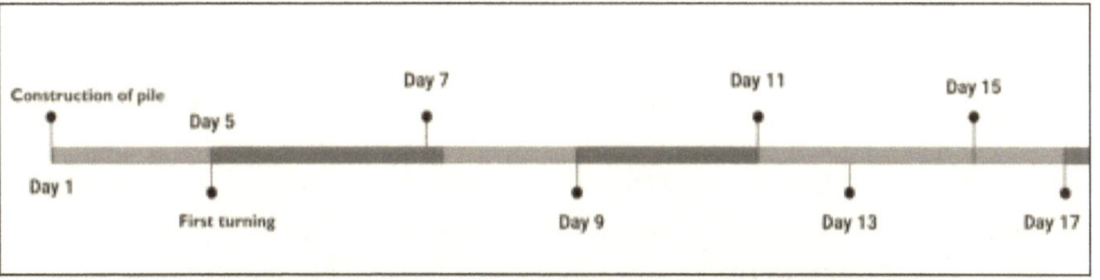

Figure 110: Timeline of compost turning schedule

10. Maintaining temperature is necessary for optimal functioning of microorganisms. In the beginning a temperature of around 20-45 °C is just right. But with increased decomposition, a warmer temperature of 50-70 °C, is ideal. These high temperatures are a sign of vigorous microbial activity. They also help get rid of pathogens (at 55 °C and above) and weed seeds (at 62 °C). Turning the compost and letting in some air will help control the temperature.

11. If the mix seems too dry, sprinkle some water. If it seems too wet add dry organic waste like dry leaf and twigs. It is generally recommended to not add fresh material once the pile starts decomposing. Microorganisms will have to start the decomposing process of fresh materials from beginning and it will affect the decomposition rate of previously available matter.

12. In cold or wet weather, protect the compost heap by covering it with a tarp or plastic sheet to prevent the weather elements from cooling down the compost.

Result

The compost will be ready in 18 days. It will be evident by the structure of the compost, which will turn into dark granular soil. Once again, it only works if you do not add new material in between.

Quantity

The total volume of a compost heap measuring 1m length, 1m width and 1.5m height is 1.5m³. The weight of the compost depends on the density[148]of materials. For example, look at the varying properties of compost made from different materials in the table below-

(Compost pile dimensions: 1.5 m high, 3 m wide, and 80 m long)

Table 24: Physical properties of different compost types based on the raw material used[149]

Compost Properties	Cattle manure (100:0)	Cattle manure and herbal plant residues (50:50)	Cattle manure and sugarcane plant residues (50:50)	Herbal plant residues (100:0)	Sugarcane plant residues (100:0)
Bulk density (kg/m³)	655.00	625.00	573.00	582.00	420.00
Moisture content (%)	25.60	23.50	30.10	31.20	32.10

The bulk density of the compost types was measured under laboratory conditions. The compost was compacted[150] for accurate results. Therefore, it should not be taken as the ideal density for compost prepared by hand. In laboratories, there is equipment which can compact a sample in a small space which increases the density. However, in everyday compost piles, materials are pressed down with hands and cannot be compacted as much.

Density of the compost varies depending on the material being used. For example, compost made with cow dung will have a higher density than one made with dry husk and food waste.

2. VERMICOMPOST

Vermicompost is a nutrient-rich, organic fertilizer produced through the decomposition of organic waste materials by earthworms. It is very similar to composting except for the presence of earthworms. It can be done in 2 ways-

    a.   Small-scale indoor composting
    b.   Large scale outdoor composting

Special kinds of worms are used for vermicomposting, as named below-

- Eisenia fetida (Manure worm/redworm/tiger worm/red wiggler worm)
- Lumbricus rubellus (Common earthworm/nightcrawler/dew worm)

How to make vermicompost?

Following is a detailed step-by-step process on how to make vermicompost.

a. Small-scale indoor composting

This is done on a small-scale, in food grade buckets. It is a good way to start if you are new to vermicomposting.

Materials required:

1. 3 buckets of same size
2. Drilling machine
3. Surgical gloves

Ingredients required:

1. Earthworms (For a household system using a standard bin size, such as the 5-gallon/ s19-liter buckets mentioned, start with around 1,000 worms or 500 grams)
   a. Eisenia fetida[151]

   or

   b. Lumbricus rubellus[152]

2. Organic waste
3. Shredded cardboard or newspaper

Steps

1. Take 3 buckets of equal size for example we are taking 3 5-gallon (19 liter) buckets[153]. A good example would be bucket sold by paint companies.
2. Leave the base of 1 bucket as it is and drill holes in the other 2 (for easy mobilization of worms).[154]

3. Next, stack the buckets with the solid base bucket at bottom and the porous base buckets on top of it (for easy understanding we are labeling these buckets 1,2 and 3 starting from the top).
4. At the base of bucket 2 create a bedding (habitable environment) for the worms using shredded cardboard or newspaper.
5. Now fill this bucket with organic wastes[155] like fruit peels, kitchen waste, cow dung[156] etc. Make sure to wear surgical gloves when handling the organic waste, to avoid contamination.
6. If the compost seems too dry, spray a minimal amount of water.

   Caution: Too much water will block the pores in the soil and oxygen flow to the worms. It will also cause difficulty in harvesting the end compost.

7. Add the previously listed type of worms to bucket 2. For 1 kg of organic waste, 2 kg of worms would be sufficient[157].
8. The worms come to the surface when there is no more organic matter for them to eat, indicating that the organic waste has turned into compost. The compost will be ready in 60-90 days.
9. The worms will move through the bucket holes to bucket 1 where a fresh supply of organic waste will be waiting for them.

Large-scale outdoor composting:

This is done on a large scale in outdoor areas. HDPE bags can be used for this purpose.

Materials required:

1. HDPE vermicomposting bags[158]
   (Dimensions: 1.219m × 0.61m × 3.66m)
   Volume = 2.7 m³
2. 8-10 sticks of same length to set up the vermicompost bag

Ingredients required-

1. Dry neem leaves
2. Dry rice straw
3. Dry cow dung/ goat manure
4. Water

5. Earthworms (450 grams of worms for every square foot of surface area)

    a. Eisenia fetida[159]

          or

    b. Lumbricus rubellus[160]

Steps[161]

1. Establish the vermicompost bags by supporting it with sticks.
2. Once in place, lay a base layer with dry neem leaves. Make sure to wear surgical gloves when handling the organic waste, to avoid contamination.
3. Add a layer of chopped dry rice straw on top of this layer and moisten it with water.
4. Add dry crushed cow dung on top of the rice straw layer. Make sure to use only old dry cow dung and not fresh ones. Cow dung gives off a lot of heat when it's fresh which can kill the worms.
5. Moisten the cow dung by adding water and add a layer of rice straw on top.
6. Repeat the steps of adding rice straw, moistening with water then adding cow dung and moistening with water until the bag is filled to the brim.
7. Once the top layer of cow dung is complete, add worms to the surface. There is no need to dig holes in the mix for the worms to go inside. They will do so automatically.
8. Cover the bag with moist gunny bags. The compost will be ready in 2-3 months.

Result

1. The finished product is dark brown in color and has a granular texture.
2. This fertilizer is essentially worm poop, also called black gold. In addition to being packed with NPK, the 3 essentials of soil, it is also rich in organic carbon and other minerals like calcium, magnesium, iron and manganese among others.

Application

Apply the fertilizer in the vermicompost to soil ratio of 1:2 (1 part of vermicompost applied to two parts of soil).

NAEROBIC ORGANIC FERTILIZERS

1.FARM YARD MANURE (FYM)

Farmyard Manure is a bulky fertilizer made from the excreta and urine of farm animals (mainly cows). It comprises decomposed mixtures of dung and urine from farm animals, combined with litter and residual materials from roughages or fodder provided to the cattle. Typically, well-decomposed farmyard manure comprises approximately 0.5% nitrogen (N), 0.2% phosphorus pentoxide (P_2O_5), and 0.5% potassium oxide (K_2O) on average.

How to make FYM?

Below is a detailed step-by-step process on how to make FYM.

Materials required

1. A shovel
2. Empty area of land to make trench
3. Surgical gloves

Ingredients required

1. Farm waste (animal excreta, straw etc.)
2. Soil

Steps –

1. Dig a trench of size 5 m in length, 2 m in width and 1 m deep.
2. Spread a layer of the farm waste (animal waste, residual straw etc.) at the bottom of the pit and cover it with a layer of soil. Make sure to wear surgical gloves when handling the organic waste, to avoid contamination.
3. Keep it covered with a layer of plastic sheet to prevent evaporation and increase the temperature and moisture within the trench for better microbial activity.
4. If the mix seems dry, sprinkle it with water.
5. Keep layering the mix alternatively with farm waste and soil. If you want to increase output, raise the trench to a height of 90 cm above the ground level.
6. When the trench is full, the top of the heap should be shaped into a dome and plastered with a mixture of cow dung and earth slurry.

Result –

After plastering, the manure is ready to be used within 4 to 5 months.

Quantity

Minimum volume[162] (dimensions – 5m x 2m x 1m) = 10m³

Maximum volume (dimensions – 5m x 2m x 1.9m[163]) – 19m³

Considering the average density of the manure to be 421 kg/m³[164]

(Bulk density varies with respect to the depth of the manure pit. It increases with increasing the depth of the manure pit. Lower bulk density can be observed in the top layer of the manure pit. This may be due to the fact that the presence of air is higher on the top surface of the manure pit.)

For 10 cubic meters:

Weight[165]= 4210kg

For 19 cubic meters:

Weight=7999 kg

Application

Apply at the rate of 4-8 tons per acre at least a month before sowing seeds[166].

- Given that each trench produces 4210 kg, the number of trenches needed to make 4 tons (4000 kg) is 1.
- Given that each trench produces 7999 kg (with an additional height of 90 cm), the number of trenches needed to make 8 tons (8000 kg) is 1.

Apply at the rate of 1-2 tons per ¼ acre at least a month before sowing seeds.

- To produce 1 ton of manure, a trench of 1.5m length, 2m width, and 1m depth will be adequate.

Volume = 1.5 x 2 x 1 = 3 m³
Taking the average density as 421 kg/m³
Total weight = 3 x 421
1,263 kg

- To produce 2 tons of manure, a trench of 2.5m length, 2m width, and 1m depth will be adequate.

Volume = 2.5 x 2 x 1 = 5 m³
Taking the average density as 421 kg/m³
Total weight = 5 x 421
2,105 kg

Please note that the numbers given above are based on the approximation of bulk density = 421 kg/m³. The numbers above can vary based on the density of your manure. This is just a standard estimate.

Precaution

1. Prevent contamination of farmyard manure with harmful substances such as disease-causing bacteria. These can be transmitted through animal waste.
   Avoid using manure from animals that have been treated with medications or have been exposed to toxic materials or are sick.
2. Store farmyard manure in a covered area to prevent leaching of nutrients due to rainfall and to maintain the quality of the manure.

Drawbacks

Since nutrients are distributed instead of being concentrated, test the farmyard manure[167] for nutrient content to determine its fertility value. This analysis helps in making informed decisions about the quantity of manure to apply based on the nutrient needs of the crops.

That being said, there is definitely a known range of NPK in farmyard manure. The general NPK content ranges from-

1. Nitrogen – 2. Phosphorus – 3. Potassium – **2. BIO ENZYME / ECO – ENZYME SOLUTION**

Bio Enzyme[168] solution is an organic solution made by fermenting organic waste like fruit and vegetable peels. The bacteria produced through fermentation can break down organic compounds. While the solution can be made from various fruit and vegetable waste, citrus[169] peels, in particular, are commonly used.

Bio-enzyme made from citrus peels has multiple uses such as:

- Used as organic fertilizer
- Used as a disinfectant and cleaner (to mop floors) for household purposes.
- Used as an insect repellent.
- To treat wastewater at domestic levels (reduces the Total Dissolved Solids or TDS of water).

*   While citrus peels, such as those from oranges, lemons, and limes, are commonly used due to their high enzyme content and pleasant fragrance, you can use a variety of fruit and vegetable peels to make bio enzyme.

We will be focusing on the first use, that is using bio enzyme solution as a fertilizer. When applied to soil, the microorganisms present in the solution break down organic matter and transform it into simpler nutrients that can be absorbed by plants.

Some Manganese (Mn), Boron (B), Molybdenum (Mo), Cobalt (Co), and Sodium (Na).

Other beneficial compounds present are enzymes (e.g., proteases, amylases, cellulases), citric acid, lactic acid, amino acids, vitamins (e.g., B-vitamins) and beneficial microorganisms.

It thereby increases the nutrients in the soil and improves soil health. When sprayed above ground, on leaves and soil, it acts as a pesticide and insecticide.

How to make bio enzyme fertilizer?

Below is a detailed step-by-step process on how to make bio-enzyme fertilizer.

Material required

1. An airtight container[170] (minimum capacity of 2 liters)
2. Weighing scale[171]
   For convenience, it is advised to use a digital kitchen scale, which can measure material quantity in grams.
3. Surgical gloves

Ingredients required

1. Pulp/peel of fruits (300 g)
2. Water (1000 ml or 1liter OR 0.2 gallon)
3. Jaggery (100 g)
4. Dry yeast (Approximately 1.5 grams or ¼ teaspoon) or curd (2 tea spoons)

Following is a list of various fruit peels that can be used for making bio-enzyme solutions along with their pH[172] and nutrients. Please note that the information given is generalized and may vary according to environment, season, size of the fruit, ripeness etc.

All the nutrients are measured in grams except for vitamin A, which is measured in micrograms (µg). The measurement of Vitamin A is extremely small, making it impractical to convert into grams (as 1 µg is equivalent to one millionth of a gram, i.e. 1 µg = 0.0000001 g).

Table 25: Nutrition in the peels of different fruits

Nutrient	Orange	Lemon	Kinnow	Banana	Pineapple	Papaya	Mango
pH	3.0-4.0	3.0-4.0	2.8-4.0	9.0-11.0	3.24-3.84	5.5-6.5	3.5-6.5
Calories	40-50	30-40	40-60	40-60	40-50	30-40	50-70
Protein	1-2	1-2	2-3	2-3	1-2	1-2	1-2
Carbohydrates	10-15	8-12	15-20	20-25	10-15	7-15	12-18 l
Sugars	5-10	2-5	8-12	12-18	5-10	5-10 l	8-12 l
Fiber	2-4	5-8	1-2	2-4	1-2	2-4	1-2 l
Fat	0.2-0.4	0.1-0.2	0.3-0.5	0.3-0.5	0.1-0.2	0.1-0.2	0.3-0.5
Calcium	0.03-0.04	0.03-0.04	0.08-0.1	0.01-0.05	0.04-0.05	0.06-0.08	0.02-0.03
Potassium	0.02-0.03	0.01-0.02	0.01-0.02	0.01-0.02	0.01-0.02	0.02-0.03	0.01-0.02
Vitamin C	0.15-0.2	0.1-0.15	0.18-0.23	0.3-0.4	0.1-0.15	0.3-0.4	0.15-0.2
Vitamin A	20-30 µg	30-40 µg	10-20µg	20-30 µg	30-40 µg	100-150 µg	40-60 µg

Steps

1. Take an airtight container, for example a 2-liter plastic bottle (made from HDPE[173] plastic). (These bottles are wasted away and end up in garbage bins anyway, it is better to reuse them for a good cause.)
2. Fill the bottle with 100 gm of jaggery, 300 gm of citrus pulp/peel (chopped), 1000 gm or 1 liter of water and ¼ teaspoon dry yeast[174] or 2 tea spoons of curd and the remaining should be kept empty. Make sure to wear gloves when handling the organic waste, to avoid contamination and infection.

    Keep the ratio of jaggery: peels: water as 1:3:10. The jaggery and yeast will speed up the process of fermentation.

3. Other fruit and vegetable peels that can be used are mango peel, banana peel, papaya peel and pineapple peel, potato peel and onion peel. Ensure that the peels are of ripe fruits as they are easier to break down.

    Discarded fruits as a whole are also welcome in the fold.

4. Keep this solution in a cool, dark area for 90 days. A standard room temperature of 27°C (80.6°F) works best for the fermentation process.

    Now, how do we attain the temperature of 27°C? Just ensure it's a dark but ventilated space.

** The airtight container should be opened once a day, and its contents stirred to let out the gas generated during the fermentation process. If this step is not performed, the container will explode from the inside because of the build-up of gas.

Remember CH4 (methane) is a by-product, which is flammable.

Result

1. Strain the liquid after 90 days. The now filtered liquid is the fertilizer we wanted.
2. Supply this solution regularly via drip irrigation to ensure optimal plant and soil health.

3. According to sources, aloe vera and chili plants thrived in the soil treated with bio enzyme solution made from kitchen waste[175].
4. Use 50 ml of this fertilizer per 5 liters of water (10 ml per liter).

* Aloe Vera requires a soil pH of 7.0-8.5 [Alkaline], while chili requires a pH of 6.0-7.0 [Mildly acidic].

Irrigation

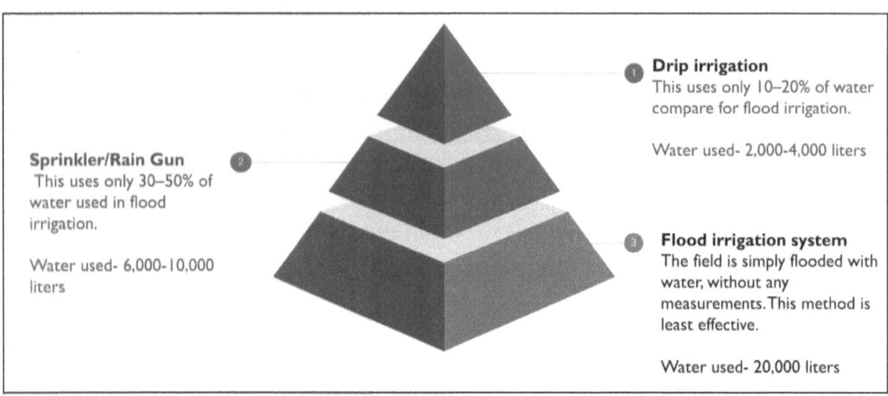

Figure 111: Different methods of irrigation and the amount of water each requires.

Irrigate 1 acre of rice/paddy crop

The amount of water required for 1 acre of crops depends on various factors like:

The type of crop grown, climate of the region, soil condition, and the soil's water retention capacity. There are different methods of irrigation, some more efficient than others. Following below are 3 kinds of irrigation systems in increasing levels of efficiency (for paddy crop):

To achieve the highest level of efficiency, it's best to opt for drip irrigation.

Application

The application rate of bio-enzyme is: Dilute 10 ml of bio-enzyme in 1 litre of water to use as fertiliser and to spray on plants in order to repel insects and pests.

Therefore, for a day of irrigation where water used is 2,000 litres, you will need 20 litres of bio enzyme. These can be made in bottles of 2 liters, so 10 bottles would suffice for the fertilizer needed for one irrigation.

Start the procedure of bio-enzyme according to the crop irrigation schedule. For example, if the crop needs to be irrigated in January, you should start making bio-enzyme in October. We can better understand with the help of the timeline given below:

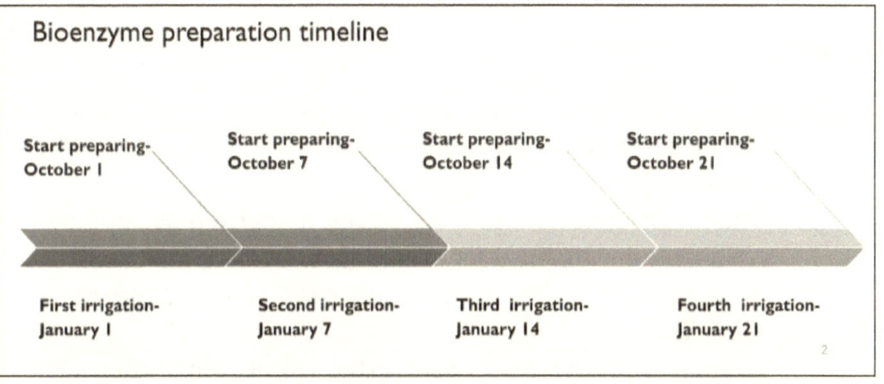

Figure 112: Bio enzyme preparation timeline according to application requirements

Precautions

1. **The liquid is not fit for human consumption**. When using citrus peels, the finished solution may look like orange juice. It is advisable to keep it in a secluded place and out of reach of children lest it is accidentally consumed.
2. When opening the container (once a day) to release gas, ensure that you open the cap slowly and keep the container at an arm's distance away from the body.
3. Anaerobic process releases lactic acid as a by-product hence the resulting solution is slightly acidic in nature. Its acidity increases with time, so the longer it is kept the more acidic it will become.
4. The pH of the solution also depends on the type of peel used. For example, citrus fruits are generally more acidic in nature than other fruits like bananas.

The pH of the bio enzyme solution can range from 5.5 to 7.5 and should be applied only after conducting a pH test of the soil, as it can be harmful. For example, if you add the bio enzyme solution to soil with a pH of 5, it will end up making it more acidic, which may harm the plants.

5. Bio Enzyme solution should always be applied after diluting and never as a concentrate or it will burn the plants.

   We restate that an ideal ratio is 10ml per liter of water. The water used should have a TDS of 300 or less ppm.

Advantages

1. Bio enzymes are effective in breaking down organic matter of the soil and speeding up the release of nutrients like nitrogen, phosphorus and potassium.
2. When the enzyme breaks down organic matter, it provides food and a habitable environment for microorganisms living in the soil.
3. These microorganisms maintain soil health and also prevent soil-borne disease.
4. Bio enzyme activity creates pores in the soil, allowing better aeration for plant roots and decreasing water logging.

3. FERTIFISH

Fertifish is an organic fertilizer made from waste parts of fish. These parts are mixed with an equal portion of molasses or palm sugar which breaks down the solid components.

Here the author wants to credit Mrs. Maheswary for her tremendous achievements in the use of fertifish. Let's get to know her better.

The Story of Mrs. Maheswary

Mrs Maheswary, a rising entrepreneur from Ernakulam, Kerala, is turning fish waste into fertilizer, which she calls 'Fertifish'. Growing up, she noticed her father using the waste parts of fish, covering them with salt, and burying them in the soil, which improved crop harvest. As an adult, she came across the training program conducted by CIFT (Central Institute of Fisheries Technology), which demonstrated how to turn fish waste into fertilizer.

After learning thoroughly about the process, she now collects fish waste from the markets and mixes it with formic acid to make fertilizer. She uses this to enrich the soil of the land where she grows bananas (required soil pH 6.5-7.5) and other vegetables. Fish waste is rich in nitrogen and molasses[176], palm sugar[177], and jaggery (commonly called 'gud' in Hindi) are rich in other essential soil nutrients as depicted in the following table:

Table 26: Selected nutrients in 100g of Molasses, Palm sugar, and Jaggery

Nutrient	Molasses	Palm sugar	Jaggery
Phosphorus	35	31	90
Potassium	390.4	1460	1056
Calcium	75	205	100
Sodium	15	37	-
Zinc	26.4	0.29	-
Iron	3.0	4.72	11

All nutrients measured in milligrams (mg).

How to make fish fertilizer/fertifish?

Below is a detailed step-by-step process on how to make fish fertilizer.

Materials required-

1. An airtight container (any plastic container, wrapped to prevent sunlight interaction)
2. Weighing scale (normal kitchen scale will work which is available online)
3. Surgical gloves (available at local pharmacy)

Ingredients required

1. Fish waste (whole fish can also be used) (1kg)[178]
2. Molasses or palm sugar or raw sugar or jaggery (1kg)

Steps

1. Collect fish waste (guts, head, skin or any other part that is not consumed and discarded). Make sure to wear gloves when handling the organic waste, to avoid contamination as well as injury.

2. Chop the fish waste into pieces and coat it with palm sugar or molasses. For 1 kilo of fish, use 1 kilo of molasses or palm sugar or jaggery.
3. Pour this mixture into an airtight container. Fill only 50% of the container and keep the rest empty.
4. Keep the container in shade for 30-40 days. Ensure no sunlight interaction occurs.
5. The air tight container should be opened once a day and its contents stirred. You should use a stick or tool which is regularly cleaned.

Result

1. The fertilizer will be ready in 30-40 days.
2. Strain the solution to get liquid fertilizer. Any remaining solid fish parts should not be reused, instead bury them near trees. Make sure to bury more than 6 feet underground or predators might catch their smell.
3. Supply this solution regularly via drip irrigation to ensure optimal plant and soil health.

Application

Dilute 1-2 tablespoons[179] of fish fertilizer in 1 gallon[180] of water, which translates to 5-10ml in approximately 4 liters of water.

Precautions

1. Fish fertilizer gives off a bad odor and Thus, it is advisable to keep it away from residential areas and in a secluded place.
2. Do not add water to the mixture or the fish will rot.
3. The kind of fish that is used affects the fertilizer. Fishes can be broadly classified into 2 types on the basis of their habitat – saltwater fish and freshwater fish.
   Saltwater fish live in the sea and are common in coastal areas, whereas freshwater fish live in inland water bodies. However, the habitat of the fish does not matter as much as its place in the food chain. How, you ask? Because of the process of bioaccumulation.

WHAT IS BIOACCUMULATION?

Bioaccumulation refers to the process by which substances, often pollutants or toxic chemicals, accumulate and build-up in living organisms over time. This accumulation occurs as a result of the organism's exposure to these substances through various sources such as food, water, or air.

As smaller organisms contaminated with chemicals are ingested, these substances accumulate and intensify in the tissues and organs of larger animals. Animals occupying the higher tiers of the food chain, including humans, are at risk of accumulating elevated concentrations of these chemicals due to biomagnification[181] process within the food chain.

BIOACCUMULATION OF MERCURY IN FISHES

Mercury is a naturally occurring element, which is toxic to humans (even in small amounts). It is released into the atmosphere by natural events such as volcanic eruptions and human activities like burning coal, industrial processes, etc. Bacteria present in the air and soil react with mercury and transform it into methylmercury, a very toxic substance.

This substance bioaccumulates in the environment. Large predatory fish are prone to elevated mercury levels because they consume numerous smaller fish that have acquired mercury by ingesting aquatic vegetation. The concentration of mercury rises with the levels of the food chain. This toxic substance can bioaccumulate in your fertilizer and through that in your soil and crops.

Thus, it is advised to use small non-predatory fishes (that feed on aquatic vegetation) to avoid the risk of mercury poisoning in your fertilizer and subsequently your crop.

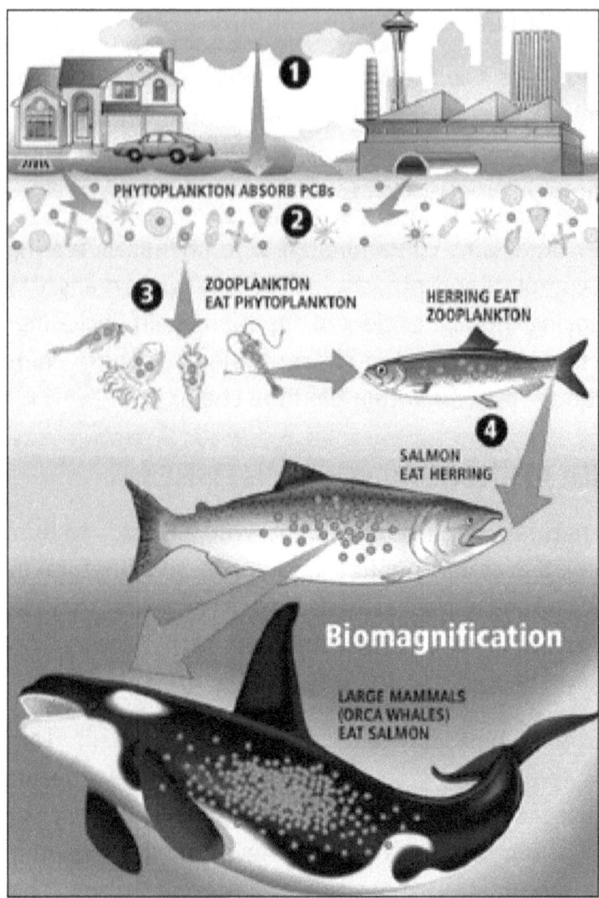

Figure 113: Biomagnification in fishes[182]

Following is a list of fish in decreasing order of mercury in their bodies, measured in parts per million[183] (ppm)[184] to give the reader an idea about the varying levels of mercury percentage in different fish in ascending order:

1. **Salmon:** 0.022 ppm (Saltwater/Freshwater)

Figure 114: Salmon

2.   **Catfish:** 0.025 ppm (Freshwater)

Figure 115: Catfish

3.   **Crayfish:** 0.035 ppm (Freshwater)

Figure 116: Crayfish

4.   **Herring:** 0.084 ppm (Salt water)

Figure 117: Herring

5.   **Cod:** 0.111 ppm (Salt water)

Figure 118: Cod

6. **Tuna:** 0.128 ppm (Salt water)

Figure 119: Tuna

7. **Marlin:** 0.485 ppm (Salt water)

Figure 120: Marlin

8. **King mackerel:** 0.730 ppm (Saltwater)

Figure 121: King mackerel

9. **Shark:** 0.979 ppm (Salt water)

Figure 122: Shark

Following is a list of some herbivorous fish found locally in India. Using fish that feed primarily on aquatic vegetation will greatly reduce the risk of bioaccumulation.

1. Catla (Catla)

Figure 123: Catla

2. Murrel (Channa spp.)

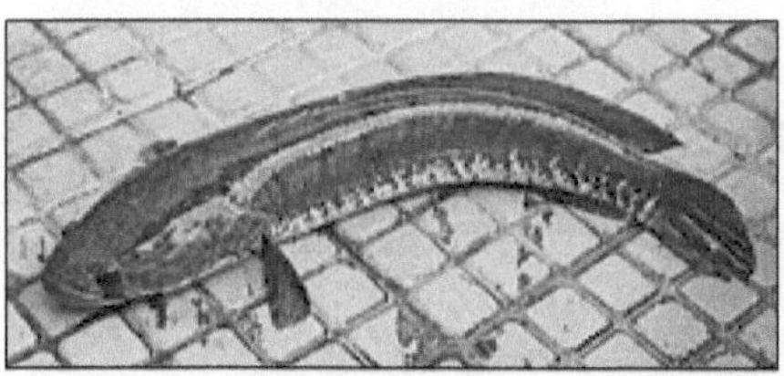

Figure 124: Murrel

3. Silver Carp (Hypophthalmichthys molitrix)

Figure 125: Silver carp

4. Mrigal Carp (Cirrhinus mrigala)

Figure 126: Mrigal Carp

5. Grass Carp (Ctenopharyngodon idella)

Figure 127: Grass Carp

HOW TO USE ORGANIC FERTILIZERS?

Until now, we have discussed five kinds of organic fertilizers, namely-

1. Compost
2. Vermicompost.
3. Farmyard Manure (FYM)
4. Bioenzyme solution
5. Fish fertiliser (Fertifish)

We have also discussed the application process of these fertilizers. However, there is a roadblock in using these fertilizers. Chemical fertilizers can be rich in one particular kind of nutrient, such as-

1. **Urea**
2. **Diammonium Phosphate (DAP)** (Contains about 18% nitrogen and 46% phosphorus)
3. **Muriate of Potash (MOP)** (Contains about 60% potassium)

This is because they are factory-made. Unlike these chemical fertilizers, organic fertilizers consist of multiple nutrients and organic matter. The only drawback being – these nutrients are present in comparatively smaller quantities or ppm. For example –

1. **Compost** (Variable amounts of nitrogen (N), phosphorus (P), potassium (K) and trace elements
2. **Vermicompost** (Nitrogen (1-2%), Phosphorus (0.5-1%), Potassium (0.5-1%), trace elements, and humic acids[185].)
3. **Manure** (Typically contains around 0.5-1.5% nitrogen, 0.2-0.5% phosphorus, and 0.5-1.5% potassium.)
4. **Bio enzyme** (Nitrogen (N), Phosphorus (P), Potassium (K), trace elements, enzymes, and organic acids)
5. **Fish Emulsion** (Contains around 5% nitrogen, 1% phosphorus, and 1% potassium).

The following table lists the ppm (parts per million) of these nutrients:

Table 27: Nutrients in ppm

Fertilizer	Nitrogen (ppm)	Phosphorus (ppm)	Potassium (ppm)	Other Components (ppm)
Compost	5,000 – 20,000	3,000 – 9,000	5,000 – 15,000	Trace elements (variable)
Vermicompost	10,000 – 20,000	5,000 – 10,000	5,000 – 10,000	Humic acids, trace elements (<1,000)
Manure	5,000 – 15,000	2,000 – 5,000	5,000 – 15,000	Trace elements (variable)

Bio Enzyme	1,000 – 5,000	500 – 2,000	1,000 – 10,000	Enzymes, organic acids (<1,000)
Fish Emulsion	50,000	10,000	10,000	Trace elements (variable)
Fertilizer	Nitrogen (ppm)	Phosphorus (ppm)	Potassium (ppm)	Other Components (ppm)

Due to the distributed nutrient content of organic fertilizers, they have to be used in considerable amounts to provide nutrition to the soil. Another drawback is using only one kind of organic fertilizer may not provide all the nutrients that your crop needs.

To solve this problem, we recommend using a multifaceted approach.

Let us understand this in detail. The area we need to cultivate for fodder crops is 1/4th of an acre (area – 1,011 sq. meters). From here on, this will be considered as the default measurement for measuring the application rate of all fertilizers.

Instead of relying on only one kind of organic fertilizer, we are going to use all fertilizers mentioned here. You can use the free space available in area 2 (where the hydroponics machine will be set up) or in area 4 (where the processing station will be set up). The structures to be built in these areas will barely occupy 40-50% of the available space.

The rest of the space can be used to make compost and manure pits and vermicompost beds. (Bio enzyme and fish fertilizer require cool shaded places; therefore, they should preferably be stored in a room and not in open areas).

Firstly, let us understand the application rates of these fertilizers. The following table will give you a general idea of the application rate.

Table 28: Application Rates and Methods of Organic Fertilizers

Fertilizer	Rate (per 1/4 acre)	Application Method
Compost	200 kg	Spread evenly and incorporate into the soil before planting.
Vermicompost	50 kg	Apply around the root zones during critical growth stages.

Farm Yard Manure	300 kg	Spread evenly and incorporate into the soil before planting.
Bio-enzyme Solution	10 liters (concentrated) diluted in 1000 liters of water	Foliar spray every 2 weeks / Supplied via drip irrigation
Fertifish	2 kg (concentrated) diluted in 100 liters of water	Foliar spray monthly / Supplied via drip irrigation

Let us now understand the detailed application details of each fodder crop that we discussed in Chapter 6.

Table 29: Detailed fertilizer schedule of fodder crops

Crop	Stage	Maturity Month	Application Method	Fertilizers
Cowpea	**Before Planting**	-	Spread evenly and incorporate into the soil.	Compost: 200 kg Farm Yard Manure: 300 kg
	Vegetative Stage	1-2 months	Apply around root zones and foliar spray	Vermicompost: 25 kg Bio enzyme: Every 2 weeks Fertifish: Monthly
	Flowering Stage	2-3 months	Apply around root zones and foliar spray	Vermicompost: 25 kg, Bio enzyme: Every 2 weeks Fertifish: Monthly
Alfalfa	**Before Planting**	-	Spread evenly and incorporate into the soil.	Compost: 200 kg Farm Yard Manure: 300 kg

Crop	Stage	Maturity Month	Application Method	Fertilizers
	Vegetative Stage	1-2 months	Apply around root zones and foliar spray	Vermicompost: 25 kg Bio enzyme: Every 2 weeks. Fertifish: Monthly.
	Flowering Stage	2-4 months	Apply around root zones and foliar spray	Vermicompost: 25 kg Bio enzyme: Every 2 weeks Fertifish: Monthly
Pearl Millet	**Before Planting**	-	Spread evenly and incorporate into the soil.	Compost: 200 kg Farm Yard Manure: 300 kg
	Vegetative Stage	1-1.5 months	Apply around root zones and foliar spray	Vermicompost: 25 kg Bio enzyme: Every 2 weeks Fertifish: Monthly
	Flowering Stage	1.5-2.5 months	Apply around root zones and foliar spray	Vermicompost: 25 kg Bio enzyme: Every 2 weeks Fertifish: Monthly
Anjan Grass	**Before Planting**	-	Spread evenly and incorporate into the soil.	Compost: 200 kg Farm Yard Manure: 300 kg
	Vegetative Stage	1-2 months	Apply around root zones and foliar spray	Vermicompost: 25 kg Bio enzyme: Every 2 weeks Fertifish: Monthly

Crop	Stage	Maturity Month	Application Method	Fertilizers
	Flowering Stage	2-3 months	Apply around root zones and foliar spray	Vermicompost: 25 kg Bio enzyme: Every 2 weeks. Fertifish: Monthly.

Using this approach, you can provide all-round nutrition to your crop. Each of these fertilizers performs multiple functions and provides all kinds of nutrients to your plants that are required for healthy growth.

Table 30: Benefits of various organic fertilizers

Fertilizer	Functions in Soil
Compost	– Improves soil structure and texture
	– Increases organic matter content
	– Enhances nutrient availability
	– Promotes beneficial microbial activity
	– Improves water retention and drainage
Vermicompost	– Enhances nutrient availability, particularly nitrogen, phosphorus and potassium
	– Improves soil structure and aeration
	– Promotes the growth of beneficial microorganisms
	– Increases organic matter content
	– Boosts plant growth and yields
Farm Yard Manure (FYM)	– Adds organic matter to the soil

Fertilizer	Functions in Soil
	– Improves soil structure, aeration and moisture retention
	– Supplies essential nutrients such as nitrogen, phosphorus, and potassium
	– Promotes microbial activity
	– Enhances soil fertility over time
Bio Enzyme	– Improves nutrient availability and uptake
	– Enhances soil microbial activity
	– Promotes healthy root development
	– Improves soil structure and water retention.
Fertifish	– Provides a rich source of nitrogen and other essential nutrients
	– Improves soil structure and fertility
	– Enhances microbial activity
	– Increases organic matter content
	– Promotes plant growth and productivity

STORE BOUGHT ORGANIC FERTILIZERS

1. THE BLOOD MEAL

Despite its ominous name, it is actually a very good fertilizer, made from the dried blood of animals. Its NPK ratio is 12:0:0, which means it exclusively contains only nitrogen and should be applied carefully.

The smell of the blood meal repels some animals like squirrels who often steal seeds, but it may also attract unwanted attention from others like dogs.

It has an acidifying effect on the soil and is a great medium for lowering soil pH. It's a long-term fertilizer in the sense that it releases nutrients slowly over a period of months (2-4 months) and therefore does not require regular reapplication. The application rate of 1.3kg per 1000 sq feet is advisable.

Figure 128: Blood meal

Drawbacks

1. Potential for Burns: If not properly incorporated into the soil or if applied in excessive amounts, blood meal can cause nitrogen burns to plants. This can manifest as scorched or brown leaves.
2. Risk of Disease Transmission: Blood meal, being an animal by-product, may carry the risk of transmitting diseases. Proper handling and processing are essential to minimize this risk.

2. THE BONE MEAL

The bone meal fertilizer is made by crushing the bones of animals to a fine powder. The NPK ratio of bone meal is 3:15:0; it has a high concentration of phosphorus and also contains nitrogen and calcium.

It releases the nutrients slowly and is a long-term fertilizer which keeps on giving for 3-4 months after application. However, bone meal fertilizer only works on soils with a pH level lower than 7, so it's necessary to get the soil tested before applying the fertilizer.

Figure 129: Bone meal

Drawbacks

1. Calcium Content: Bone meal contains calcium, which can contribute to soil alkalinity. In soils that are already alkaline, the use of bone meal may further raise the pH level.
2. Risk of Contamination: Bone meal can be sourced from animal bones, and there may be concerns about contaminants or diseases. Proper processing and quality control are essential to minimize these risks.

3. THE KELP MEAL

Kelp meal is another good source of potassium. It is made from dried seaweed and has an NPK ratio of 1:0:4. It releases nutrients slowly over time and should be added when preparing soil for cultivation.

Figure 130: Kelp meal

In this chapter, you learned:

Coming up...

Hydroponics
History
Hanging gardens of Babylon
William Gericke
Tomato plants
Purpose
Fodder
Macronutrients
Major components
Sealed structure
Controlled environment
Location
Secluded
Sunlight
Tray
Plastic
Lightweight
Does not react
Slightly inclined
Holes on one end
AC/ heater
Irrigation
Sprinkler
Manual
Exhaust
Benefits
Requires less
Land
20 x10m
Water
Labor
Increased yield
Environment friendly
Quality fodder
Available all year
Crops
Maize
Cowpea
Wheatgrass
Horsegram
Process
Pre-seed treatment
7 day growing

CHAPTER 8

Hydroponics

TO SUMMARIZE CHAPTERS 4 and 6, we have covered two essential elements of nutrition so far-

1. Micronutrients
2. Roughage

In this chapter, we are going to discuss the third component of nutrition – Macronutrients.

Before delving into the details of macronutrients, let us look back for a moment. We started this book with a problem – the problem of the decreasing area of land and the danger of farmers becoming landless in the future.

At present, the phenomenon of land fragmentation poses an immediate danger to the farmers who live on the very periphery of society – <u>marginal farmers</u>. However, this issue will not confine itself to wrecking the lives of only marginal farmers. It's like wildfire; unless immediate and strong measures are taken, it will keep spreading until it burns everything down to ashes.

This metaphor depicts the problem of decreasing land needing an urgent fix. It also shows how nature will be unbiased in who it takes down. A wildfire will burn everything from the smallest grass to magnificent tall trees. To correlate, at present only marginal farmers are at risk of becoming landless, but it is evident that in the coming future (due to land fragmentation) even large farmers with land sprawling over hectares will have descendants falling into the marginal category and losing their lands.

This will escalate the issue of land dispute among families. This headline from an article published in the newspaper 'India Today' will bring the issue of land dispute into perspective-

'Farmer hangs himself from a tree in Gurugram over a land dispute with family'[186]

It is about a farmer who clashed with his brother over land ownership and ended up committing suicide. This is not a remote incident but one among hundreds that take place every day.

The contents of this particular chapter of our proposed solution if talked about individually might seem like a utopian way out to the problem of decreasing land. However, using this method, a farmer can grow fodder without soil.

Yes, you read that right!

Hydroponics (the third component of the self-sustainable land project) means growing plants without using soil. Instead, we use water to provide nutrients to the plants. It might sound unreal at the moment, and questions like the following are obvious:

- How can a plant be cultivated without using soil?
- Where will the seeds be planted?
- What will the roots hold onto?
- What about gravity? Without soil, how will the plants stand?
- What about water type?
- What about the weather?
- What types of crops and plants can be grown?

The proposal of growing crops without soil might sound baffling, and the idea must seem absurd. As we progress further, we will understand how this is not only possible but also sustainable.

WHY HYDROPONICS?

Why should a farmer opt for hydroponics instead of the traditional method of growing fodder? What advantages does hydroponics have over the traditional methods of growing fodder? Listed below are the major advantages, answering this question of why.

1. SOLUTION TO DECREASING LAND

This book is dedicated to discussing the decreasing area of land for agriculture and pasture use due to various reasons like land fragmentation, urbanization, industrial use, etc. The traditional method of farming requires a large area of land to produce bulk fodder, whereas in hydroponics, the same amount of fodder can be produced on a ridiculously low area of land.

Using hydroponics technology, about 600-1000 kg of maize fodder can be produced daily in a 7-8 day growth cycle, in only a 45-50 m2 area compared with one hectare required in traditional farming. Hydroponics uses vertical farming, for example towers of trays stacked on top of each other to produce more fodder in less area.

It is a logical solution for farmers who own less than one hectare of land. The minimal land required for hydroponics is only 10m x 5m to grow 600-650 kg of fodder per day.

In the traditional method, roots of plants spread out in the soil and hence require more space between each plant to sustain growth. But in the hydroponics system, the roots of plants are very short and do not need such spacing. This means more plants per unit space can be grown.

2. WATER CONSERVATION

Water is a major component of hydroponic farming. It is the substitute for soil, the single most crucial element to grow any plant. Even so, it is actually needed in very small amounts. The water is directly sprayed onto the roots and only about

1.5-2 liters are needed to produce 1 kg of green fodder hydroponically in comparison with traditional methods which use up to 65 liters on average for 1 kg of traditional fodder.

This system minimizes water wastage and increases the efficiency of using available water. The runoff water from the trays can be collected and reused to water trees and crops. Before reusing, it is recommended that the water be treated or filtered. A simple charcoal and sand-based filter can ensure small bacteria do not stay suspended in the water.

This results in a no-waste system. Thus, hydroponics is a boon for areas with water shortage like arid and semi-arid areas of the world.

3. NO ADDITIONAL INPUTS

Plants in hydroponics are grown in a controlled environment in a sealed room; this reduces the risk of a disease outbreak significantly.

In contrast to plants grown traditionally, the plants in hydroponics do not need huge investments in pesticides, insecticides, or herbicides. The resulting fodder is thoroughly organic without any traces of pesticides or insecticides.

Since traditional farming relies on soil and an open environment, the chance of disease and insects ruining the crop is high, resulting in a high capital investment going into preventing them. In hydroponics, even if a fungal infection or other disease breaks out, it can be easily eliminated.

Farmers should keep in mind to use only fresh or low TDS water to minimize the risk of waterborne diseases. TDS of up to 250 is acceptable, but the pH should be as close to 7 as possible.

4. INCREASED YIELD

Water is sprayed directly onto the tray. This water contains trace amounts of minerals, so no energy is wasted in seeking out nutrients by the roots. This is in contrast to traditionally grown plants whose roots seek out nutrients in the soil and have to convert them before consuming.

Because nutrients are supplied directly to the plant roots, it increases plant growth and accelerates fodder production by 25%. One kg of un-sprouted seed yields 4-5 kg of green fodder in 7 days. The author has been able to get as much as 6 kg with extreme control over the environment and by using a semi-automatic hydroponics machine.

5. QUALITY FODDER

Since hydroponic fodder is only 7-8 days old when it's fed, it's bursting with nutrients. It is observed that when we compare the ready fodder with the original seed on a Dry Matter (DM) basis, the crude protein (CP), neutral detergent fiber (NDF), acid detergent fiber (ADF), and calcium content are higher in the fodder. Additionally, the organic matter (OM) and non-fibrous carbohydrates (NFC) content decrease.

Hydroponic fodder is also a great source of vitamins, antioxidants, and bio enzymes. Altogether, it has more positives compared to the dry grain.

6. Since hydroponic fodder is grown in a controlled environment, it can be grown all year round without any problems. The same crop, like maize, can be grown without the need for crop rotation.

This ensures that the fodder produced is consistent not only in quantity but also in quality. When the farmer grows his own fodder, they can be assured of the quality. Feeding good quality fodder all year round increases the health and output of the livestock. The author has consumed hydroponically grown gram saplings himself.

7. ENVIRONMENTALLY FRIENDLY

In chapter 1, we talked about the environmental damage done by the use of pesticides and fertilizers, which not only degrade the soil but also pollute water bodies nearby. The breakdown of fertilizers results in the emission of greenhouse gases. In contrast, hydroponics has a reduced carbon footprint and is environmentally friendly. None of the materials used are wasted as even the produce is consumed whole (seeds, root mat, etc.) by the animals, leaving no residues.

8. THINGS TO TAKE CARE

- Try feeding the fodder on the 5th day itself. This will prevent any insects from getting into the roots.
- Regularly check the root mat starting from the 4th day to see if there are larvae at the base. If so, wash the tray and feed the fodder on the very first day of larva sighting.
- Ensure all trays are washed and sun-dried after every use.
- Water pH level should not be acidic.
- Treat the water to ensure zero contamination.

Before delving into the how and what details, let us step back in time and understand the history of hydroponics.

HISTORY OF HYDROPONICS

(The Hanging Gardens of Babylon & other wondrous stories)

To take a momentary stroll down the etymology[187] lane, the term 'hydroponics' comes from the Greek words:

Hydro + Ponos = Hydroponics

(Water) + (Labor) = Process of growing plants without soil

Hydroponics is the process of growing plants without soil, with only water as nutrition.

The history of hydroponics dates back to the ancient fable of the *'Hanging Gardens of Babylon'*.

Babylon was, at one time, the largest city of the ancient world, situated in southern Mesopotamia, present-day Iraq. The Hanging Gardens of Babylon are said to have been built on the banks of the Euphrates River by King Nebuchadnezzar II for his wife, Amyitis, who missed the lush green landscape of her home.

It is considered one of the 7 wonders of the ancient world, mostly because of the technology that was used to build a sprawling vertical garden at a time when cultivation was done purely for the purpose of food and not decoration[188].

Yes, the naysayers can complain that hydroponics were just decorative.

But, this ancient wonder has many theories to its name and has historians in a knot. How exactly were these gardens 'hanging'? Were they built through terrace farming? What was the system of irrigation? It is theorized that hydroponics could be an answer to this riddle. According to this theory, the hanging gardens were built in a structure resembling a mountain slope, and water was supplied to the plants through an irrigation system based in the center of the structure.

The slope would ensure that the water was continuously running, which would inhibit the growth of any bacteria due to stagnation. The plants grew perhaps solely through the nutrition they absorbed from the water of the Euphrates River. And so, ancient Babylon gave the world the legendary 'hanging gardens' with technology that could rival modern techniques at present.

And all of this was done by a king, so in love with his queen, that he constructed a vertical garden to cure her homesickness. And perhaps no hands were chopped off post-construction (Pun intended).

The term 'hydroponics' was officially coined in 1937 by William Frederick Gericke, a physiologist at the University of California, also known as the father of hydroponics.

Gericke authored "The Complete Guide to Soilless Gardening," published in 1940. This book was one of the first comprehensive guides on hydroponics and detailed the methods and benefits of soilless plant cultivation.

It remains a seminal work in the field and is often referenced by those studying or working with hydroponics.

Figure 131: William Frederick Gericke[189]

Figure 132: Mr. Gericke on a ladder, harvesting his hydroponically grown tomato plants and his wife standing at the base of the ladder[190]

It was difficult for people back then to believe that plants could be grown without soil, with only water, and even his own colleagues doubted his logic. However, he proved the theory right by growing 7.6 meters high tomato vines in his backyard with only a mineral nutrient solution. Would you like to take this challenge? The author has achieved this by using his own invention of a PVC pipe-based vertical grower.

Although it's a technique that has been around since ancient times, its importance in human history has never been more prominent than at present.

The decreasing area of land under cultivation has resulted in decreased green fodder production. Pasture land is being converted into housing complexes, industries, or becoming unusable due to overgrazing. Farmers choose to cultivate commercial or food crops instead of fodder crops because of greater demand and higher profit rates of the former.

In the author's own village Daurai, Ajmer, there has been a corruption scandal where government pasture land was illegally transferred to some villagers.

Traditional fodder crop cultivation is a labor-intensive and time-consuming process. It often necessitates hiring additional labor for various tasks, such as cutting and chaffing. Harvesting these crops also demands significant time due to their voluminous nature, which complicates transportation. Additionally, like other crops, fodder crops face challenges such as water scarcity for irrigation.

These problems will only increase in magnitude in the coming future, therefore it is necessary to find an alternative. Hydroponics provides a long-term, sustainable solution to this problem. How? Let us analyze the process of growing fodder through hydroponics to understand its place as a sustainable alternative.

Before we dive into details, let us understand the process of growing hydroponic fodder in very simplified terms. The first basic necessity to grow any kind of crop is seeds. Fresh, disease-free viable seeds of the crop that the farmer wants to grow.

Now, since soil is not used, there has to be an alternative to give the seeds a base. In this case, trays made of plastic are used. Why only plastic? We will get to that question in the next few pages.

So instead of soil, the seeds are spread on a tray which is kept in a sealed structure with a controlled environment. They are sprinkled with water from time to time. The fodder is ready to be harvested after 7 days and can be fed to the livestock as a whole – roots, seeds, and leaves.

This is an overly simplified explanation of the process, just to give the reader an idea. Let us now analyze the details of the process along with the major components involved.

MAJOR COMPONENTS OF HYDROPONIC STATION

1. SEALED STRUCTURE

The first major component of a hydroponic station is a sealed structure. We do not mean a vacuum structure, but do lay emphasis on being airtight, where humidity is non-transferable.

Figure 133: Front view of hydroponics station[191]

There is a very particular reason behind the emphasis for this structure to be 'sealed'. When a farmer grows crops traditionally i.e. in soil, in an open environment, the crop is susceptible to many risks. From sowing the seeds to harvesting the crop, there are many things that could go wrong and damage the crop or destroy it completely.

1. Soil itself becomes a major threat, not by nature but because of mismanagement by the farmer.
2. Use of chemical fertilizers destroy the natural fertility of soil, making it barren in the long run. Soil loses humus and pH balance as well as natural nutrition.
3. Excessive use of water causes soil erosion.
4. Strong winds or dust storms also contribute to soil erosion.
5. Attacks from insects or pests and stray animals like cows eating the crop.
6. Sudden weather changes like rain or storm.
7. Attack of pests as well as underground mounds of ants and termites etc.

All these elements prevent the crop from reaching its full potential in terms of harvest. These factors are manageable but cannot be wholly eliminated from the traditional farming system. The farmer uses risk prevention methods like using fertilizers for the soil, insecticides, and pesticides to protect the crops and fencing to keep away stray animals. But these solutions are heavy on the pocket and have to be repeated for every crop season in increasing quantities of either time, money, effort, or all 3.

The reason hydroponic crops are grown in a sealed structure is:

1. To eliminate the risks and threats involved in traditional farming.
2. The sealed structure will establish a controlled environment[192] with minimum temperature variation.
3. The sealed structure provides an environment which is 99% free of any foreign material introduced by external factors. This includes the visible threats of insects and pests but also threats which are invisible to the naked eyes like bacteria.

In fact, the structure is so enclosed that it does not even allow natural air to flow freely, unless the farmer wants it to.

What does this mean? It means that in traditional farming, the farmer is at the mercy of external factors which are beyond their control. It may rain or not, and the fate of their crop is dependent on this 'maybe'.

But in the sealed structure of hydroponics, they are no longer reliant on unpredictable factors. The sealed structure gives them control over every aspect of the environment within, increasing the success rate to almost 100%.[193]All the potential dangers of the traditional system can be significantly reduced in this structure.

The structure ensures that:

1. The weather outside has no effect on the temperature inside.
2. No insects or other animals can enter.
3. The chance of soil-borne bacterial infections is completely out of question since there is no soil. This provides an optimal environment for the plants to grow and reduces the risks, otherwise involved in traditional farming to almost negligible.
4. Proper thermal insulation and earthing also ensures mishaps are minimal.

Even better news? This structure can be built in a space as small as 10m x 5m. In our proposed solution (of 1 acre land), this structure will be built on a space measuring 20m x 10m in area 2 (1011 sq. m). This means that the farmer has much more than the minimum area required to carry out hydroponics.

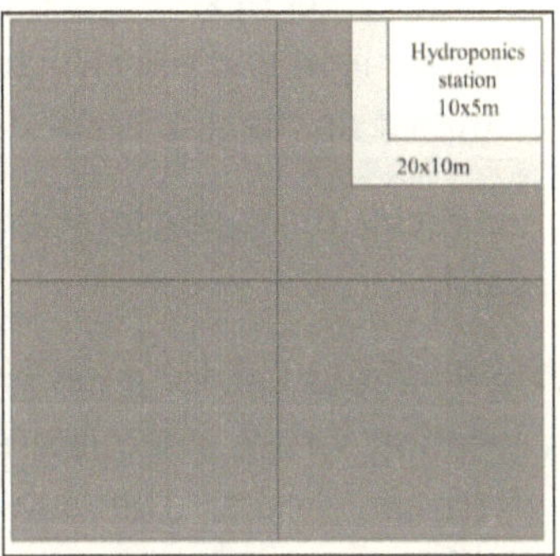

Figure 134: Diagrammatic representation of Area 2 where a hydroponics station will be set up

Additional benefit: Even after the construction of the structure, there will be ample vacant land in Area 2 that can be utilized for other purposes, like digging compost pits.

2. LOCATION... LOCATION... LOCATION

The second major component is the location of this structure. Building the structure without assessing the environment will have negative effects on the growth of plants. Remember that we are in control of the environment within the structure. To establish this control, the location of the structure is very important.

Figure 135: Sunlight filtering through the windows of a hydroponics station[194]

For example, if the farmer wants to control the amount of sunlight that the plants receive within the structure, they can do so by building windows in strategic locations.

But for this to happen, the structure should be first located in an area that receives sunlight from multiple directions. If it is built in an area with trees around it, the trees will block sunlight and the structure will remain in shade, thus having a not so great impact on the growth of plants.

So how does the farmer decide on a good location? There are a few things that can help us in this regard:

1. Sunlight is extremely important for good growth and the structure should be in a location where adequate sunlight reaches during morning and afternoon hours. The sunlight should enter the structure from 3 sides via glass windows, meanwhile one side will remain windowless with no sunlight.
So, we should have the possibility of light entering from the east, west, north, or south.

2. Build on a spot near the boundary (but not in the shade of trees) to ensure that there are no disturbances near the structure, like farm animals going near it.
3. The secluded area will also ensure the structure does not become an obstacle, sitting in the middle of the land and disrupting the daily work carried out on the farm.
4. The prime location of the structure in area 2 means that there will be no cost of transporting the fodder to reach the livestock.

3. TRAY

Plastic trays are the next crucial component of hydroponics-based fodder development. In the beginning of this chapter, we made a statement that fodder can be grown without soil.

Therefore, before proceeding further, let us clear up a few burning questions.

Firstly, yes, soil is not needed to grow plants. The reader might wonder, if not soil, what will be the base where seeds are placed? The tray will provide the base.

The roots hold on to themselves, making a mat inside the tray, using each other as a source of tension to grow against the force of gravity. Multiple seeds have their roots grab onto each other, thereby mutually benefiting from the mat that gets created.

The missing element of soil in hydroponics changes the procedure of growing fodder significantly. *The plants that can be cultivated using hydroponics are limited.* This is because in the absence of soil to support the stems of the cultivated plant, it becomes tough to sustain such plants once they gain weight. Also, the type of roots the plant has is a key requirement to make mats.

According to the laws of physics, for the plant to grow tall, which is against the natural gravitational pull of Earth, it needs to exert a force that is equivalent and slightly greater than the gravitational pull of Earth. This force requires the roots to have a grip, which is negligible in hydroponics. Therefore, we cannot grow plants that need stem strength; instead, we grow leafy plants or grass.

Figure 136: Trays assembled in racks inside a hydroponics station[195]

Plastic trays are the base where the plant mat will be grown; this is the substitute for soil in this system. There are a few things to keep in mind while buying trays for hydroponics.

a. The first is their material. Plastic trays are a good option because they are cheap and long-lasting, lightweight, easy to move and will not get damaged from continuous exposure to water via sprinkler system.

Table 31: Standard sizes of hydroponic trays along with the materials they are typically made of

Tray Size	Dimensions (L x W x H)	Material
Small Tray	10" x 20" x 2.5"	High-Density Polyethylene (HDPE), Polypropylene (PP)
Medium Tray	24" x 48" x 6"	High-Density Polyethylene (HDPE), Polypropylene (PP)
Large Tray	36" x 72" x 6"	High-Density Polyethylene (HDPE), Polypropylene (PP)
Extra Large Tray	48" x 96" x 6"	High-Density Polyethylene (HDPE), Polypropylene (PP)
Propagation Tray	21" x 11" x 2.5"	High-Density Polyethylene (HDPE), Polypropylene (PP)
Flood and Drain Tray	48" x 48" x 7"	High-Density Polyethylene (HDPE), Acrylonitrile Butadiene Styrene (ABS)
NFT Channel Tray	78" x 6" x 3"	UV-stabilized PVC, Polypropylene (PP)
Deep Water Culture (DWC) Tray	36" x 36" x 12"	High-Density Polyethylene (HDPE), Polypropylene (PP)

b. Special trays are available for growing hydroponics fodder[196]. Trays made from other material, like iron, cannot sustain water damage and end up getting rusted. They do not handle temperature well thus are not suitable for our purpose.

c. Plastic trays are easy to clean. Trays used in hydroponics should be washed after every use (every 7 days)

d. Plastic trays are less reactive to temperature change.

e. The next important thing to keep in mind is that the trays should not have a linear base but should be slightly inclined (around 5 degrees) toward one side. The reason behind this is very simple.

In hydroponics, as the name suggests, water or 'hydro' is essential as it provides the nutrition that is required to grow plants. The water is provided through sprinkling.

The slight incline (approximately 5 degrees) of the tray ensures that excess water can be drained at one end and thus is not collected at the base of the seed. If collected, it will stagnate and result in the rotting of the seed, or worse, it will lead to fungal or bacterial infection.

Notice how a very small structural detail like the slight incline of the tray can change the entire course of plant growth. This is just a small reminder that every such small detail in this book is present because it has a purpose. It is not present by chance, and if ignored, it can easily bring down the entire plan. As the story goes, even an ant can bring down an elephant.

f. The inclined end of the tray should have 3-4 small holes. This is to dispose of excess water. Make sure to leave the space above the holes free, otherwise it will lead to blockage. Stagnant water can ruin the plant mat.

g. The general measurement of a tray is 2 feet in width and 1 inch in height. Out of the 2 feet, 3inch space should be left on the corner of the tray where water will collect and disposal of excess water will happen at this end. As for the height of the tray, only 50%, that is half inch should be filled with seeds. Rest of the space should be left for plant growth[197] because as roots grow they will first spread in a linear direction and then vertical and when they grow vertical that's when the fast growth happens.

4. WATER

The seeds grown in hydroponics do not require much watering. Just 2-3 liters of water can produce 1 kg of lush green fodder. They do require occasional sprinkling of water to maintain humidity. This can be done manually by the farmer on a small-scale; for larger projects, a sprinkling system can be set up with a timer.

Using distilled water is advised to sprinkle plants because it does not contain any chemicals or minerals which might interfere with the plant growth. The excess water will travel through the holes in the tray, via pipes to a water tank where it can be stored.

This water should not be reused to water the plants grown in hydroponics as it increases the risk of infection or disease in the plants. However, the runoff can be used to water crops and trees without any problem. This means no water is wasted in this system. We need to decontaminate this water before reusing it.

The use of neem oil, 10ml per 100 liters of water, will ensure bacteria and larvae don't form in water storage tanks. If possible, using UV LED lights can also ensure that the bacterial and viral infections are under control.

It is suggested not to let this water stay unused as bacteria form very quickly due to the available nutrients in the water.

5. EXHAUST FAN

A couple of exhaust fans should be placed for the inlet and outlet of air. This will ensure that there is a means to enable the flow of air in the room. This is necessary for many reasons.

Stale and humidified air will give rise to disease and bad odor and thus must be avoided. The growing seeds/saplings will need a steady supply of carbon dioxide to grow, hence proper airflow is required for optimal plant growth.

6. HEATING/COOLING ELEMENTS

Heating/cooling elements such as an air conditioner and heater are required to maintain and control the temperature of the hydroponics room. This ensures that the outer temperature does not affect the inner temperature of the room.

The temperature inside the room must remain constant regardless of the temperature outside. The temperature should range between 15-32°C, and each seed has a specific temperature range.

Now that we have explained the major components of the hydroponic station, it is now time to understand how it will work.

The structure has windows on 3 sides – east, west, and north, while the south side remains windowless. It also has 2 doors on opposite ends facing east. One door is to insert the tray on day 1, while the other is to move trays as they proceed through the channel.

GROWING HYDROPONICS FODDER

1. Pre-soak seeds before spreading them on the mat. These are generally soaked in water from a few hours to 24 hours, depending on the type of crop seed. For example, soaking maize seeds for 4 hours is enough.
   Soaking time for various crops is provided in Table 4.

2. Seeds should be whole, healthy and viable, disease, infection and insect free. Damaged seeds will hamper the end production so it's necessary to get good quality seeds.

3. The seeds should be tied tightly in a gunny bag and kept for at least 24 hours to allow for the heat generated within to propagate germination. Time to time keep pouring water on the bag.

4. The farmer spreads the germinated seeds on the tray. Consider this as Day 1.
   (Seed application differs from crop to crop. For maize, a seed rate of 6.4-7.6 kg/m2 is sufficient. If seed density is high, the possible risk of microbial contamination in the root mat increases, which will have a negative effect on fodder growth).

5. On Day 1 the seeds should be kept away from the sunlight, in the windowless area of the structure.

6. From here on, every day the tray will be shifted one place further in the line toward the northern part of the room (where windows are placed). As it moves through the line it will get an increasing amount of sunlight every day, as is required for optimal growth.

7. On day 7, the plant mat is ready and can be freshly fed to the livestock.

Figure 137: Progression of hydroponics fodder over 7 days[198]

Figure 138: Finished plant mat[199]

Figure 139: Feeding hydroponically grown fodder to livestock[200] [201]

REQUIRED TIME TO SET UP

The hydroponics station can be set up in the span of a month. Once it's set up, the farmer can immediately start producing hydroponic animal fodder, which only takes 7 days to grow (per individual tray). There are some things to take care of on a daily basis in the hydroponics room. The author recommends feeding as early as 5-day-old trays but never going beyond 7 days.

1. The first is the daily shifting of trays. Each tray will start at the southern dark corner of the Acre room and should be shifted one space ahead each day until it reaches the northern side on day 7.

2. Water sprinkling is to be done on a daily basis, keeping in mind not to overwater the plants because then it becomes a habitat for bacteria and fungi. The trays should have small holes to dispose of excess water.

3. Inlet and outlet of air must be ensured daily to maintain continuous airflow to disperse any humidified air that builds up inside. Also, plants growing inside need an adequate amount of carbon dioxide to grow.
4. The trays must be cleaned on a regular basis, after every 7-day process is complete.

Remember that we are trying to grow a seed in an artificial environment. Thus, any deviation from recommendations can and most likely will have a negative impact on the results. Here is a checklist of daily, weekly, and monthly tasks to keep your hydroponics station up to date.

Table 32: Daily Checklist

Task	Details
Check Water Levels	Ensure the reservoir has enough water; refill if necessary.
Monitor pH Levels	Check the pH of the water; adjust if necessary (optimal range 5.5-6.5).
Inspect Plants	Look for signs of pests, diseases or nutrient deficiencies.
Shift Trays	Move trays to ensure even light distribution and air circulation.
Ensure Sunlight	Verify that plants receive adequate natural sunlight (at least 6-8 hours).

Table 33: Weekly Checklist

Task	Details
Clean System Components	Clean reservoirs, grow trays, and other system parts to prevent algae and build-up.
Inspect Roots	Check plant roots for health, looking for signs of rot or discoloration.
Prune Plants	Trim dead or yellowing leaves and manage plant growth.

Table 34: Monthly Checklist

Task	Details
Deep Clean System	Thoroughly clean the entire hydroponic system, including pumps and tubing.
Calibrate Meters	Calibrate pH meters to ensure accurate readings.
Review Plant Growth	Assess the overall plant health and growth; adjust care practices if necessary.
Check for Leaks	Inspect the entire system for any leaks or potential issues.

MACRONUTRIENTS

In this chapter, we are taking the example of 4 fodder crops which can be grown hydroponically, i.e. maize, pulses, wheat, and horse gram, to show the nutritional level of hydroponically grown fodder.

As Micronutrients are being provided by trees, and the roughage is being provided by the field crops, hydroponics fodder will provide the macronutrients. Thus, in order to sustain the nutritional value, the resulting fodder generated from the Hydroponics plant should be given within 7 days of sprouting.

The best nutritional value comes if the fodder is fed within 7 days of sprouting when the grass is green and still standing, and the roots have formed a mat.

Following is a table listing the requirements for growing fodder in hydroponics:

Table 35: Requirements for growing fodder in hydroponics

Crop	Seed Quantity (per square meter)	Optimal Temperature (°C) [°F]	Seed Soaking Time (hours)	Light Hours (per day)	Water pH Level
Maize	25-30	20-25 °C [68-77 °F]	4-5	14-16	6.0-6.5

Pulses	25-30	20-25 °C [68-77 °F]	6-8	12-16	6.0-7.0
Wheat	30-35	18-24 °C [64-75 °F]	8-12	12-16	6.0-6.5
Horse Gram	25-30	20-28 °C [68-82 °F]	8-10	12-14	6.0-7.0

The macronutrients present in each of the hydroponically grown fodder crops are as follows:

Table 36: Macronutrients present in hydroponically grown fodder

Nutrient	Maize (%)	Cowpea (%)	Wheatgrass (%)	Horse gram (%)
Protein	9 – 14	23 – 25	15 – 25	22 – 25
Fiber	2 – 7	6 – 10	25 – 30	5 – 6
Ether Extract (Fat)	4.5 – 5	1 – 2	< 2	1.5 – 2
Ash	1.5	3 – 4.5	5 – 6	3 – 4
Carbohydrates (NFE)	72 – 73	55 – 60	3	60 – 65

Total:

Each row sums to 100%, which represents the total compositional makeup of each plant in terms of moisture plus dry matter. Dry matter itself includes protein, fiber, fat, ash, and carbohydrates.

Table 37: Total compositional makeup of each plant

	Maize (%)	Cowpea (%)	Wheatgrass (%)	Horse gram (%)
Dry Matter	87 – 90	88 – 90	10 – 15 (Fresh)	88 – 90
Moisture	10 – 13	10 – 12	75 – 85 (Fresh)	10 – 12
TOTAL	100%	100%	100%	100%

In this chapter, you learned:

Coming up...

DC
AC
Inverter
Solar panels
Electricity
Section 1
Storage
Room 1
Living quaters
Room 2
Section 2
Structure
The shed
Disease risk elimination features
Food and water borne
PP plastic containers
RO water filter
Predators/ air borne
Elevation
Cold winds
Roller curtains
Soil borne
PP slats floor
Direct transmission
Separate sections

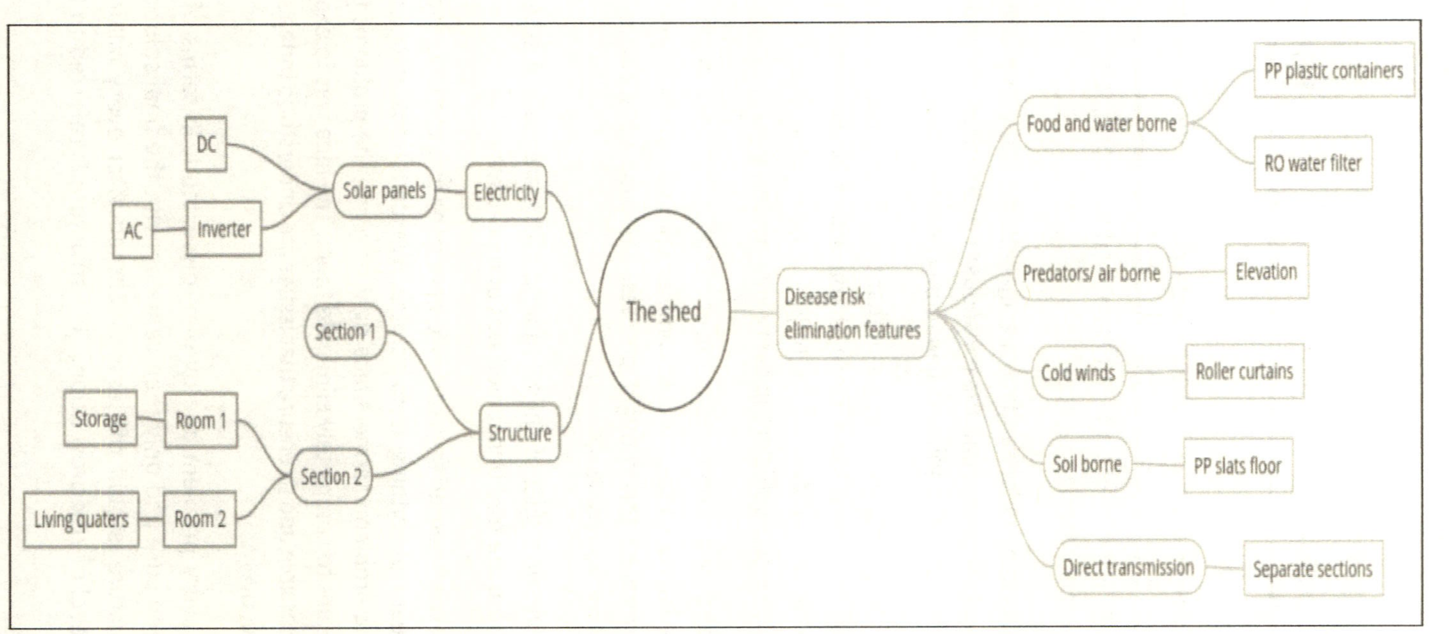

CHAPTER 9

The Shed

IN THIS CHAPTER, we delve into the centerpiece of our sustainable land project: The Shed. By addressing the critical challenges faced by marginal farmers, we aim to provide a self-sufficient and long-term solution through innovative livestock rearing practices.

When we began understanding the magnitude and complexity of the problem of decreasing land and the consequent destruction of livelihoods of farmers, we knew that the solution had to be comprehensive.

In saying 'comprehensive', we mean that the solution would be complete in every sense. Imagine it like a circle, if you will. It would ensure that the farmer family becomes independent, requiring no external help and can run a business which is self-sufficient in every way conceivable.

It would be a long-term investment, something that once in place would sustain generations to come. It would come as a permanent fix to the farmers' problem and through this thought process, we came up with the idea of animal rearing as the solution.

However, in our model of animal rearing, there are many elements that are different from the traditional methods of this activity.

We have experimented for years. We have gone into the field and reared livestock to learn everything from scratch. We undertook this activity to understand the problems farmers face right now and the problems that can arise in the future to completely eliminate them. The idea was to experience every hurdle possible and to ensure that issues are understood independently as well as collectively.

We took every problem one by one, dissected it in terms of origin, prevention, and cure and only then came up with the final solution. The resultant structure is built off lessons learned after every failure, with the highest level of risk prevention. This structure is referred to here as the shed.

We will talk in detail about every component of the shed, but before that, the reader needs to understand the problem with traditional methods of rearing. Only then will we be able to understand and appreciate the unconventional yet logical and meticulously engineered shed.

THE RISK OF DISEASE IN LIVESTOCK REARING

The first risk we encountered in raising livestock was disease. Since they are herd animals, infectious diseases can do tremendous damage and can take down an entire farm quite quickly. Let us begin with understanding the types of diseases generally seen in livestock and how they originate.

Diseases of livestock can be separated into 4 categories:

1. Soil-borne diseases
2. Food and waterborne diseases
3. Airborne diseases
4. Diseases transmitted through direct contact with infected animals.

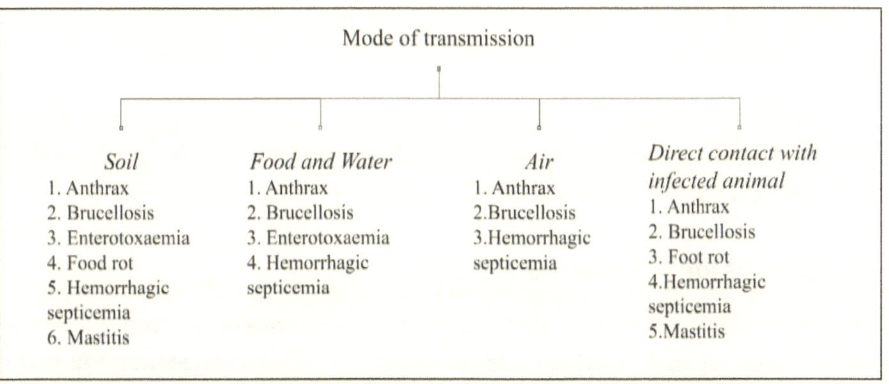

Figure 140: Mode of transmission of different diseases

Traditional enclosures typically lack solid flooring, and livestock generally walk directly on a soil base. Animals excrete urine and feces directly onto this ground, where it accumulates.

This accumulation can create damp conditions that lead to bacterial growth. From here on, the bacteria can easily get into the hooves of the ruminants who stomp around in the moist environment. The result is a disease called foot rot.

In the beginning, the foot rot is benign and only causes inflammation and reddening of soft tissues between the toes.

If not taken care of, the bacteria enter the hard part of the hoof and starts to digest the hard-outer covering which protects the soft internal tissues.

In the worst-case scenario, the hoof horn becomes rotten and can separate from the hoof wall.

This disease is infectious in nature and can easily spread among all the inhabitants living in close quarters.

It results in lameness, affects reproductive capabilities, and reduces appetite, which dramatically affects milk production and wool production. The affected animal is reluctant to move around and will stay in the same place for long durations. The disease is difficult to spot from day one as the animal will only start showing symptoms like limping when the bacteria has done significant damage.

The cure is both labor and capital-intensive, and the disease can re-emerge if the ruminants are repeatedly kept in moist conditions.

This is just an example to show one of the many diseases affecting livestock that emerge from unhygienic conditions. These diseases can be easily tackled by creating a hygienic environment.

FOOD AND WATER BORNE DISEASE

The fodder fed to livestock is emptied into large containers, from which the animals can eat accordingly. These containers are often not cleaned regularly, thus becoming a thriving environment for all sorts of bacteria that can gain easy access to the ruminant's stomach and make them ill. This has been a historic reason for animal disease-related deaths.

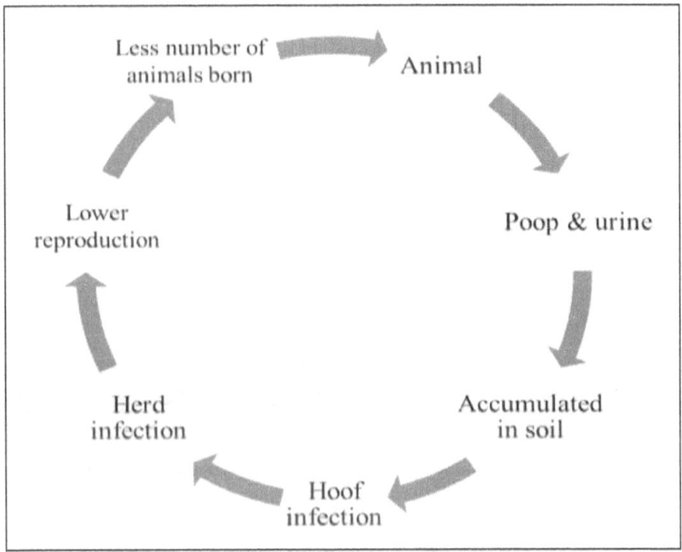

Figure 141: Cycle of disease

Next are waterborne diseases – Evident from the name, such diseases spread through contaminated water. For example, uncovered water sources that are not changed regularly thus become stagnant and turn into breeding grounds for mosquitoes and all sorts of bacteria.

When this water is supplied to livestock, they fall ill. Goats and sheep need continuous access to fresh water for good health. If the water container is not clean or the water itself is unhygienic, it can affect the health of the animals. Continuous supply of poor-quality water is detrimental to the overall health and efficiency of the livestock. Such water causes liver and kidney infections, leading to hepatitis and renal failure.

AIRBORNE DISEASE

The last category of disease is airborne diseases. More often than not, the livestock are kept in poorly ventilated closed spaces which promote airborne bacterial infections.

Poor ventilation leads to a build-up of bacteria due to stagnant conditions. Many times, pathogens from other animals like cattle are carried through the air and can infect the goats and sheep. In summer, closed spaces with no airflow can cause distress in the animals. Since furry animals do not have sweat glands in their skin, they panic and try to cool through their hooves, which can lead to chaos and stampede.

THREAT OF PREDATORS

Apart from diseases, the threat of predators is another major risk involved in rearing livestock. In rural areas, jackals and wild dogs often attack farms and take away baby goats and even adults.

Even fencing the area off fails, as they squeeze their way in through the fence or dig a hole in the ground to gain access to the goats. Preventing the entry of these predators is a tedious task. The damage done by them is considerable and results in huge losses for the farmer. There are hundreds of instances of such attacks every year in the writer's district itself.

DIRECT CONTACT WITH INFECTED ANIMAL

Contagious diseases spread through direct contact with infected animals. Traditional rearing systems often do not have a secluded space to isolate infected animals from the herd. In such cases, the infected animal becomes the problem and spreads the disease to the whole herd. Most diseases are transmitted because of contaminated environment or from the infected to healthy goats. Usually, sick animals are tied separately in the open, and that is a 50-50 approach.

This is a summarized explanation of the major risks involved in rearing goats and sheep. Our knowledge of these risks comes from first-hand experience in rearing goats.

Which is why we worked hard to ensure that the concluding solution should be a structure built with the aim of not only reducing but completely eliminating these risks from the root level. Dear reader, we finally present to you, the Shed.

Note: The use of 'we' instead of 'I' is because this idea's implementation required a dozen-plus set of hands and feet, each one equally important.

STRUCTURE OF THE SHED

The shed will be built in area 3 of the land. Area 3 is to be further divided into 2 subsections. The shed will be built in Section 1, and Section 2 will be an area with a dry sand base for the goats to roam around. This sand base has to have a good drainage system as well.

Section 2 will also have 2 small rooms. Room 1 will be used to store fodder, and Room 2 will be used as living quarters or guard quarters by the family as the goats should be monitored 24x7. So, sentry duty is a must.

The following pictures will give the reader a more concrete idea of how this space will look.

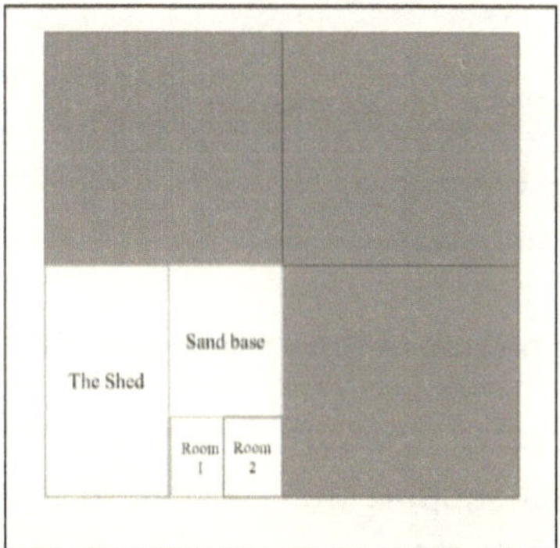

Figure 142: Diagrammatic representation of Area 3

Figure 143: Structure of Area 3[202]

As shown in Figure 143, the shed is strategically divided into 2 sections, providing both an elevated living space and a sand-based roaming area for the goats.

FEATURES OF THE SHED

SECTION 1

1. ELEVATION

Figure 144: Elevated structure of the Shed supported by pillars as seen from far[203]

The shed is an elevated structure. The base ground is of concrete on which pillars are erected that support the elevated living quarters of the livestock. This elevation serves 2 purposes.

1. Firstly, it greatly reduces the risk of soil-borne disease as the elevation ensures zero contact with the ground[204].
2. It also secures the animals inside, not only from predators like jackals or wild dogs but also from reptiles like snakes.

Figure 145: Close-up picture of pillars supporting the shed[205]

Figure 146: Additional space provided by the shed[206]

In addition to eliminating diseases and predators, the elevation provides supplementary space below which can later be used for other purposes, like storage.

The elevation is accessed via a ramp.

Additionally, we have left a space of 4m all around the structure so that it is not cramped and has enough space in case any activity related to the structure, such as repairing or painting, has to be done.

2. FLOORING

As we enter the space where the goats will be kept, the first thing that catches our attention is the flooring. This is very interesting. When choosing the type of floor an elevated surface should have, there are many things to keep in mind.

- As this space will be used to keep goats and sheep, the flooring should be sturdy and capable of bearing weight.
- Since it does not have ground support, the material needs to be really tough to endure the weight of the animals at elevation.
- The flooring should not accumulate excreta or urine. It should facilitate proper disposal of the waste and simultaneously ensure that the hooves of the animals do not get stuck in them. Otherwise, it could result in hoof damage, and we certainly want to avoid that.
- The flooring should be easy to clean in order to eliminate risks related to hygiene.
- It should not be made of a material that absorbs water because that would defeat the whole purpose of the elevation. If the material absorbs water, it will provide a moist environment for bacteria, resulting in bacterial infections all over again.

After giving all these factors much thought and consideration, we decided to use strong, durable plastic slats shown in the following picture to make the floors.

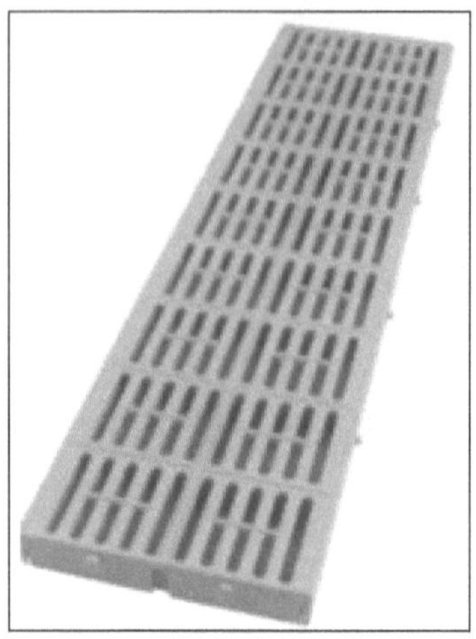

Figure 147: Polypropylene slats[207]

Figure 148: Ramp leading up to the living quarters[208]

The same is used on the ramp as well.

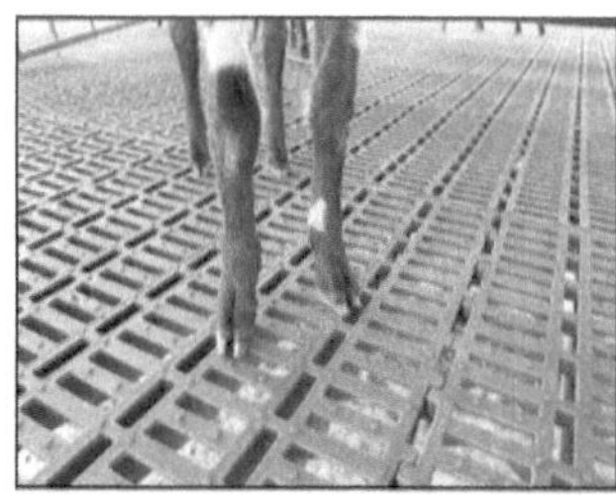

Figure 149: Goats coming down the ramp[209] **Figure 150: Goats can easily walk on these slats without hooves getting stuck[210]**

These are made up of a special type of material called polypropylene. It is a tough and rigid thermoplastic. The material has many advantages. It is water-resistant and absorbs less than 0.01% of water if soaked in it.

Along with being highly impermeable, it is also heat resistant and can withstand temperatures up to 90°C[211] (194°F). In the author's village, Daurai, Rajasthan, India, temperatures in peak summertime can reach up to 45°C (113°F), even 50°C (122°F) in some districts. In that scenario, this material works best because the warm temperature will not damage it, nor will it get heated up and injure the hooves of the goats.

Not only is it chemically inactive, which means that it is resistant to most elements like acids, bases, salts, etc., but a close-up image of the slat will show the special design of holes in it.

Figure 151: Openings to facilitate easy movement of excreta and urine[212]

Figure 152: Slat openings as seen from below[213]

Although it is lightweight, each individual slat can bear a weight of up to 500 kilograms.

These are perfect for easy flow of waste while not being large enough for hooves to get stuck in. Lastly, the material does not require much cleaning as waste does not accumulate on the surface, and even in case it gets wet, it dries off very quickly.

The complete floor structure is not leveled but is a little slanted from both sides, which meets at the center. This ensures that fluid from all sides is collected at the center.

Also, the hive structure of the design ensures that the weight-related stress distribution is spread evenly across the entire slab, ensuring a long-lasting & sturdy footing.

3. SEPARATE SECTIONS

The next prominent feature of the structure is the different sections, separated by iron bars.

This is done to segregate the goats based on

1. Age (baby, adult, and old)
2. Health (healthy and sick)
3. Gender (male and female)
4. Pregnant goats.
5. Temperament (some goats show aggressive behaviour and indulge in fights and may even injure fellow goats).

Figure 153: Separate sections inside the structure[214]

Each category of goat has different needs. Separate sections allow the farmer to monitor different goats efficiently.

- Pregnant goats need more care than others in terms of nutrition, regular check-ups, medical needs, etc.
- Baby goats are much more energetic than adult goats and thus more prone to creating havoc. They might even pick a fight with male adult goats, which may end up in them getting injured. They also tend to pester their mothers at all times, which can lead to irritation and unrest in the female goats. It is best to keep them in a separate section until they are mature enough.

- Sick goats must be separated from the rest to prevent the disease from spreading and to help them recover. It is for the herd's benefit. Being separated from the rest will give them proper rest, which is necessary to recover. The separate sections also eliminate the risk of disease transmission.

4. FOOD AND WATER CONTAINER

Each section has its own feeding tray and water container. The food tray is made from a special type of plastic. There is an interesting story behind choosing this particular material.

In the initial stage when we were still experimenting and learning, we used trays made of iron for feeding the livestock. But the iron trays were heavy and not easy to move around. They were not easy to clean either as the food would stick to their surface. Another drawback was iron rusting over time, which meant it could not be used as a long-term solution.

After understanding the drawbacks of using metal trays, we chose a material that had none of the problems of the former. Thus, we decided on the plastic tray shown in the picture below. For the concerned parties about plastic use, we want to confirm these are food grade multiple-use plastics.

Figure 154: Food container[215]

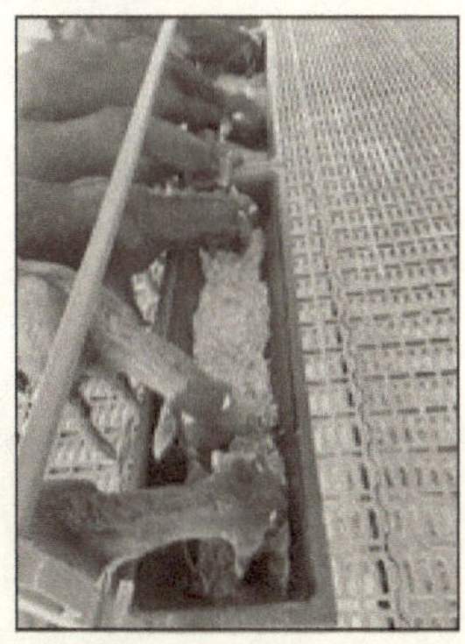

Figure 155: Goats eating from the container[216]

Figure 156: Close-up picture of goats eating from the container[217]

This tray is lightweight but sturdy and can be easily removed for cleaning. The surface is smooth, and leftover fodder can be easily cleaned. Because it can be easily cleaned, the risk related to foodborne disease is eliminated.

Along with having a separate food tray, each section has a separate water container, also made of plastic.

Figure 157: Water container[218]

These are kept on a tripod-like stand, giving it a little elevation so that the container does not get contaminated from its surrounding environment, such as droppings and stray pee droplets.

Figure 158: Water coming from the tap and goats drinking[219]

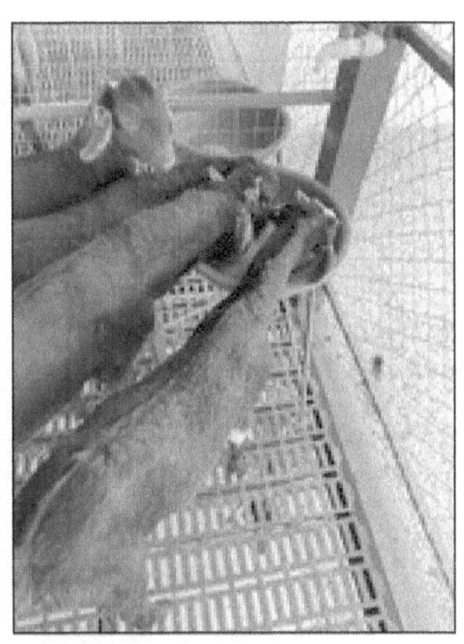

Figure 159: Goats drinking from the container[220]

5. RO (Reverse Osmosis) WATER PURIFIER

Previously, we talked about the risk of waterborne diseases, originating from unhygienic containers or contaminated water. To eliminate this risk at the root level, we set up an RO water purifier system for water supply.

Figure 160: RO water purifier[221]

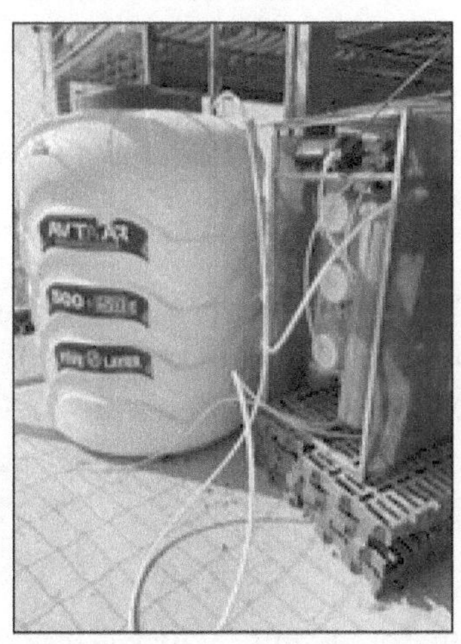

Figure 161: RO water purifier connected to tank[222]

In a water purifier, water is purified through the process of Reverse Osmosis (RO). This process removes solute[223] particles like salts, minerals, and organic compounds from the solvent[224] (in this case, water) and gives clean water (with a reduced number of solutes[225]).

To understand the process of reverse osmosis, we must first understand the process of osmosis. Osmosis[226] is the movement of water from a higher concentration (of water) to a lower concentration (of water) through a semipermeable[227] membrane. Water has a *natural tendency* to move from higher concentration to lower concentration. We can better understand this with the help of the diagram below:

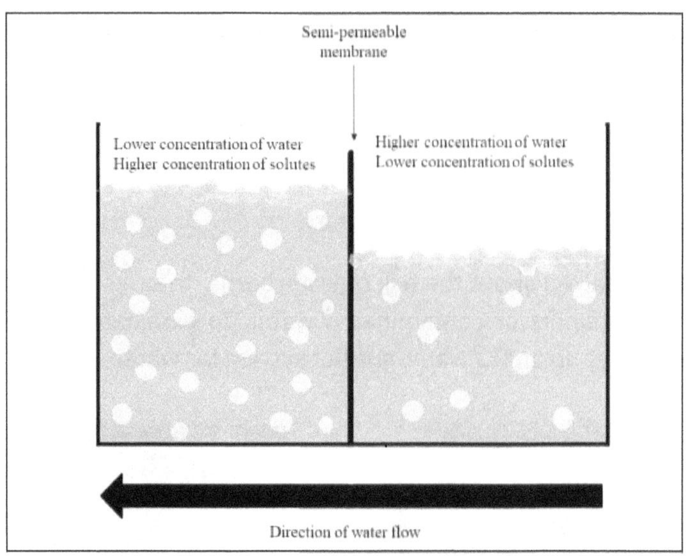

Figure 162: Diagrammatic representation of osmosis

The container is divided into 2 halves by placing a semi-permeable membrane in the middle. Side A contains freshwater, while Side B contains saltwater. The concentration of water is higher on Side A than on Side B, hence water from Side A will move through the semi-permeable membrane to Side B. Particles of salt are too big to pass through the membrane, so they stay where they are.

In some time, you will notice that the level of water on Side A has decreased as water has moved to Side B where the level has increased. This depicts the process of osmosis.

A real-life example of osmosis is the process of water absorption by plant roots. When a plant's roots are in contact with soil, water moves from an area of higher water concentration (soil) to an area of lower water concentration (plant roots) through a semi-permeable membrane. This osmotic process allows plants to take in water and essential nutrients needed for their growth and survival.

The natural flow of water is from freshwater (high water concentration, low solute concentration) to saltwater (low water concentration, high solute concentration).

In reverse osmosis[228] (RO), we *artificially* reverse this flow. Water mixed with solutes (salt, minerals, etc.) is forced through a semipermeable membrane by applying pressure which is greater than the osmotic pressure to obtain freshwater. The membrane allows only water molecules to pass through it and retains the solutes on the other side, giving fresh water as the final product.

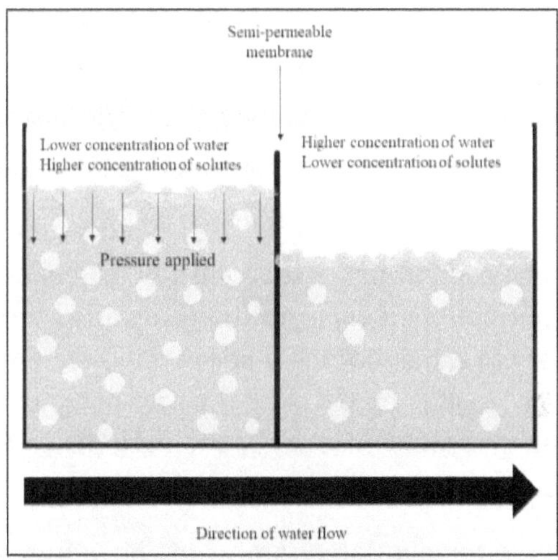

Figure 163: Diagrammatic representation of reverse osmosis

The RO on our farm has a capacity of pumping out 500 L of water every hour, but this capacity is variable depending on the TDS (Total Dissolved Solids) of the water. TDS refers to the total amount of dissolved solids (salts, minerals, and other impurities) present per liter of water.

Total dissolved solids (TDS) are measured as a volume of water with the unit milligrams per liter (mg/L), otherwise known as parts per million (ppm)[229] For example, at our farm[230], we receive water with a TDS ranging from 280-300 ppm. Goats can drink water with a maximum TDS of 120; lower quantities are even better. Thus, the required TDS of water received at the end of purification is 120 ppm. On this basis, the purifier pumps out approximately 500 liters per hour.

A goat consumes approximately 1-3 gallons[231] or 5 to 13 liters. of water every day[232]. Let's consider the maximum amount (3 gallons) for ease of calculations. The proposed structure of the shed can accommodate up to 50 goats[233]. It is necessary to calculate the runtime of RO (and all appliances, as a matter of fact) because electricity generated via solar panels is limited and thus should be used very carefully.

A higher concentration of TDS in the water results in less clean water output as the filter will generate more wastewater (water with solutes). If the level goes higher than 120, it will be harmful for the goats in the long run. The wastewater pumped out by the filter can be used for watering the trees and crops.

Water with a maximum TDS of 700 can be used to water plants. Furthermore, each section has a separate tap, all connected to one water tank which supplies purified water to the goats at all times. This step might seem unnecessary to some, but the reader should remember that the aim of this structure is not to just 'get by' or do the bare minimum. It is to completely eliminate any risk that could arise at its root level. Hence, the use of RO water purifiers is advised.

Question: If we remove salts from water, how do goats get the desired salts?

Answer: We provide them with bricks of rock salt which they lick to their satisfaction.

6. VENTILATION

The next threat to eliminate was that of airborne diseases. To achieve this, we had to ensure that the area had proper ventilation, and by proper ventilation, we mean that there should be continuous airflow throughout the whole space. For this purpose, we had fans installed on the ceiling of the structure and also at the corners, as shown in the picture below. The wiring of all fans was securely placed within plastic enclosures to avoid any damage.

Figure 164: Fans placed inside the structure[234]

It is worth mentioning that each enclosure has a separate high-voltage plug (16 A) provided to facilitate the use of any electronic items if needed. This will ensure that the animals do not have to be moved from one enclosure to another in case of an emergency that requires electricity (like medical procedures).

The fans would facilitate cross ventilation of air in summertime and reduce the heat effect on animals.

Since the enclosure is made up of steel mesh instead of solid walls, it allows the free flow of air in and out of the space. The steel mesh would also facilitate sunlight to reach every corner of the enclosure, which is beneficial for the ruminant's well-being and overall health.

Moving air not only keeps the environment cool during summertime, but it also prevents the build-up of odor and bacteria. The elevated surface, combined with proper ventilation, eliminates the risk of airborne diseases.

7. ROLLER CURTAINS

While the use of steel mesh was advantageous for airflow, it had some drawbacks too. Its quality of allowing a free flow of air is good for summertime, but the same quality becomes harmful when seasons change, and the cool summer breeze is replaced with the cold winds of winter.

These winds could very well become the reason for cold-induced diseases in the animals. To combat this problem, we found a way to prevent the direct entry of winds during winters or rains without replacing iron net with solid walls since ventilation is essential all year round. The solution we have come up with is roller curtains made from polyester fabric.

These curtains are placed on all sides of the enclosure and can be rolled down during winter nights or when it rains. The polyester fabric ensures that winds do not get past the curtains, and the animals inside stay warm even during windy nights.

It also proves useful for the rainy season as polyester is water-resistant, and water just rolls off the surface of the curtains. This ensures that the livestock inside will not get drenched in rain, which otherwise leads to the birth of many moisture or humidity-related infections like fungi.

Figure 165: Roller curtains[235]

Figure 166: Roller curtains as seen from outside[236]

8. SOLAR PANELS

The shed is covered with metal sheets on the upper areas and has a <u>gable</u>[237] roof (as shown in the image).

Figure 167: Slanted roof covered with metal sheets which are zigzag in shape[238]

Since the beginning, we have emphasized greatly on this project being a self-sufficient end-to-end solution. It means that the farmer should not have to depend on any outside help, and that includes the supply of electricity too.

The farmer would need electricity for multiple purposes, and thus, self-sufficiency is necessary to ensure an uninterrupted flow of electricity for the smooth execution of all activities. To achieve that, we covered the roof of the shed with solar panels.

Figure 168: Solar panels on the roof[239]

There are 3 kinds of solar systems which are in general use while the book is being written.

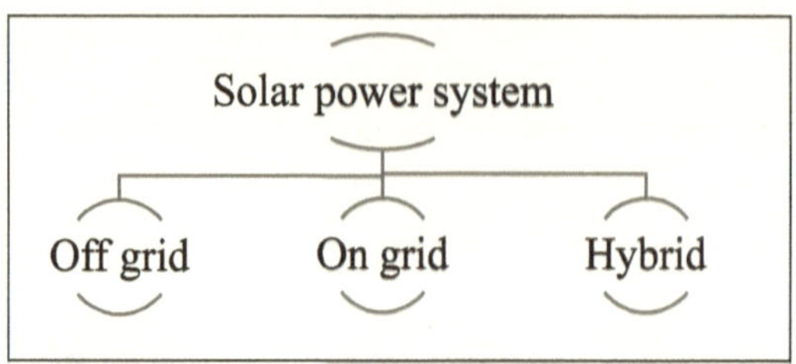

Figure 169: Types of solar power systems

The 'grid' here is the power grid that supplies electricity generated in power plants to households, companies, etc. By this fact,

1. 'Off-grid' means a solar power system which is completely independent and not connected to the grid for electricity. In an off-grid system, solar energy is the sole source of electricity which is either directly used or stored in batteries to be used later. Since it is not connected to the grid, there is no electricity bill.
2. Similarly, 'On grid' means a solar power system which is connected to a grid. Such as the grid of your local sub – station.
   In an on-grid system, the solar power system is connected to the power grid, which does 2 things-

   a. Supplement electricity in case electricity generated by solar panels fall short and cannot meet the consumption requirements.
   b. In case extra electricity is generated which exceeds the consumption level, it is supplied back to the grid.

This excess electricity is generally compensated through net metering. Net metering is when the utility company compensates or credits your account for electricity generated by your solar system and sent to the grid. Then, whenever you need to draw energy off the grid, you'll be drawing on those credits to get your electricity without racking up charges on your electricity bill[240].

3. Hybrid – The hybrid solar system is linked to the grid using net metering and is equipped with a battery backup for power storage. The energy captured by solar panels is processed through a hybrid solar inverter to produce electricity.

One of the key advantages of a hybrid solar system is its capability to provide power backup. This ensures uninterrupted electricity usage, even in the event of power outages. The battery backup plays a crucial role in storing excess power generated by the solar system during peak hours.

We recommend installing an 'Off-grid system' because of the following reasons-

1. It is a one-time expense. Since it's not connected to the grid, you will not get any electricity bills (on grid or hybrid system will have a component/bill generated).
2. It will not be impacted by the dynamics of market prices. For example, if the cost of electricity per unit rises, it will have no effect on you.
3. The costs are identifiable, with the only risks being potential manual errors or unforeseen events that are beyond our control (force majeure).
4. Planning for risks can prevent the challenges that arise due to unavailability of sunlight. The power generated through off-grid systems is limited. If exhausted you cannot source additional power from the grid. To avoid a power outage, one must properly plan the running time of appliances. Thus, having some basic management shall ensure a smooth-running enterprise.

The slanted roof provides an increased area to plant solar panels, in addition to preventing waterlogging during the rainy season. Solar panels can be categorized into two types:

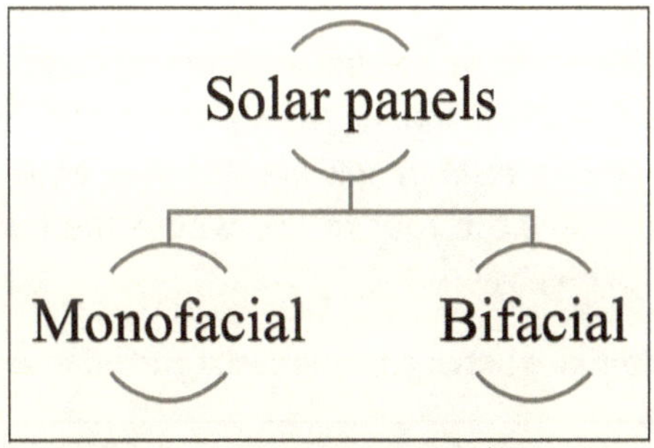

Figure 170: Type of solar panels

Monofacial solar panels

Monofacial solar panels have solar cells on only one side.

1.   **Bifacial solar panels:**

Bifacial solar panels have solar cells on both sides. At the base of the solar panel, a reflector is installed to reflect light onto the solar cells situated on the other side.

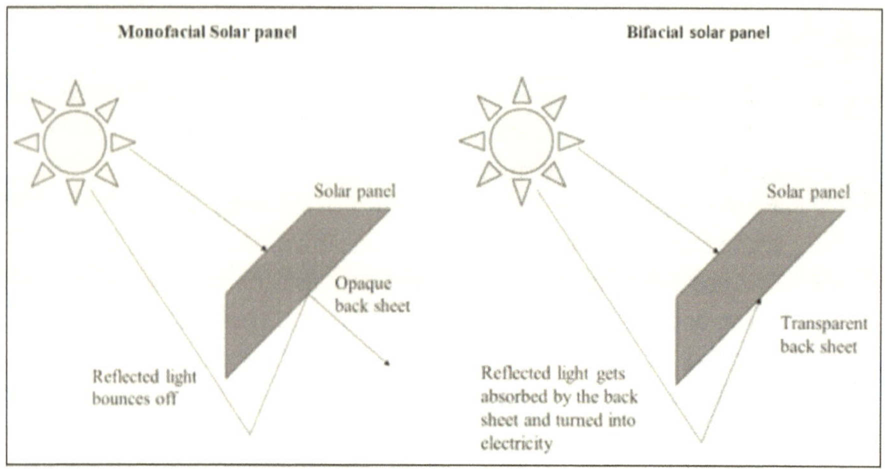

Figure 171: Difference between the functioning of bifacial and monofacial solar panels

We recommend installing monofacial solar panels as they cost less than bifacial solar panels. Bifacial solar panels require a reflector at the base and support to uphold the panels. The requirement of this structure adds an additional ₹20,000-30,000 to the cost of the structure.

They also require some space between each panel for the sunlight to reach the reflective surface. Installing the structure of bifacial panels will cost you more, whereas monofacial panels are not only equally efficient but will cost less, and we do have the roof to use where the installation of bifacial panels is not going to be easy.

Table 38: Difference between monofacial and bifacial solar panels

Properties	Monofacial	Bifacial
Solar cells	Solar cells are present on only one side of the panel.	Solar cells are present on both sides of the panel.
Efficiency percentage[241]	16-21%	17-24%

Properties	Monofacial	Bifacial
Cost of a solar panel (in India)	₹25-₹30/Watt[242]	₹30-₹35/Watt
Production of one panel per day[243]	300-350 Watt	320-450 Watt

The shed that we built has 15 solar panels on the roof, each capable of generating 335 watts of electricity. Collectively, they can produce 5 kW (kilowatt) of energy every day.

Out of the 15 solar panels, 10 are used for immediate present needs like the mulching machine. The remaining 5 are connected to batteries which store their electricity that can be used later. These panels have a warranty of 25 years[244] and come as a long-term solution.

They need to be cleaned once every week; otherwise, the collected dust will have a negative impact on their performance. Machines that require high-voltage, like the mulching machine or the grinder, should be used one at a time, or it will overload the panels.

Following is a breakdown of the electrical appliances used in the shed we currently have and the amount of electricity they need to give the reader an idea.

The appliances can either be used consecutively[245] or concurrently[246]. Machines that require high-voltage like the grinder or chaff cutter (mulching) should be used one at a time. Both of them cannot run at the same time.

Other appliances like a fan, tube light, etc., are low-voltage machines and can run parallel to each other. It is important to adjust the runtime of all appliances in accordance with the total output that the solar panels can generate.

Table 39: Electricity requirement of appliances

Appliance	Quantity	Volt[247]	Estimated usage time per day (hours)	Concurrent or Consecutive
Grinder	1	2200 V	1	Consecutive
Chaff cutter	1	2200 V	1	Consecutive

Packing machine	1	1000 V	1	Consecutive
Water motor	2	375 V	1	Concurrent
RO water filter	1	450 V	3	Concurrent
Fans	7	60 V	8	Concurrent
Tube light	5	20 V	8	Concurrent
LED light	2	40 V	8	Concurrent

Table 40: Use of the appliances

Appliance	Use
Grinder	Used to grind solid goat manure, wood chips, neem bark, etc., for manufacturing products.
Chaff cutter	Used to shred goat feed items like green forage and dry forage.
Packing machine	Used for packing products made on the farm.
Water motor	To supply water from RO to the water tank, from where it can be accessed through taps placed in every section.
RO water filter	Used to purify water for the goats.
Fans	Used for air circulation and reducing heat inside the shed during summertime.
Tube light	Used for visibility inside the shed during nighttime.
LED light	Used for visibility inside the shed during nighttime.

Most of these machines run on AC / alternating current. What exactly is AC and why do most appliances run on this type of current? To begin with, there are 2 kinds of current:

1. Direct current or DC is an electric current flowing in one direction only.
2. Alternating current or AC is an electric current that changes its direction at regular intervals many times a second.

The flow of current can be better understood with the diagram below:

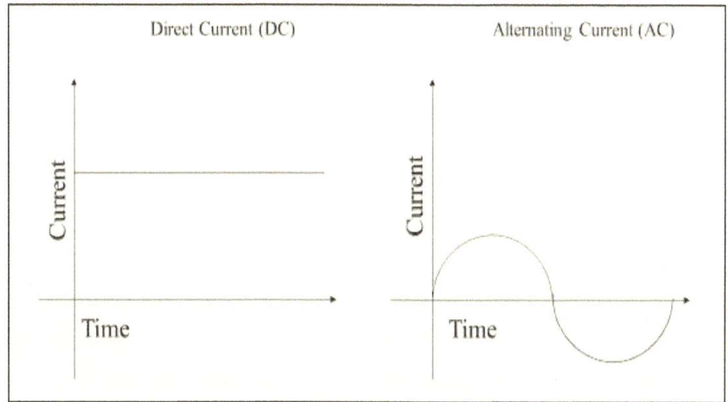

Figure 172: Diagrammatic representation of DC and AC

Most appliances around you, such as the refrigerator, washing machine, fan, etc., run on AC, while DC has limited applications (for example, trains).

This is because AC has more advantageous properties than DC when it comes to low-voltage appliances. AC voltage[248] can be easily increased or decreased making it suitable for transmission over long distances. Unlike alternating current (AC), it's challenging to alter the level of direct current (DC) voltage without significant energy loss and the risk of fire.

Thus, DC cannot be transmitted over long distances without losing significant power.

Solar panels generate electricity in the form of Direct Current (DC). This can be used either directly or stored in batteries which is then turned into alternating current (AC) by an inverter.

The type of current (DC OR AC) to be used depends on the appliance. If it's an appliance that consumes more energy it's better to supply it with DC. In case of appliances that require less energy and can be powered via batteries, AC is more suitable.

Following this, here is a division of appliances listed in Table 2 based on the type of current they run on:

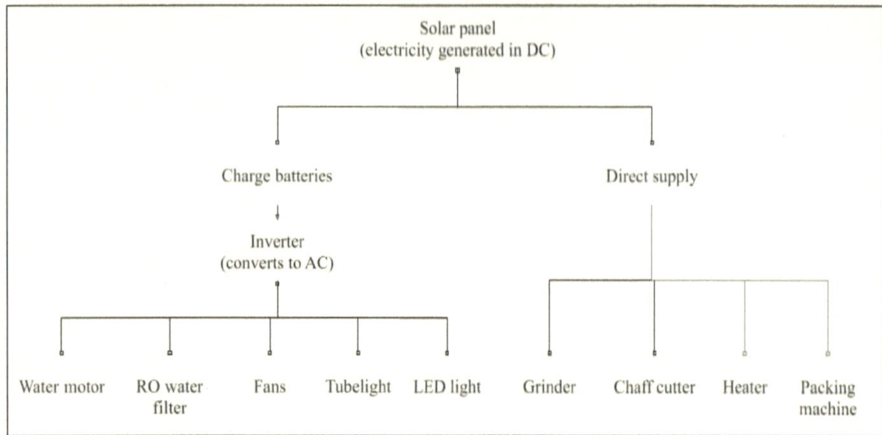

Figure 173: Appliances and type of current they run on

The machines that run on direct supply can be used only one at a time. So, if the grinder is in use, the chaff cutter cannot be used. Meanwhile, machines that run on stored electricity converted to AC can be run in parallel to each other.

Since AC is being used for the majority of appliances, we cannot compromise on its quality. One might compromise on the quality of solar panels[249] but not on the quality of the inverter.

A good quality inverter efficiently converts DC into AC. If its quality is compromised, the energy lost during conversion will be more, thus less electricity will be available. Also, low-quality inverters may not be able to bear the voltage of incoming DC and might heat up very quickly. They will eventually short the circuit when the wire can no longer take the heat and melt.

Therefore, for safety measures and to avoid a power outage, the inverter should be of the best quality available.

This completes the structure of the shed.

SECTION-2

Section 2 is fairly simple. It is the area parallel to the shed and is mostly empty space with a sand base, with 2 additional rooms at one end.

Now the question arises, why dry sand? Goats and sheep are not stationary animals, they love to move around, and it is necessary for their health too. The flooring that we provided in the elevated space will not harm them, but it is also not advised to have them walk on only artificial flooring, which does not have the same firmness as land.

They need a natural surface to stomp on and walk around. Soil is out of the question because of the potential risks of disease that come with wet soil. Hence, we came up with the solution of using dry sand as the natural base for the animals to roam around.

We filled Section 2 with dry sand as it is a much better alternative than normal soil. For one, it does not retain moisture as much as normal soil. Additionally, it does not get stuck in the hooves of the animals and provides a soft bedding for them to walk on. Sand is not easy for plants/weeds to grow in.

1. ROOM 1

One of the 2 rooms built on the edge of Section 2 must be used as a storage room to store fodder and the mulching machine. The mulching machine creates mulch from dry and green fodder, which is easy for the animals to eat. The room will also have a mini fridge to store medicines for the livestock. This will ensure that medicines are always readily available and at hand in case of any emergencies. The fridge keeps the medicines cool and dry.

2. ROOM 2

The second room will be used as living quarters capable of accommodating one person, complete with basic necessities. This is because one person should be available 24/7 at the farm to take care of the goats. This can be done in shifts or by one person; it all depends on the farmer.

Lastly, the whole area should be sealed off with a fence. This enclosure is not to keep predators out but to keep the goats in and to prevent them from escaping or running off. Predators should be prevented from entering the 1-acre fence itself; thus, the perimeter solution has to ensure that animals cannot come there.

CHECKLIST FOR SHED MAINTAINCE AND LIVESTOCK CARE

Table 41: Daily Checklist

Task	Details
Livestock Health	Check all animals for signs of illness or injury.
	Ensure sick animals are isolated in designated sections.
	Monitor the food and water intake of each animal.
Food and Water	Clean and refill water containers.
	Check and refill food trays.
	Ensure the RO water purifier is functioning properly.
Cleanliness and Hygiene	Remove any waste from the elevated floor.
	Ensure the slats are free of blockages.
	Clean any spills or messes in the feed and water areas.
Ventilation and Temperature	Check that fans are operational and providing adequate airflow.
	Monitor the temperature inside the shed.
Safety and Security	Inspect the fencing and ensure there are no breaches (openings for predators to get inside the shed).
	Check the roller curtains and roll them up or down as needed based on weather conditions.

Table 42: Weekly Checklist

Task	Details
Livestock Management	Conduct a thorough health check on all animals.
	Weigh animals and monitor growth rates.
Equipment and Infrastructure	Clean all feeding and watering equipment thoroughly.
	Inspect the flooring and ramp for any signs of wear or damage.
	Check the storage rooms for cleanliness and organization.

Task	Details
Solar Panels and Electrical Systems	Clean the solar panels to ensure maximum efficiency.
	Inspect the wiring and inverters for any issues.
	Ensure all fans and lights are operational.
General Maintenance	Check for and repair any minor structural damage.
	Ensure that the shed and surrounding area are free from any potential hazards.

Table 43: Monthly Checklist

Task	Details
Health and Nutrition	Schedule veterinary check-ups for the animals.
	Review and adjust the feeding plan as needed based on health and growth assessments.
Water Purification System	Perform a thorough inspection of the RO water purifier.
	Replace filters or other components as necessary.
Structural Inspection	Conduct a detailed inspection of the shed's structural integrity.
	Check the condition of roller curtains and replace if necessary.
Equipment Maintenance	Perform maintenance on all major equipment such as the grinder, chaff cutter and packing machine.
	Test and ensure the water pump is functioning correctly.
Record Keeping	Review and update records of livestock health, growth and productivity.
	Update maintenance logs and address any recurring issues.

CONCLUSION

This concludes the complete structure of area 3. Every aspect of this structure is made in a certain way after careful thinking and detailing. You can add suggestions on top, but do not cut costs.

It took us months and many failures to understand each and every risk involved and even more time to come up with a solution that could eliminate all of them and achieve an optimal level of efficiency.

We did this so that the person reading does not have to go through the same procedure of trial and error that we went through. Through our mistakes, we perfected the structure of this shed so that you could have a present-at-hand plan to implement. It is our firm belief that if a person follows the recommendations, they will achieve a level of self-sufficiency with a small area of land.

In this chapter, you learned:

Coming up...

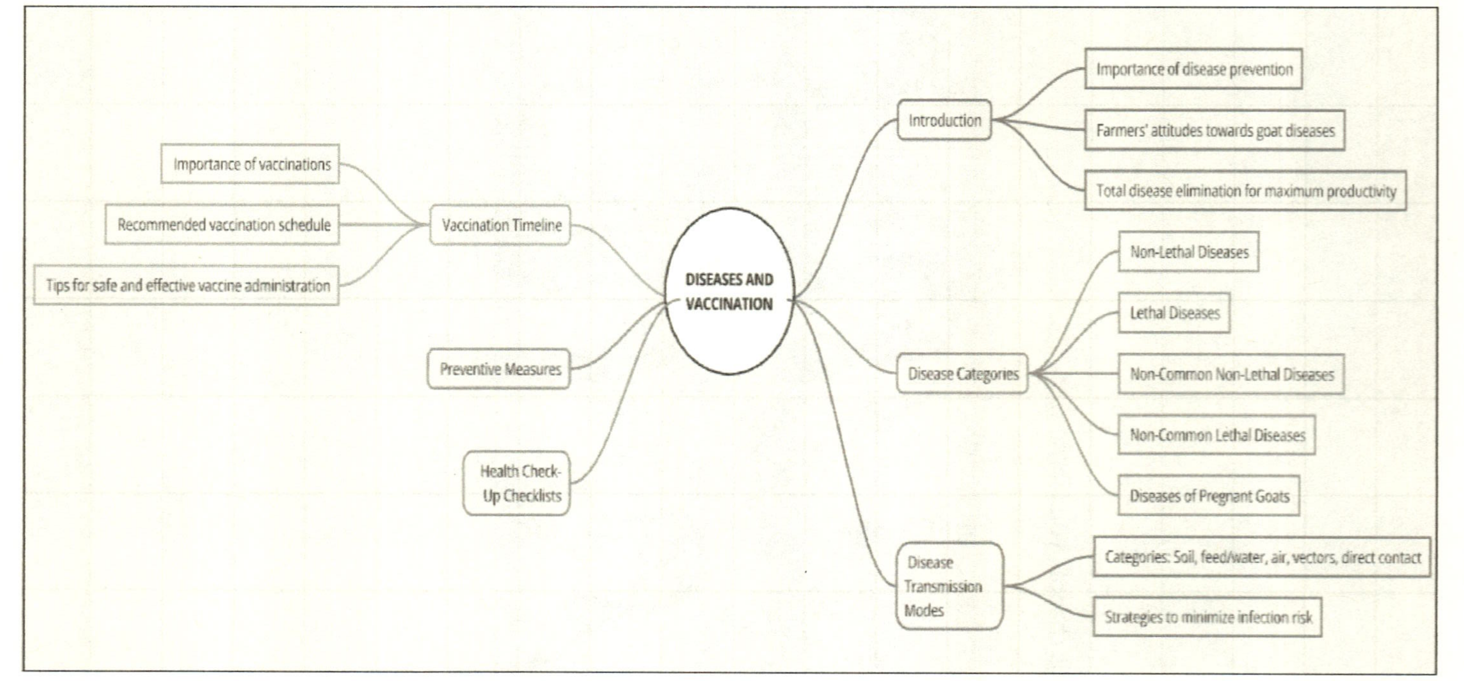
DISEASES AND VACCINATION
Introduction
Importance of disease prevention
Farmers' attitudes towards goat diseases
Total disease elimination for maximum productivity
Disease Categories
Non-Lethal Diseases
Lethal Diseases
Non-Common Non-Lethal Diseases
Non-Common Lethal Diseases
Diseases of Pregnant Goats
Disease Transmission Modes
Categories: Soil, feed/water, air, vectors, direct contact
Strategies to minimize infection risk
Vaccination Timeline
Importance of vaccinations
Recommended vaccination schedule
Tips for safe and effective vaccine administration
Preventive Measures
Health Check-Up Checklists

CHAPTER 10

Diseases and Vaccination

DISEASE IN HERD animals like goats and sheep can prove lethal if not handled and eradicated quickly. Although they are significantly less prone to falling ill than other ruminants, still the risk of disease is not completely eliminated.

Farmers often have a careless attitude and exhibit a lax approach to preventing diseases in goats and sheep due to the infrequency of illnesses in these animals. However, the total elimination of disease is necessary to achieve maximum output. In this chapter, we are going to talk about the common diseases of goats, both lethal and non-lethal.

For more information regarding transmission and prevention of the listed diseases and non-common diseases (lethal and non-lethal) of goats, please check dauraiwala.com.

Goats can be affected by a variety of diseases, which can be broadly categorized into non-lethal and lethal diseases. Non-lethal diseases, while not immediately life-threatening, can significantly impact the health and productivity of the herd. On the other hand, lethal diseases require urgent attention as they can quickly lead to fatalities.

The following tables list various kinds of diseases in goats along with their symptoms. Each table has symptoms listed in the form of a checklist. This way, you can easily assess if your goat is suffering from a particular disease by checking against the given symptoms. These tables will help you quickly identify potential health issues in your herd.

Before each table, we have included a brief description of the disease listed.

First, let's examine the common non-lethal diseases that can affect goats.

COMMON NON-LETHAL DISEASES

While these diseases are not fatal, they can cause considerable discomfort and reduce the overall health and productivity of the herd. Identifying and managing these diseases promptly is crucial.

1. Coccidiosis (Endoparasitic):

A parasitic disease affecting the intestines, causing diarrhea and weight loss, particularly in young goats.

2. Roundworm (Endoparasitic):

Parasitic worms in the intestines cause weight loss, diarrhea, and anemia.

3. Tapeworm (Endoparasitic):

Intestinal parasites causing weight loss, potbelly, and anemia.

4. Tick/Lice/Flea Infection (Exoparasitic):

External parasites causing itching, hair loss, and a rough coat.

5. Goat Polio (Vitamin Deficiency):

A neurological disease caused by thiamine deficiency, leading to a pressing head, seizures, and blindness.

Table 44: Common Non-Lethal Diseases and Their Symptoms

Symptom	Coccidiosis कोक्सीडियोसिस	Roundworm गोल कीड़ा संक्रमण	Tapeworm फीटाकृमि संक्रमण	Tick/Lice/ Flea Infection चीचड़ संक्रमण	Goat Polio बकरी पोलियो
Diarrhea	✔	✔	✔	✘	✘
Weight loss	✔	✔	✔	✘	✘
Itching	✘	✘	✘	✔	✘
Seizure	✘	✘	✘	✘	✔
Signs of blindness	✘	✘	✘	✘	✔

1. Foot Rot (Bacterial):

A bacterial infection causing lameness, swelling, and foul odor in the hooves.

2. IBK (Bacterial):

Infectious Bovine Keratoconjunctivitis, a bacterial eye infection causing swelling, discharge, and reduced appetite.

3. Pneumonia (Viral):

A viral infection causing coughing, fever, and reduced appetite.

4. FMD (Viral):

Foot-and-mouth disease, a viral infection causing blisters, reduced appetite, and swelling.

5. Sore Mouth (Viral):

A viral disease that causes blisters and sores around the mouth and nose.

Table 45: Common Non-Lethal Diseases and Their Symptoms

Symptom	Foot rot (Bacterial) खुर सड़न	IBK (Bacterial) आंख की सूजन	Pneumonia (Viral) न्यूमोनिया	FMD (Viral) खुरपका-मुहपका	Sore mouth (Viral) मुंह में घाव
Lameness	✔	✘	✘	✘	✘
Swelling	✔	✔	✔	✔	✔
Foul odor	✔	✘	✘	✘	✘
Discharge	✘	✔	✔	✘	✘
Blisters	✘	✘	✘	✔	✘
Hesitation to urinate	✘	✘	✘	✘	✘
Coughing	✘	✘	✔	✘	✘
Fever	✘	✘	✔	✘	✘
Reduced appetite	✘	✘	✔	✘	✘
Wound	✘	✘	✘	✔	✔

COMMON LETHAL DISEASES

Lethal diseases pose a significant threat to your herd's survival and require immediate attention. Recognizing the symptoms of these diseases early can prevent fatalities and the spread of infection to other animals.

1. Anthrax:

A serious bacterial infection causing fever, swelling, and sudden death.

2. Enterotoxaemia:

Also known as overeating disease, caused by Clostridium bacteria, leading to sudden death and bloody discharge.

3. CCPP:

Contagious Caprine Pleuropneumonia, a bacterial lung infection causing fever, labored breathing, and sudden death.

4. HS:

Haemorrhagic Septicemia, a bacterial infection causing fever, swelling, and sudden death.

5. BL:

Bluetongue, a viral disease which causes fever, swollen lips and mouth, and weight loss.

6. PPR:

Peste des Petits Ruminants, a highly contagious viral disease that causes fever, mouth ulcers, and sudden death.

7. Goat Pox:

A viral disease that causes skin lesions, fever, and swelling.

Table 46: Common Lethal Diseases and Their Symptoms

Symptom	Anthrax गर्जिक रोग	Enterotoxaemia अचानक मृत्यु रोग	CCPP संक्रामक बकरी फेफड़े की सूजन	HS गला घोंटू बुखार	BL काला पांव रोग	PPR	Goat Pox बकरी चेक
Fever	✔	✗	✗	✔	✔	✔	✔
Bloody discharge	✔	✗	✗	✔	✗	✗	✗
Anemia	✗	✔	✔	✔	✔	✗	✔
Swelling	✔	✗	✔	✗	✗	✗	✔
Sudden death	✔	✔	✗	✔	✗	✗	✔

NON-COMMON NON-LETHAL DISEASES

Some diseases are less common but still important to recognize and manage. These uncommon non-lethal diseases can cause significant health issues if left untreated.

1. CAE:

Caprine Arthritis Encephalitis, a viral disease that causes swollen knee joints, weakness in the rear legs, and facial paralysis.

2. Listeriosis B:

A bacterial infection causing loss of appetite, walking in circles, and facial paralysis.

3. Urolithiasis:

A condition causing difficulty in urinating and bloody urine due to stones in the urinary tract.

Table 47: Non-Common Non-Lethal Diseases and Their Symptoms

Symptom	CAE गठिया रोग	Listeriosis b घूम रोग	Urolithiasis मूत्र पथरी
Loss of appetite	✗	✔	✗
Walking in circles	✗	✔	✗
Facial paralysis	✗	✔	✗
Bloody urine	✗	✗	✔
Swollen abdomen	✗	✗	✔

NON-COMMON NON-LETHAL DISEASES

In addition to the more commonly known lethal diseases, there are several less common but equally dangerous diseases that can affect your goats. Early identification and treatment are critical to preventing severe outcomes.

1. Blue Tongue:

A viral disease that causes fever, swollen lips and mouth, and nasal discharge.

2. Scrapie:

A fatal neurodegenerative disease that causes incoordination and tremors.

3. Tetanus:

A bacterial infection causing muscle stiffness, spasms, and difficulty eating.

4. Q Fever:

A bacterial infection causing fever, lethargy and weight loss.

Table 48: Non-Common Lethal Diseases and Their Symptoms

Symptom	Blue tongue नीली जीभ रोग / कैटर्रल फ़ीवर	Scrapie	Tetanus धनुस्तंभ	Q fever
Fever	✔	✗	✗	✔
Swollen lips/ mouth	✔	✗	✗	✗
Mouth ulcers	✔	✗	✗	✗
Nasal discharge	✔	✗	✗	✔
Incoordination	✗	✔	✗	✗

DISEASES of PREGNANT GOATS

Pregnant goats are particularly vulnerable to certain diseases that can affect their fertility and the health of their offspring. Monitoring for these specific conditions is essential to ensure successful pregnancies and healthy kids.

1. Brucellosis:

A bacterial infection causing abortion, reduced fertility, and vaginal discharge.

2. Chlamydiosis:

A bacterial infection causing abortions, stillbirths, and vaginal discharge.

3. Mastitis:

An infection of the udder causes a swollen, painful udder and a foul odor in the milk.

4. Pregnancy Toxaemia:

A metabolic disease in late pregnancy causing loss of appetite, muscle tremors, and difficulty standing.

Table 49: Diseases of Pregnant Goats and Their Symptoms

Symptom	Brucellosis गर्भपात रोग	Chlamydiosis	Mastitis थनैला	Pregnancy Toxemia गर्भावस्था विषाक्तता
Abortion	✔	✔	✗	✗
Reduced fertility	✔	✗	✗	✗
Swollen udder	✗	✗	✔	✗
Foul odor in milk	✗	✗	✔	✗
Loss of appetite	✗	✗	✗	✔

DISEASE TRANSMISSION MODES

Understanding how diseases are transmitted is vital for implementing effective prevention and control measures. Different diseases spread through various means such as soil, feed, water, air, vectors, and direct contact.

The following table outlines the modes of transmission for both lethal and non-lethal diseases, helping you to devise strategies to minimize the risk of infection in your herd:

Table 50: Diseases and their modes of transmission

Disease	Category	Soil	Feed/ Water	Air	Vector	Direct Transmission
Haemorrhagic Septicemia	Lethal	✔	✔	✔	✗	✔
Anthrax	Lethal	✔	✗	✗	✗	✔
Black Quarter	Lethal	✗	✔	✗	✗	✗
Goat Plague (PPR)	Lethal	✗	✔	✔	✗	✔
Goat Pox	Lethal	✗	✗	✔	✔	✔
Contagious Caprine Pleuropneumonia (CCPP)	Lethal	✗	✗	✔	✗	✔

Disease	Category	Soil	Feed/Water	Air	Vector	Direct Transmission
Q Fever	Lethal	✗	✗	✔	✔	✔
Blue Tongue	Lethal	✗	✗	✗	✔	✔
Scrapie	Lethal	✗	✗	✗	✗	✔
Foot Rot	Non-lethal	✔	✗	✗	✗	✗
Foot-and-mouth Disease (FMD)	Non-lethal	✔	✔	✔	✗	✔
Pizzle Rot (Urethritis)	Non-lethal	✔	✗	✗	✗	✗
Sore Mouth	Non-lethal	✔	✔	✗	✗	✔
Brucellosis	Non-lethal	✗	✔	✗	✗	✔
Listeriosis b	Non-lethal	✗	✔	✗	✗	✔
Infectious Bovine Keratoconjunctivitis	Non-lethal	✗	✗	✗	✔	✔
Tick/Lice/Flea Infestation	Non-lethal	✗	✗	✗	✗	✔
Caprine Arthritis Encephalitis (CAE)	Non-lethal	✗	✗	✗	✗	✔
Mastitis	Non-lethal	✗	✗	✗	✗	✔

VACCINATION TIMELINE

Vaccination is one of the most effective ways to prevent serious diseases in goats. Regular vaccination schedules help protect your herd from outbreaks and ensure long-term health and productivity.

The following section provides an overview of essential vaccines for goats, including recommended schedules and tips for administering vaccines safely and effectively. By adhering to these guidelines, you can significantly reduce the risk of disease and promote the overall well-being of your goats:

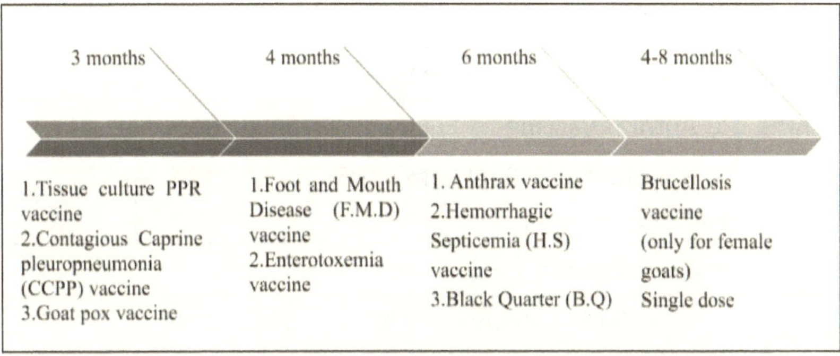

Figure 174: Vaccine timeline for goats

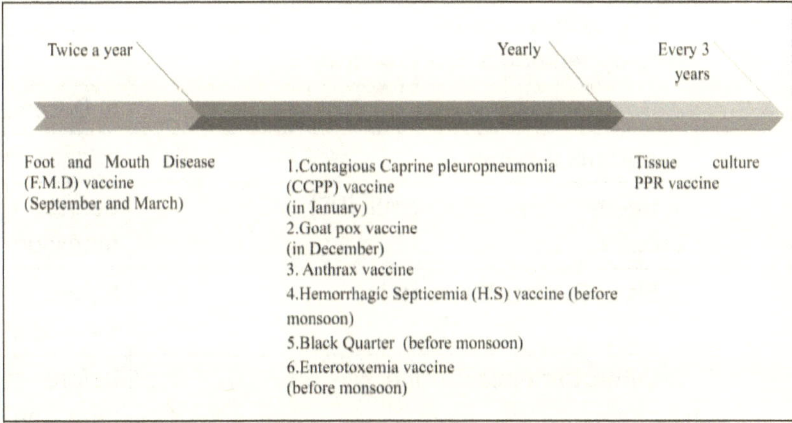

Figure 175: Vaccine booster dose timeline

Table 51: Vaccination Timeline for Goats

Age/ Stage	Vaccine	Frequency	Notes
3 months	1. Tissue culture PPR vaccine	Single dose	
	2. Contagious Caprine Pleuropneumonia (CCPP) vaccine		
	3. Goatpox vaccine		

Age/ Stage	Vaccine	Frequency	Notes
4 months	1. Foot and Mouth Disease (FMD) vaccine	Single dose	
	2. Enterotoxaemia vaccine		
6 months	1. Anthrax vaccine	Single dose	
	2. Haemorrhagic Septicemia (HS) vaccine		
	3. Black Quarter (BQ) vaccine		
4-8 months	1. Brucellosis vaccine (only for female goats).	Single dose	
Twice a year	Foot-and-mouth disease (FMD) vaccine	Twice a year	September and March
Yearly	1. Contagious Caprine Pleuropneumonia (CCPP) vaccine	Annually	In January
	2. Goatpox vaccine		In December
	3. Anthrax vaccine		
	4. Haemorrhagic Septicemia (HS) vaccine		Before monsoon
	5. Black Quarter (BQ) vaccine		Before monsoon
	6. Enterotoxaemia vaccine		Before monsoon
Every 3 years	Tissue culture PPR vaccine	Every 3 years	

After reading through the tables, the reader will notice that most diseases have their origin in contaminated environments like soil, water, or feed. This is the primary breeding ground of most bacterial and viral infections. While this may seem like a problem, it actually makes our work easier.

Because after having identified the primary source of illness, it is easy to strategize on how to eliminate it. Eliminate the source and the disease will be automatically eliminated, which will ensure that the goats reach the optimal health goal. The reader might be thinking – but not all diseases are fatal and thus, obviously won't kill the animal. That is true. Many of these diseases are not deadly, but they do impact the ruminant's health significantly.

Our goal behind making the structure of the shed, as illustrated in Chapter 9, was not just to provide a living space for the goats and sheep. The goal is to provide a completely threat-free environment to its inhabitants so they can thrive. When the farmer provides a space that is completely free of dangers and has everything, from nutritious food and clean water to hygienic living spaces, it boosts the livestock's health by folds. Understand it in this way – in the traditional system, many threats still prevail. These can be related to overcrowding, unhygienic living conditions, not enough food or water, and the threat of predators like jackals.

In such a stressful environment, most of the ruminant's energy goes into surviving. If the animal is continuously in survival mode, it will never reach the pinnacle of health, and that will end up being a loss for the farmer. In this system, we have taken care of everything, eliminated every possible risk, and provided every possible comfort to the animal, which means there is no longer a need to 'survive'. The reader will be amazed to see the transformation an animal goes through when it is no longer fighting to survive.

Another factor that should be taken into consideration is the contagious nature of many diseases listed in this chapter. Goats and sheep are herd animals, which means that one infected animal can easily spread the disease to the whole herd. This is another reason why regular cleaning and maintaining a hygienic environment is important. To prevent disease transmission and limit it to one corner of the shed, we built separate spaces. These are not only effective in limiting disease transmission but also in segregating goats.

Segregating the livestock also helps in keeping track of individual health conditions. Marking individual goats and performing regular check-ups ensures that the onset of a disease is immediately noticed, resulting in swift and effective treatment. Below is an example of a checklist to tick off on an everyday basis to keep track of the livestock's health:

Table 52: Daily Health Check-Up Checklist

Date	01/01/2024	02/01/2024	04/01/2024
Temperature			
– Normal range: 38.5°C to 39.7°C (101.3°F to 103.5°F)			
Skin			
– Check for wounds.			
– Check for lice and ticks			
Coat			
– Consistent and shiny coat			
Eyes			
– Check for excessive discharge and swelling.			
Nasal Discharge			
– Check for a clean nose			
Mouth			
– Check for ulcers and swelling.			
– Check gum color for anemia (dull pink indicates anemia)			
Hoof			
– Check for infections (hoof rot).			
– Regular trimming			
Lethargy			
– Check for alertness (lethargy indicates potential health issues).			

Date	01/01/2024	02/01/2024	04/01/2024
Fecal Consistency			
– Check for diarrhea (sign of trouble)			
Udder (for mother goats)			
– Check for swelling or redness.			
– Check the milk consistency and color			

Table 53: Weekly/Monthly Health Check-Up Checklist

Date	01/01/2024	08/01/2024	15/01/2024
Weight			
– Check for overweight or underweight conditions			
General Health			
– Isolate new goats and those returning from the market for a few days to monitor for infections			
Vaccinations			
– Ensure all goats receive regular vaccination shots			

This is just an example of what all things can be included in a daily checklist. Every goat should be numbered and have a separate checklist accordingly.

Here is some context for the things listed above:

1. The ideal body temperature of a goat should range between 38.5°C–39.7°C (101.3°F–103.5°F).
2. The skin should be checked for wounds caused by diseases or injuries due to other reasons as they provide easy entry for bacteria. Regular checking of lice and ticks is done to eliminate the parasites as soon as they emerge.

3. A healthy coat should be consistent (no hair loss patches) and have a shine. If it's dull and rough, it is probably because of a deficiency of minerals like calcium, iron, or magnesium.
4. Eyes should be checked for excessive discharge and swelling. Healthy eyes are clean.
5. Discharge from the nose is a symptom of many diseases like pneumonia and causes difficulty in breathing. The animal should have a clean nose.
6. The mouth should be checked for ulcers and swelling as it prevents the animal from eating properly, which can lead to several issues.
7. Check the gum colour for signs of anaemia. If the gum is a dull pink color, the animal is probably anemic and should be treated accordingly.
8. Hooves should be kept clean and checked regularly for infections on the surface and in between the soft tissues. They should also be trimmed regularly as lengthy hooves result in trouble when walking.
9. Signs of lethargy should be checked as it is a symptom of many diseases. A healthy goat is always alert to its surroundings. If it's being lethargic, there is probably something wrong.
10. Fecal consistency is another thing to check on a daily basis. If the goat has diarrhea, it is a sign of trouble.
11. Udder health should be regularly checked in mother goats for signs of swelling or redness.
12. Also, check the consistency and colour of milk to determine health.

The checklist above is just an example to give the reader an idea. The reader can make their own checklist, suitable for their farm. Apart from daily check-ups, there are some other preventive measures that should be done on a weekly or monthly basis. These can include weighing an individual goat to check if it's overweight or underweight.

Table 54: Ideal weight of the Sirohi breed of Rajasthan at different stages

Category	Minimum Weight (kg)	Maximum Weight (kg)
Birth Weight (Kids)	2	3.5
6 Months Weight (Kids)	15	30
Adult Weight (Male Bucks)	30	50
Adult Weight (Female Does)	25	40
Older Goats Weight	25	50

Regular vaccine shots should be ensured on a yearly basis. Another effective method of disease prevention is to isolate new goats from the herd for a few days to check for possible infections they may be carrying.

If the goats are transported to the market and brought back to the farm without being sold, they should also be isolated for a few days as they might have picked up a disease from the open environment of the market. Taking this simple step can significantly decrease the likelihood of disease transmission in goats.

Lastly, the reader will notice that nowhere in the following tables have we written anything about the 'cure'. We have only written about the source, symptoms, transmission, and prevention of the diseases. The absence of a column labeled 'cure' is not because of ignorance but has a very logical reason behind it.

More often than not, the farmer tries to diagnose the animal, be it a goat, sheep, or cattle, at home and subsequently attempts to cure it on his own. Trying home-based remedies not only results in a delay for effective treatment but these remedies may make the disease worse or make treating them difficult afterwards.

Moreover, if the farmer follows this manual word by word and follows the instructions on how to build a shed, many of these diseases will automatically be eliminated. If the very environment in which bacteria thrive, like wet muddy soil or unhygienic feed containers or contaminated water, is wholly eliminated, the diseases that originate from them are also eliminated. Another important detail to keep in mind is vaccines.

Vaccination is the most – and we are emphasizing on the word 'most' – effective way of prevention against fatal diseases that have a high mortality rate, like anthrax or goat plague. These diseases do not give time for treatment, and animals often die in a few days after being diagnosed.

If it's contagious, the death of an animal is only the first in the series of deaths that follow. It could take down an entire herd, and if the disease is zoonotic – that is, it can be transmitted from animal to human – even the farmer and people around him are at risk.

After considering this, is it not better to invest in vaccination and proper infrastructure than regularly spending on treatment and living with the uncertainty of a deadly disease taking over your farm?

Our purpose behind giving these ominous warnings is not to scare the reader. The end goal that we want you to achieve from this manual is a successful running farm with maximum efficiency and output.

To ensure that, it is necessary for the reader to understand the complications of dealing with diseases on their own. It is not only harmful to the animals but also economically perilous for the farmer. To reach the pinnacle of productivity, risk control measures and their understanding are of essence. Thus, it is insisted that the reader does not play doctor and goes to a vet for professional medical advice.

In this chapter, you learned:

Coming up...

Potting soil
Primary ingredient
Soil
pH
Acidic
Neutral
Basic
Fertilizer
Manure
Processed
Finely crushed goat poop
Organic matter
Nitrogen
Phosphorus
Potassium
Urine
Processed
Crystallized matter
Nitrogen
Phosphorus
Potassium
Humidity
Mulch
Wood chips
Tree bark
Packaging
Quantity
1 and 5 kg bags
Label sticker
Polythene bags
Prevention
Neem oil
Neem kernel powder
Neem bark
Onion peels
Risk
Indoor plants
Disease
Powdery mildew
Root rot
Plant rust
Sooty mold
Outdoor plants
Disease
Powdery mildew
Root rot
Plant rust
Sooty mold
Pests
Aphids
Mealybugs
Mites
Whiteflies
Ants
Basic requirement
Indoor plants
Sunlight
Indirect
Less evaporation
Water
Once a week
Soil
Granular
Nutrients
Macro
N,P,K,Ca,Mg,S
Micro
Fe,Zn,Mn,B,Cu,Cl
Planting space
Pots
Mulch
Not needed
Outdoor plants
Sunlight
Direct
More evaporation
Water
Multiple times a week
Soil
Lumpy
Nutrients
Macro
N,P,K,Ca,Mg,S
Micro
Fe,Zn,Mn,B,Cu,Cl
Planting space
Pots
Soil
Mulch
To maintain humidity

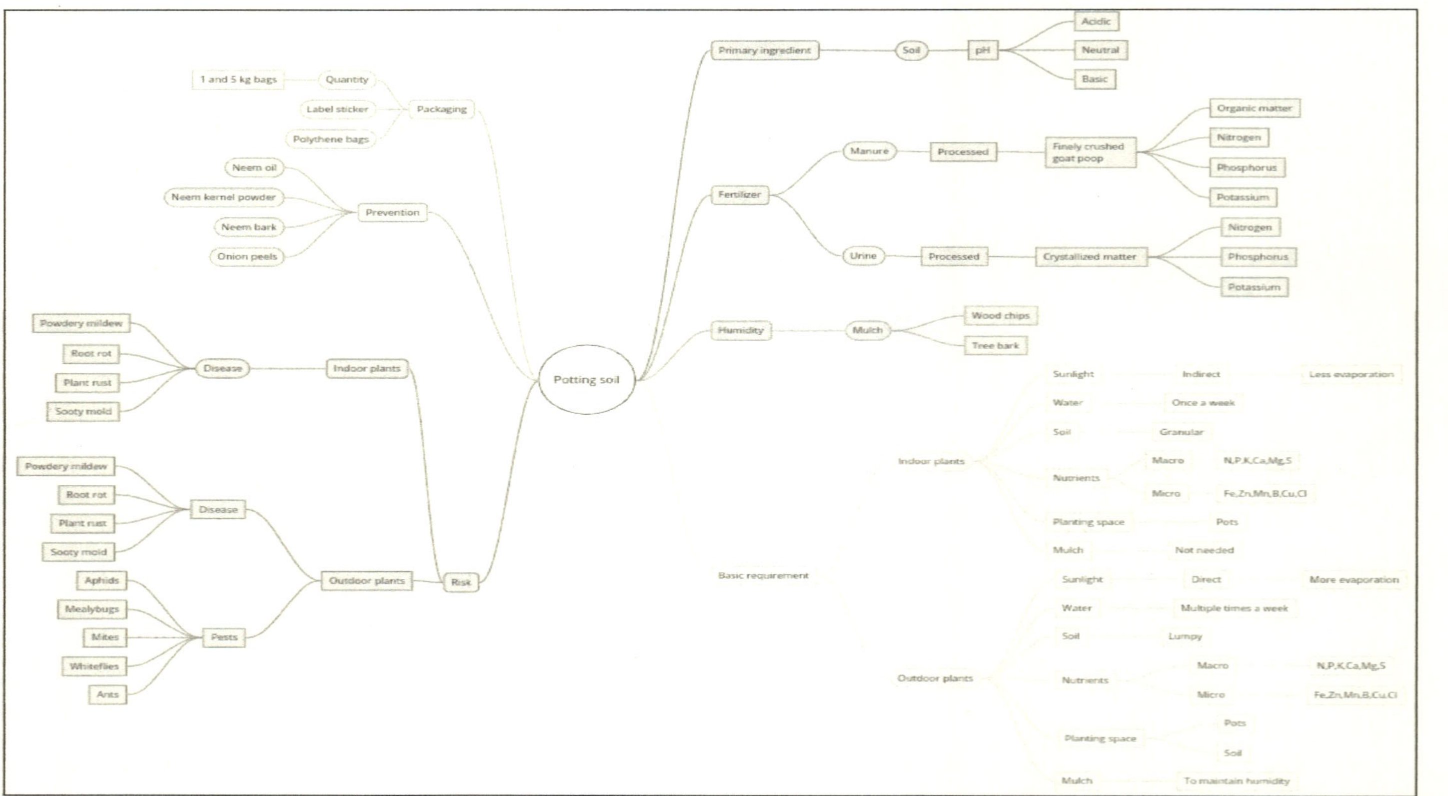

CHAPTER 11

Potting Soil

UNTIL NOW WE HAVE DISCUSSED EVERYTHING ABOUT THE LIVESTOCK, I.E. GOATS AND SHEEP, FOR THE GOAL OF HAVING A SUSTAINABLE LIVELIHOOD. WE HAVE COVERED QUITE A BIT, RANGING FROM WHY GOATS AND SHEEP ARE THE BEST CHOICE OF LIVESTOCK TO THEIR FOOD SOURCES AND DISEASE MANAGEMENT.

Let's now indulge in understanding how we can generate a regular source of income via them.

Most people who rear these animals are unaware of a great resource that they produce, which can be monetized and sold. The said resource is actually a waste product, and yes, you are thinking right, we are referring to the excreta and urine of the livestock.

Before we talk about the details, let us first understand the difference between active and passive sources of income.

Active income can be defined as "income that requires the recipient to actively participate in an activity or trade to earn money. This typically includes wages, salaries, commissions, and any other earnings where labor or services are directly exchanged for compensation."[250]

On the other hand, passive income can be defined as "earnings derived from a rental property, limited partnership, or other enterprise in which a person is not actively involved."[251]

This type of income typically requires minimal effort to maintain once the initial setup or investment has been made.

In this chapter, we will discuss the passive source of income.

'ONE MAN'S TRASH IS ANOTHER MAN'S TREASURE'

During our 5-year-long research on livestock rearing, we talked to farmers who reared these animals. In one of the conversations, we became very curious about what they do with the excreta of the animals.

Now, before we tell you their response, let us revert for a moment to Chapter 9 where we discussed the traditional methods of livestock rearing. In this method, animal quarters do not have solid floors; instead, they have a soil base. They urinate and excrete on this floor.

In most cases, the excreta is collected and used to fertilise soil on their agricultural land. People who do not have their own land sell it, and a one-ton trolley of manure can fetch them ₹4000-5000 ($48-60).

If one thinks about it, this is not a very optimal use of the manure. Goat and sheep manure are rich in NPK (nitrogen, phosphorus, and potassium), which are essential minerals for soil fertility. The average ratio of NPK in goat poop is 3:1:2.

Goat urine contains primarily nitrogen. Precisely, the nitrogen content ranges between 0.9% to 1.5%, phosphorus content is between 0.1% to 0.2%, and potassium is between 0.5% to 1%. Additionally, it contains trace elements like zinc, copper, iron, and manganese. It is generally alkaline and helps neutralize acidic soils.

Both the solid and liquid waste are therefore high in minerals and can be used as fertilizers, which farmers normally do. But that's not what we are talking about. Instead, we strategized that the most optimal way to use this manure was to sell it in the market as *potting soil*.

We will now explain the market demand for potting soil and how manure from the farm can be marketed to supply this demand.

BUSINESS CASE OF POTTING SOIL

1. LAND USE IN VILLAGE VERSUS CITY

The first thing the reader needs to understand is the different ways in which land is used in villages and cities. Presently, if one goes to a village, apart from land used for building houses, most of the land goes into agriculture-related activities.

One can see acres of land dedicated to growing crops or used for big animal farms, with animals like goats, cattle, etc. Thus, it is going to be very difficult for someone from a village to believe when we state that in cities, people pay to buy soil.

In cities, close to zero land is used for agriculture. Instead, land is used for building housing complexes, apartments, industries, malls, offices, etc. As a result of these man-made activities, nature is pushed into a corner, and even finding normal soil to grow plants is a difficult task. Construction activity renders the soil infertile, and it is not suitable to grow most kinds of plants.

Cities and towns also lack patience, thus anything organic is tough to sustain. Fast is the lifestyle.

2. FARMING AS A SOURCE OF LIVELIHOOD VERSUS HOBBY

Secondly, from the scale on which land is used for farming activities in villages, one can easily tell that it is a source of livelihood and income.

But in cities where people have limited space to live in and limited time from their jobs, growing plants becomes a hobby. It is no longer a necessity but is done purely for the aesthetics. The following tree structure will help us to understand it better.

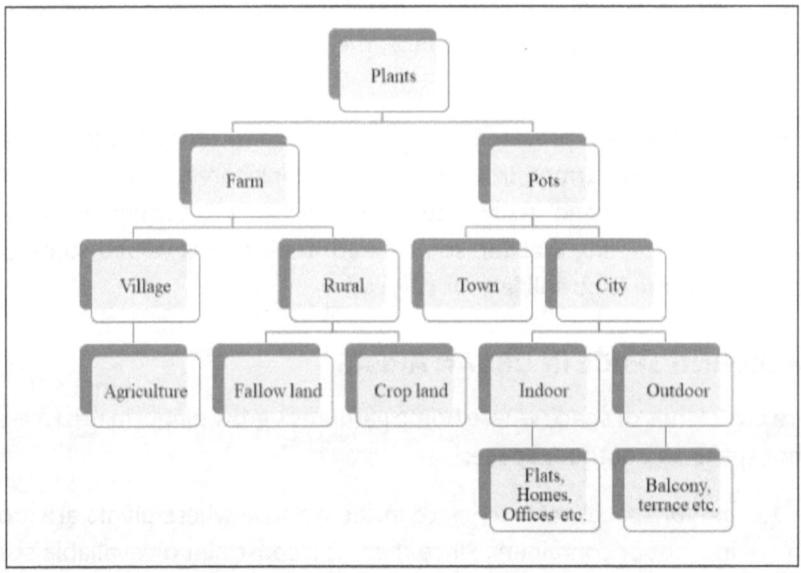

Figure 176: Tree structure

Take a flat for example. Someone residing in a flat has limited space where they can grow plants. This could be their balcony because it fulfills the requirements of sunlight, air, and an open atmosphere for the plant. The balcony has very limited space.

Unlike in villages where you can plant the seed in the soil in an open area, if a city person wants to grow plants, they have to first buy a pot, soil, fertilizers, etc. They cannot just go out and scoop soil from outdoors because there is no fertile soil present.

Perhaps it is because of their abundance that farmers underestimate the market in cities that would readily take organic fertilizers such as these.

3. ONLINE SHOPPING FOR EFFECTIVE TIME MANAGEMENT

In the city, any person having a job generally only gets time for their hobbies on weekends. Thus, a person living in the city who grows plants as a hobby is more focused on time management than the money they spend. For example, for acquiring soil for the pots, it is more feasible for them to have it delivered to their doorstep rather than going to a nearby village and procuring it from there.

Our intention behind listing these differences is to ensure that the reader understands the potential market for the manure produced on their farm. At its place of origin, due to its abundance, the manure might seem like it is not worth much.

However, once it is processed, it will turn into a commodity that can bring huge profits to the farmer. In villages, soil is considered as something that is naturally available and easily accessible, which is why farmers might have a hard time processing that the soil beneath their feet is valued so much in cities where there is no soil left for cultivation.

GARDENING SPACE IN URBAN AREAS

There are 2 kinds of space where home gardeners grow plants in urban areas: indoor space and outdoor space.

1. Indoor spaces refer to space inside a house where plants are grown in a pot or containers. Since there is a constraint on available space, the variety of plants grown is also limited. These plants are the ones which do not need direct sunlight.
2. Outdoor spaces refer to space outside the walls of the home. It could be a balcony, a porch, a small garden etc. Here the plants can be grown either in a pot or directly in the soil.

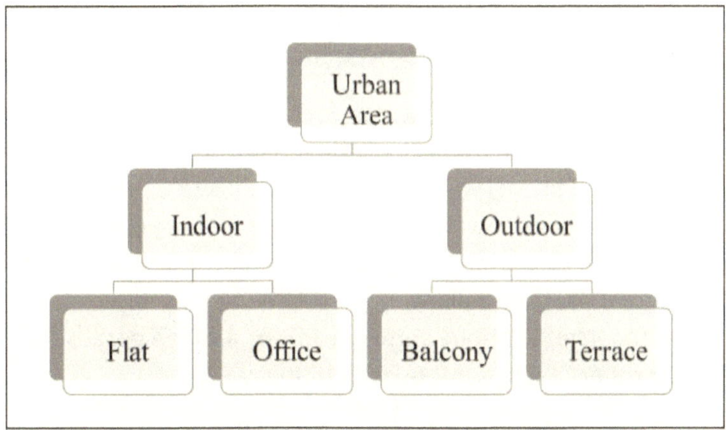

Figure 177: Tree structure focusing on urban areas

Determining the appropriate pot size is crucial for a plant's growth. If the pot size is too small, the plant will not be able to reach its peak growth. Small pots limit root growth and inhibit plant growth.

For example, look at the following pictures of spinach grown in a small pot versus spinach grown directly in the soil (where it had enough space to grow properly).

Figure 178: Spinach grown in a small pot versus spinach grown in open ground[252]

You will notice that the leaves of spinach grown in the pot are comparatively smaller than those grown in the soil. This proves that pot size matters if you want your plant to reach optimal growth.

Similarly, if a plant is grown in a pot that's too big for its size, it will result in deteriorating health. Here are some scenarios that can occur in this case:

a. The soil will hold the water for a longer duration, resulting in dampness around roots all the time. This will cause root rot, a fungal infection in plants, which cuts short the life of a plant.
b. A lesser amount of water will cause the soil to dry out quickly because of increased volume. Dry soil will result in hampered growth and eventual death of a plant.
c. The soil itself will start getting acidic or alkaline because the excess water is not being synthesised optimally.

Thus, it is very important to decide the appropriate pot size for your plant.

Below is a table of pot size (in inches) and the kind of plant it is suitable for. The table also provides information on how much soil is needed for a pot this size.

Table 55: Pot size chart and recommended plants for each size[253]

Pot Sizes (inches)	Pot Equivalent (Gallons/Liters)[254]	Suitable Plants	Soil Needed and Weight (Pounds/ grams)[255]
4' pot	0.125 gal / 0.473 L	Nursery plants/ Seedlings	0.137 lbs./ 60 g
5-6" pot	0.25 gal / 0.946 L	Small succulents	0.27 lbs./ 120 g
7-8" pot	1 gal/ 3.78 L	Larger succulents	1.1 lbs./ 490 g
10' pot	3 gal/ 11 L	Small herbs, such as spring onions	3.3 lbs./ 1490 g
12' pot	5 gal/ 19 L	Lettuce / spinach	5.5 lbs./ 2490 g
14' pot	7 gal/ 26 L	Larger herbs such as rosemary	7.7 lbs./ 3490 g
16' pot	10 gal/ 38 L	Small shrubs/ small fruits such as strawberries	11 lbs./ 4980 g

Note: All figures are estimates, and exact specifications largely depend on the manufacturer.

SOIL TEXTURE

The soil texture also varies for indoor and outdoor plants. Indoor plants need soil with a granular texture and good drainage. Granular and crumb structures are individual particles of sand, silt, and clay grouped together in small, nearly spherical grains[256].

Figure 179: Granules of soil[257]

Since indoor spaces do not receive much sunlight, the moisture level in the soil remains unchanged. Soils with good drainage ensure that the soil retains moisture but not in an excessive amount, which otherwise causes root rot.

Outdoor plants need soil which has a lumpy texture with good water retention capacity. Outdoor plants receive more sunlight and hence experience more evaporation. Therefore, soil type with good water retention ensures moisture is maintained.

INGREDIENTS OF POTTING SOIL

Now that we have explained the market demand for potting soil, we will now proceed to how the said potting soil is to be produced. Please note that the information here is personally implemented and researched by the author.

There are 4 main ingredients that go into making potting soil, as listed in the diagram:

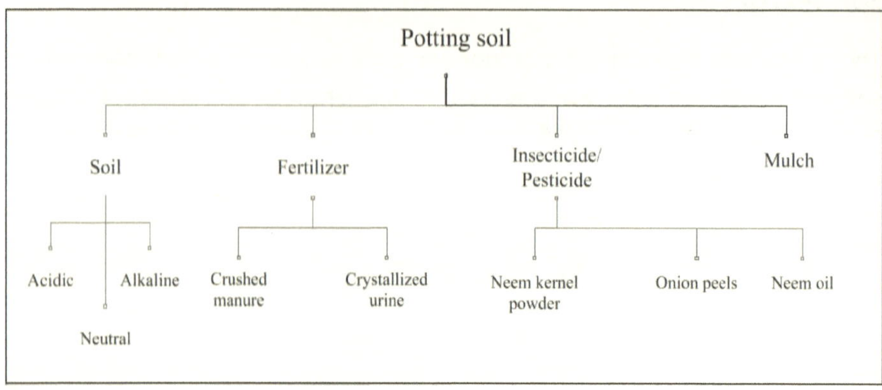

Figure 180: Ingredients of potting soil

1. SOIL

The farmer can source soil needed for the potting soil from their land itself. In our proposed land project, only area 1 is being cultivated for fodder crops. The topsoil of areas 2, 3, and 4 is not required as there are no cultivation activities taking place on them.

Thus, the farmer can remove the topsoil of these areas up to a depth of 1 inch and use it as an ingredient for the potting soil.

Soil can be divided into 3 types based on its pH:

1.   Acidic
2.   Neutral
3.   Alkaline

On a pH scale of 1-14, acidic soils fall below 7, down to 5. A pH value lower than 5 is too acidic for plants to survive, other than a few exceptions. Neutral soil falls exactly on a pH scale of 7. Alkaline (basic) soil type has a pH value greater than 7, and up to 8 is good for plants.

Different plants need different kinds of soil pH for healthy growth. For example, plants like onions, potatoes, and tomatoes grow well in acidic soil, while others like peas and cabbage prefer alkaline soils, and others like pomegranate and celery prefer neutral soil.

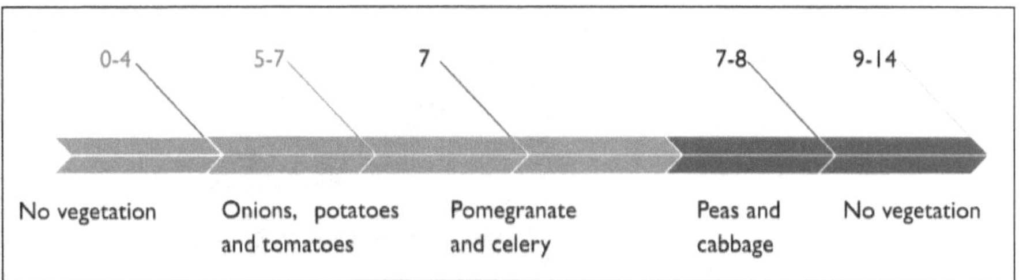

Figure 181: pH scale with a range of 0-14, depicting the pH levels required by different plants

To cater to the consumer's demand, the farmer should have soil of all 3 types.

2. FERTILIZER

The excreta and urine of livestock animals are going to be the fertilizer for this soil. Goat urine is alkaline in nature, so it can be used to reduce the acidic pH or increase the alkalinity as well.

Remember, diluted and pasteurized urine is to be used.

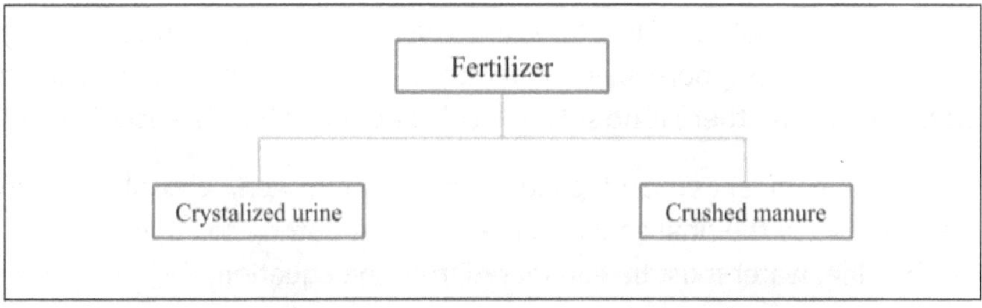

Figure 182: Two kinds of fertilizer obtained from goat waste

In Chapter 9, we discussed the structure of the shed where the livestock will be kept. The structure has a special feature to collect the manure and urine that the animals excrete.

The floor is slanted from both sides to meet at the center so that the urine is collected in the middle. The slats that make up the floor have small openings in them to allow manure to pass downward and get collected.

Figure 183: Space in slats for easy passage of excreta to pass downward[258]

Figure 184: Collected excreta[259]

Since the process of collecting the manure is now clear, let me describe the next course of action. Firstly, the liquid and solid animal waste should be segregated.

a. CRYSTALLISED URINE

The urine will be collected in a tank, and the manure in a separate container. From here on, they both have separate processes to go through. In the traditional system, there is no setup to collect urine, which is wasted away.

The urine of sheep and goats is rich in nitrogen, phosphorus, and potassium. Since the final goal is to manufacture potting soil that can have a long shelf life, water must be eliminated from the equation.

It is a fact that water provides a habitable environment for bacteria and fungi to develop and will terminate the shelf life of the final product. The reader might be thinking, but urine exists in a liquid state, how can we take water out? The answer is through the process of crystallization.

Crystallization is a common method used to extract and concentrate valuable components from urine, through evaporation, where the urine is allowed to dry, and the remaining solids form crystals. The collected urine should be spread out in a container to speed up evaporation. The remaining crystals are packed with nitrogen-rich extract, along with potassium and phosphorus and will be one of the components of the potting soil.

The author recommends the process of using a solar cooker to evaporate the water. Even the distillation process can be used, where the water is also collected and used in solar batteries as distilled water.

b. CRUSHED MANURE

Now comes the solid excreta. Goat poop is rich in organic matter, nitrogen, phosphorus, and potassium. Just like urine, water should be eliminated from the solid waste as well. The solid waste should be dried in the sun for a period of 5 days to reduce the moisture content to zero.

There is another option of using a sundryer. Basically, have a rectangular box made of some metal and its top be of glass. The sun's rays will come through the glass. The inner surroundings must have a black colored surface so it can absorb more heat. Ensure there is an escape channel for moisture. There's your basic sundryer.

Afterward, the dried waste should be crushed into a fine powder. For this purpose, we have a crusher on the farm, and we advise the reader to have the same.

Figure 185: Grinder to crush dry excreta and turn it into fine powder[260]

Figure 186: Solid dry goat excreta and finely crushed powder of goat excreta

The machine will do a much better job of finely grinding the excreta than if it's done manually. If the process is done manually, it will require labor, and the final product will take more time to produce.

The machine quickly completes the work which is otherwise labor and time-intensive. It is a long-term investment, like everything else on the farm and also the best way to maximize production. When the final product is out in the market, this machine is a feasible way to ensure that it keeps up with the increasing demand that's going to roll in.

SOIL TO MANURE RATIO

The ratio of ingredients in potting soil will be 77:5:5:4:9. For every 77 parts of soil, the farmer should supply 5 parts of granules, 5 parts of pesticide, 4 parts of coconut coir, and 9 parts of fertilizer. So, 77 kg soil + 5 kg granules + 5 kg pesticide + 4 kg cocopeat + 9 kg fertilizer = 100 kg potting soil.

So, for example, the farmer got a trolley of 1 ton of soil. Out of this 1 ton, only 770 kg will be used for the potting soil. That leaves the farmer with 230 kg more soil, which they can convert into potting soil in the same ratio.

3. INSECTICIDE/PESTICIDE

An essential element is a natural insecticide and pesticide, organically sourced, which will make the soil pest and insect repellent. Indoor and outdoor plants are both at risk of getting infected with fungal diseases like:

1. Powdery mildew
2. Root rot
3. Plant rust
4. Sooty mold

We can even say that indoor plants are more at risk because it's easier to accidentally create a humid environment inside the house, where sunlight reaches partially and the air is stale.

The chance of a pest infection is higher in outdoor plants because that is a more habitable environment for them. To avoid the plants from getting infected by pests, the farmer should add crushed neem (Azadirachta indica) bark, which is obtained by the process of crushing neem bark and kernels. Neem kernel cakes are also used for the same purpose.

Moreover, this is an additional source of NPK (5.2% N, 1.0% P, 1.4% K) and enhances soil fertility and structure. Neem is a natural insecticide and pesticide. Adding fine powder of neem to the soil will make it immune to 700 plus insects and pests. Neem oil can be used as a substitute for neem powder. However, neem oil must be used as prescribed, based on the concentration levels.

Figure 187: Neem bark and crushed powder of neem bark

Following is a list of common garden insects that neem products repel:

5. Aphids
6. Mealybugs
7. Mites
8. Whiteflies
9. Ants
10. Thrips

Along with neem bark powder or oil, dried and powdered onion could be added. Onion acts as a natural insect repellent as its smell is pungent for plant-eating insects.

4. MULCH

Mulch is a material (for example, decaying leaves) that you put around a plant to protect its base and its roots, to improve the quality of the soil, or to stop weeds growing[261]. It is made from natural materials that decompose over time, adding organic matter to the soil and improving its fertility. Examples of organic mulch include shredded bark, wood chips, straw, leaves, grass clippings, and compost.

Mulch also ensures harmful solar UV rays don't hit the topsoil, thereby keeping microbial activity ongoing.

Figure 188: Dry leaves[262]

Along with dry leaves, we are also going to use coconut coir as mulch. Coconut coir is the fibrous part of the coconut and is extracted from the outer husks. This can be easily sourced from temples and coconut vendors.

Crushed powder of coconut coir acts as mulch and maintains humidity in the soil. It has natural antifungal properties, which can help prevent soil-borne diseases and pests. The fibrous texture of coconut coir allows for air pockets to form in the soil and regulates aeration. This promotes the growth of healthy microorganisms and root health.

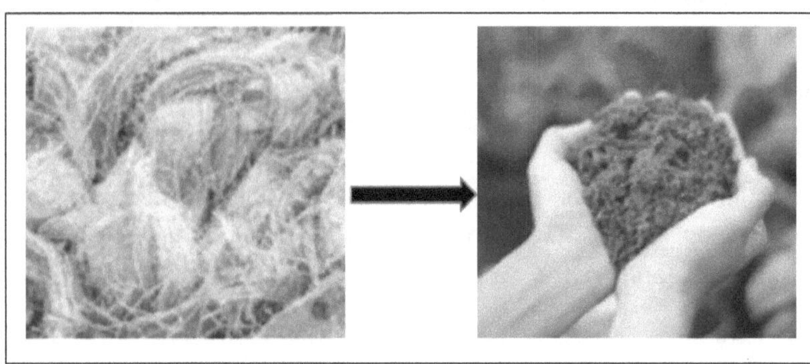

Figure 189: Coconut coir and Powdered coir[263]

Adding a layer of mulch over the potting soil will help to retain moisture, thus increasing soil fertility.

The process of making potting soil can be summarized as shown in the diagram:

COST INVOLVED IN PRODUCTION

When a product is manufactured, there are 2 main costs that go into the manufacturing process – capital expenditures and operating expenses.

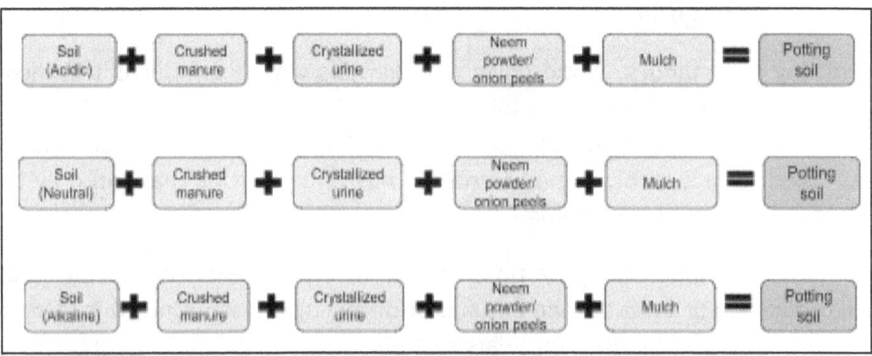

Figure 190: Ingredients and process of making potting soil

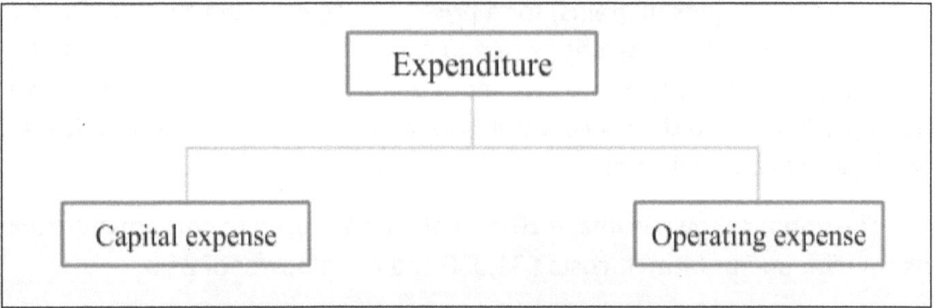

Figure 191: Two kinds of expenditure involved in production

Capital expenditures are major, long-term expenses, while operating expenses are day-to-day expenses. Examples of CapEx (Capital expenditures) include physical assets, such as equipment and machinery. Examples of OpEx include employee salaries, rent, and utilities[264].

CAPITAL EXPENDITURE

In the case of potting soil, the capital expenditure includes machinery to process raw materials such as the grinder, packaging machinery, storage facility, etc.

1. GRINDER/ CHAKKI

Purpose: The grinder is used to crush solid goat excreta that has been dried in the sun for at least 2 days. The dried waste is then put into the grinder, which crushes it into a fine powder as shown in image 11.

Crushing the manure, wood chips, and kernels with a grinder is the most efficient way of turning them into finely crushed powder. This method not only saves time by providing a huge output in limited time but also eliminates the need to hire labor. The end product has fine particles that can only be achieved if done by a machine.

Cost: A grinder is a one-time long-term investment. This means that you only have to invest in the initial cost of buying it once. Once it is in your possession, it can be used for years to come, and the only other cost will be its maintenance (which comes under operational cost).

In India, you can get a grinder or chakki (generally used for making flour out of different kinds of grains) for a price ranging between ₹12,000-32,000. The horsepower (hp), chamber size and capacity (how much weight can the grinder crush at once), electricity requirement (how much voltage does it need per hour), and the space it will take (according to dimensions of length, width, and height) will vary.

The grinder shown in image 10 is what we have used to crush manure and neem bark on our farm. It costs £32,000 and has a power of 2 hp.

2. THERMAL PRINTER

Purpose: A thermal printer is different from your regular printer that one might see in offices, photocopy shops, etc. While a regular printer uses ink to print on pages (of varying sizes like A4 or A5), a thermal printer uses heat to print on a special kind of paper.

The purpose of a thermal printer in our case is to print shipping invoices for each product that we are going to sell. A shipping invoice is a document provided by a seller or shipper to the buyer or recipient of goods being shipped. It contains various kinds of information.

Information to include on a shipping invoice:

1. Seller's address – This does not mean your own address but the address of the storage or warehouse from where products are shipped.

2. Buyer's address – This means the address of the buyer (that the buyer will provide when they make a purchase)
3. Seller's email – provide the company's official email in case the buyer wants to reach back to you.
4. GST Number – Provide the official GST number registered under your company's name for authentication.
5. Ship Date – the date on which the product was shipped.
6. Product details – Include the following details regarding your product:

    a. Product name.
    b. Serial number (in the case of multiple products)
    c. Product quantity.
    d. Price of the product (in the case of multiple products, mention each individual price and then the total price)
    e. Unique barcode (A unique barcode should be provided for each product shipped. This enables easy tracking of the shipment)
    f. Manufacture date and expiry date

These are the basic things that you should include in the shipping invoice.

Cost: the price of a thermal printer in India can range between ₹5,000-10,000. This can also be outsourced to online print and ship companies like Printo.in.[265]

3. WEIGHING SCALE

Purpose: to weigh product quantity and provide precise information about your product's weight to the consumer. It is also necessary to keep the appropriate weight of each object according to the composition ratio.

For example, potting soil consists of ingredients in the ratio 77:5:5:4:9. of soil: granules: neem powder: mulch: manure. So, you will need to determine the weight of individual ingredients according to the total weight of the palace.

So, for 5 kg of potting soil, you will need 3850 g of soil, 450 g of fertilizer, 250 g of pesticide, 250 g of granules, and 200 g of coco peat. You will also need a weighing machine to weigh the exact amount of each ingredient.

Cost: The price of a weighing scale in India can range between ₹500 and ₹2500.

OPERATIONAL EXPENDITURE

In the case of potting soil, operational expenditure includes the cost of raw materials, labor costs, utilities like electricity, transportation costs, and the share of money that will go to the online platform, also known as the middleman, where you will sell your potting soil.

1. RAW MATERIALS

All the ingredients used to make potting soil are freely available to the farmer. The soil will be procured from their land. The manure will be procured from animals on the farm. Neem bark/kernel can be procured either from trees growing on their land or from neem trees present in nature on fallow land.

This means that they would not have to spend money on buying the basic inputs. At the same time, they would be producing potting soil as an output, which will generate revenue. So, their production cost is incredibly decreased while the product cost remains the same.

Manure will be supplied continuously, all year round, for years to come, so the farmer can carry on the process of manufacturing without any worry. The very basic materials are provided to them for free, so they not only save a lot of money but also do not have to depend on external networks to get the raw material.

2. LABOR

This business is part of our sustainable land project, which aims to provide employment for a family of at least 4 people at home. The goal is that they do not have to leave their homes and wander into cities in search of a job. We want to ensure that they can stay connected to their roots while having a source of income.

The labor, therefore, will be provided by the family members. Labor work includes gathering goat waste, spreading it in the sun to dry, grinding it using the grinder, packaging, etc.

Please keep in mind that just because it's your family doesn't mean you can withhold payment from them. You have to ensure that each member is paid a decent amount for the work they are doing.

Also, remember, the author is not asking you to quit your job. The request is simply for those who currently have land and do not have a decent, well-paying job.

3. ELECTRICITY

Since the electricity requirement on our land project is fulfilled by solar panels (see Chapter 9 for more details), you will not have to pay electricity bills every month. Thus, you will save on this operational cost.

4. PACKAGING MATERIAL

For packaging the product, it is recommended to use transparent Ziplock bags of 1 and 5 kg. Ensure that the bags are food grade. Food grade Ziplock bags are plastic bags designed specifically for storing food items.

The term "food grade" indicates that these bags are made from materials that are safe for direct contact with food and are approved for use in food packaging according to regulatory standards.

Since our product's potting soil can be compared to flour (food) in texture, it can be safely transported in these bags. It will ensure that the product inside remains untouched, does not have the risk of contamination (which can happen in case the bag splits open) and safely reaches the consumer.

The other operational cost required in packaging is buying the special print paper needed for printing shipping invoices via a thermal printer.

Cost: These are available for under ₹500 (in a set of 6 or more rolls) in India.

MIDDLE MAN

After the production part is done, comes the selling part. There are 2 options for selling your product. You can either sell it directly to the consumer. This will require you to build a website for your company, list your products there, invest in marketing and advertising your products, and transporting them to the consumer.

The other way is to employ a middleman who will take the products and ship them to the consumer on your behalf. This is where online shopping sites like Amazon and Flipkart come into the picture.

To sell your product on any online site, you will need a registered GST number or PAN number for your company. From here on, you can list your products on the site to sell them. Aggregator sites provide 3 options for shipping to the seller:

1. Fulfillment centers – The seller needs to send their products to one of the fulfillment centers. From there on the aggregator will take care of storing, packing and shipping their orders as per customer demand.
2. Easy ship – The seller has to store and package their orders. The aggregator will pick the packaged order from the seller's location and ship them to customers.
3. Self-ship – the seller has to ship the orders themselves. The aggregator will only showcase their products on the website.

Breakdown of various fees generally charged by an aggregator:

1. REFERRAL FEE

A referral fee is a commission paid to the person or entity that facilitated a deal by linking up a potential customer with an opportunity[266].

For each product sold, the aggregator charges a referral fee, which varies by-product category and is calculated as a percentage of the total selling price of the product.

For example, according to Amazon's seller website[267], the percentage of referral fee on potting soil is as follows:

a. <= ₹300 – 9%
b. >₹300 and ≤₹15,000 – 10%
c. >₹15,00 – 5%

2. SHIPPING FEE

Shipping fees refer to the fees the aggregator charges to ship your product to the consumer. It is calculated based on item weight and distance. Shipping fees are computed on volumetric or actual weight, whichever is higher[268].

Different fee rates are applicable based on distance:

- Local rate will be applicable where the pickup and delivery happen in the same city, i.e. intra-city pickup and delivery.
- The regional zone consists of 4 regions. The regional rate will apply if the shipment moves within the same region and the service is not within the same city.

For example, look at the list of shipping regions according to Amazon:

- Region 1 – (Chandigarh, Delhi, Haryana, Himachal Pradesh, Jammu and Kashmir, Punjab, Rajasthan, Uttar Pradesh – Zone A and Uttarakhand).
- Region 2 – (Dadar and Nagar Haveli, Daman and Diu, Gujarat, Madhya Pradesh, Maharashtra)
- Region 3 – (Andaman and Nicobar, Andhra Pradesh, Goa, Karnataka, Kerala, Puducherry, Tamil Nadu, Telangana, Lakshadweep).
- Region 4 – (Arunachal Pradesh, Assam, Bihar, Chhattisgarh, Jharkhand, Manipur, Meghalaya, Mizoram, Nagaland, Odisha, Sikkim, Tripura, Uttar Pradesh-Zone B**, West Bengal).
- National rate will apply if the shipment moves across the region

Table 56: Shipping charges based on weight and distance

Standard Size	Local	Regional	National
Up to 500 g	₹44	₹53	₹74
Each additional 500g (up to 1kg)	₹13	₹17	25
Each additional kg after 1 kg	₹21	₹27	₹33
Each additional kg after 5 kg	₹12	₹13	₹16

CLOSING FEE

Closing Fee is charged every time your product is sold on the aggregator's website based on the price range of the product. This fee also varies based on the fulfillment channel you are using. Here is a breakdown of closing fees for easy ship sellers on Amazon:

Table 57: Closing fees based on item price (including Shipping Charges)

Item price	Closing fees
₹ 0 – 250	₹ 3
₹ 251 – 500	₹ 6
₹ 501 – 1000	₹ 30
₹ 1000+	₹ 56

So, for example, you chose the easy sell option of shipping. Now you have your product, 1 kg of potting soil that you are going to sell for ₹300 and ship to a consumer from Rajasthan to Delhi. So, the commission of Amazon on this product will be:

Referral Fee + Shipping Fee + Closing Fee

Referral fee – 9% of 300 = ₹27

Shipping fee – ₹53 (for 500 gm) + ₹17 (for an additional 500 gm) = ₹70

Closing fees – ₹6

Total fees= ₹97

This is the commission you will have to give to Amazon, also known as the middleman, on 1 kg of potting soil that is priced at ₹300.

Note: this is just an example to explain the commission fees and not a precise rate.

PACKAGING

For the ease of the consumer, the packaging of the potting soil is going to be separate sachets for each item, as shown in the following diagram:

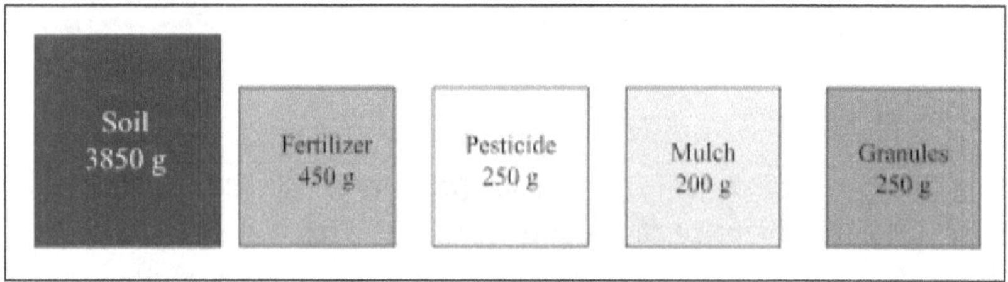

Figure 192: Diagrammatic representation of packaging of 5kg potting soil

Table 58: Individual weight of each ingredient according to the previously mentioned pot size (in the ratio 77:5:5:4:9 of soil: neem powder: granules: mulch: fertilizer)

Pot Size	Soil (g)	Neem Powder (g)	Granules (g)	Mulch (g)	Fertilizer (g)
4" pot	46	3	3	2	5
5-6" pot	92	6	6	5	11
7-8" pot	377	25	25	20	44
10" pot	1147	75	75	60	134
12" pot	1917	125	125	100	224
14" pot	2687	175	175	140	314
16" pot	3835	249	249	199	448
18" pot	5760	374	374	299	673

NOTE: The volume of each item differs based on the density. 500 g of neem bark will not take the same space as 500 g of fertilizer as the density of both items is different. Thus, we have taken the actual weight as the standard measure for measuring these ingredients instead of measuring them by volume.

This kind of packaging has many benefits, such as:

1. CONSUMER ENGAGEMENT

This type of packaging makes mixing potting soil into a little Do It Yourself or DIY project for the consumer. It engages them in the process of making potting soil by mixing each of the items given below. It deepens the consumer's connection with their soil and, as a result, their garden.

2. SEPARATE SACHETS

The separate sachets are made to cater to the demand of the consumer. They now have the option to:

a.   Mix the contents of the soil at once and have 5 kg of potting soil.
b.   Mix the contents in the ratio we provide to make small amounts of potting soil based on their needs.
c.   Use the ingredients separately. This means they can use the ingredients not as one mix but instead as individual items. So, fertilizer can be used for a different plant and mulch for a different one.

The separate sachets also mean that they can be sold individually. For example, the farmer can provide separate packets of each ingredient so that the consumer can order either the whole potting soil mix or individual ingredients like mulch according to their needs.

The farmer will need a packing machine to seal the plastic bags that contain the ingredients. Additionally, they should have stickers made with their label to put on these packets. The expiry date and ingredients of the mix should also be mentioned.

IS SELLING POTTING SOIL PROFITABLE?

A business is sustainable only when you have a considerable margin between the production cost and selling price while being available at affordable rates to the consumer. For example, if you are producing a pen for ₹40 but have to sell it for ₹20, you will be at a loss.

At the same time, if the production cost is ₹40 and the selling cost is ₹30 but you have to pay ₹10 for transportation, the profits are zero. At this rate, your business will not sustain.

The main aim of selling potting soil is not to earn profits as income. The aim is to use the money earned through selling potting soil to sustain your farm and animal husbandry business. So, do not make the mistake of focusing solely on profits by comparing product quality or employees' (your family's) salaries.

Also, the money earned has to be sufficient to pay for the operational expenses, which we assume will be around ₹50,000 ($596) per month in total.

1. OPTIMAL USE OF AVAILABLE RESOURCES

As mentioned previously in the chapter, in the traditional method of livestock rearing, manure is not optimally used. In most cases, the manure is collected and used to fertilize soil on the farmer's agricultural land. People who do not have their own land sell the manure, and a trolley of one ton can fetch ₹4000-5000 ($48-60). [269]

This method fails to utilize the produce in the most optimal way possible. Our approach asks the farmer to utilize manure for making potting soil, which is much more sustainable and profitable to them.

Understand it this way, earlier the farmer sold 1 ton of manure for a small amount. By following this method, from 1 ton of manure they can make many packets of potting soil. Following the previous ratio of ratio 77:5:5:4:9 of soil: neem powder: granules: mulch: fertilizer, for every 5 kg packet of potting soil, the farmer will need 0.45 kg or 450 g of manure. So, they can make approximately 2222 packets of potting soil with 1 ton (1000 kg) of manure.

2. REVENUE GENERATION

The average amount for a 5kg packet of organic potting soil is ₹250-500 ($3-6)[270]. If we take the average price of a 5 kg packet at ₹375 ($5), 200 bags will fetch a decent amount of ₹75,000 ($895).

The end amount may differ based on the price the farmer decides for the products, and the final profit can be calculated after deducting the fees for transportation and other resources used. Assuming that ₹25,000 ($298) is the operational expense in procuring the raw input plus the packaging and sales commission, the farmer still makes a profit of ₹50,000 ($596) per ton.

This is just an example to explain how manure, which is present in abundance and free of cost, can be processed to make a commodity that will fetch the farmer huge profits. The only cost they will have to bear is of packaging, shipping, transport, and marketing, as we will explain in the next chapter.

Additional note: The Indian government has published numerous schemes such as the Mudra loan, which can be used to set up this part of the business. As of 2024, the Mudra loan can be disbursed for 20 lacs. More details can be sought from the Government of India website[271].

Similarly, National Bank for Agriculture and Rural Development (NABARD) also has various schemes for buying livestock[272].

In this chapter, you learned:

Coming up...

Producer
Consumer
Product
What is Selling
Opex costs
Why are we selling
Disadvantage
Physical stores
Direct
Online platform
Modes of selling
Selling potting soil
Process of registration
Registering as a seller on aggregator sites
Business connections
Filling forms
Documents required
B 2 A
B 2 B
B 2 C
Self
Hire someone
PAN Card
Email account
Current bank account
GST
Shops and Commercial Establishment Act
Self ship
Easy ship
Fulfillment centers

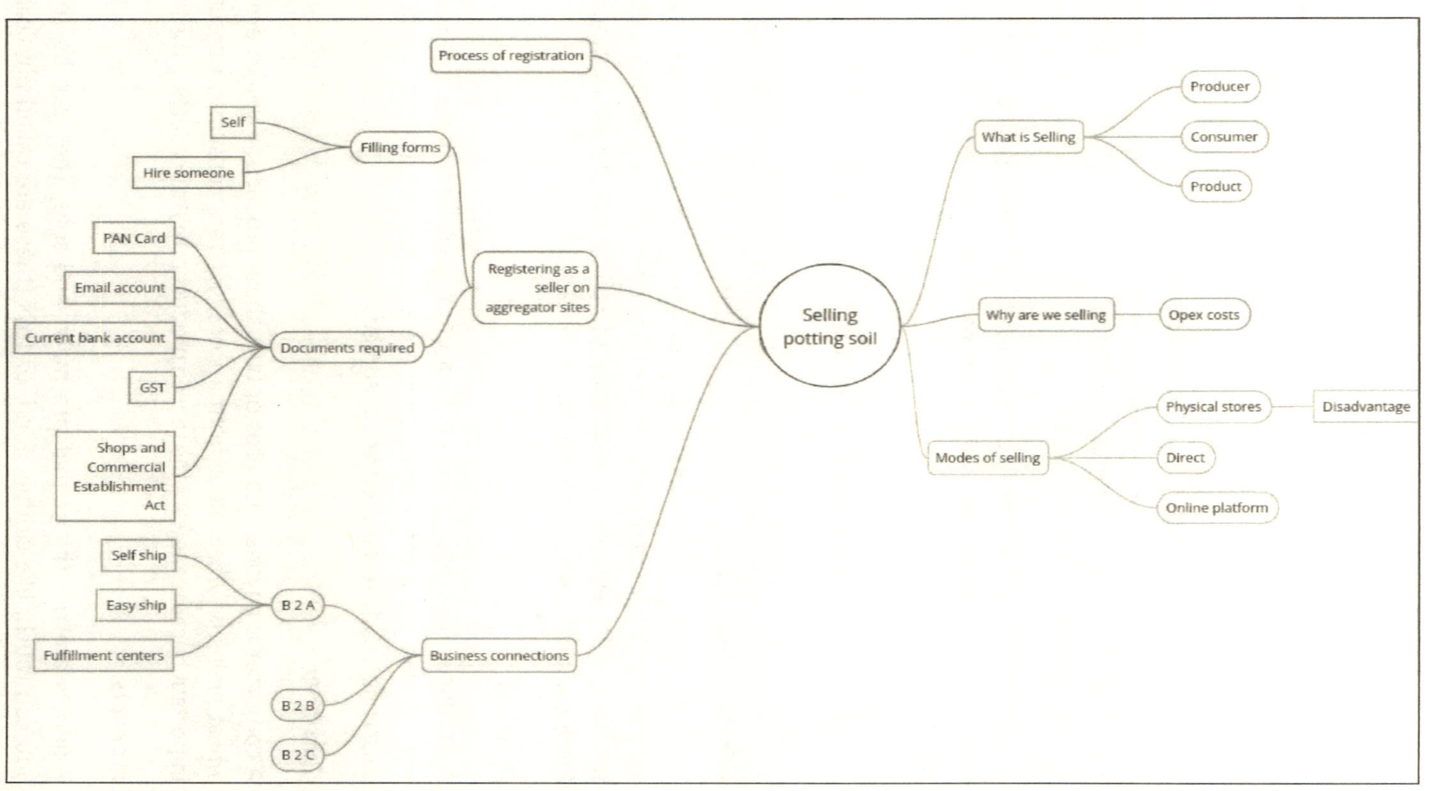

CHAPTER 12

Selling

IN THE PREVIOUS CHAPTER, we explored a passive source of income that can be used to fund the operational costs of running your farm – potting soil. We learned the process of producing potting soil, the ingredients required, and how to package it in order to sell.

In this chapter, we will be focusing on the 'selling' part. As we progress through the chapter, we will be answering 3 questions related to selling: what, why, and how.

1.   What is selling?
2.   Why are we selling?
3.   How are we swelling?

WHAT IS SELLING?

To 'sell' by definition means to give or hand over (something) in exchange for money[273]. In our context, we are selling 3 products – organic potting soil, fertilizer, and pesticide. The activity of selling has 3 major components – Producer, Consumer, and Product.

Producer

A producer is someone who makes or creates something. For example, a farmer who produces wheat. They are the ones who bring a product into existence, ready to be used or consumed.

Consumer

A consumer is anyone who uses or buys these products. If you've ever bought wheat grains or wheat flour from a store, you're a consumer. Consumers are important because they are the reason producers make products in the first place.

Products

Products are the things that are made and sold. They can be something you can touch, like clothes, food, or toys (these are called physical goods).

Products can also be services, which are things you pay for but can't touch, like a haircut, a movie streaming subscription, or a ride in a taxi.

MODES OF SELLING

1. Direct Selling: This happens when producers sell directly to you without a store in between. This could be through a salesperson visiting your home or even online through the producer's own website.
2. Physical Stores: This is the traditional way. You walk into a store, pick what you want, pay for it, and take it home. Examples include grocery stores, clothing stores, and bakeries.
3. Online Stores: Here, you use the internet to buy products. You go to a website, choose what you want, pay online, and then the product is shipped to your house. Amazon and eBay are examples of online stores.

Now that the concept of selling is clear, let's move on to the purpose of selling.

WHY ARE WE SELLING?

The first question to ask before we start selling is the purpose – why are we selling potting soil? Selling potting soil is not your principal source of income but instead a passive source. What is the difference between a principal source and a passive source of income?

The word 'principal' by definition means the most important or main. In this context, the principal source of income means the main source of income. Meanwhile, a passive source of income can be defined as an additional source of income apart from the main income. It helps to earn a little extra cash in addition to the cash from your primary source of income.

When we say that the business of selling potting soil, fertilizer and mulch is a passive source of income, we mean that it's not the primary business that you should be focusing on. The primary source is animal products from the animals (goats and sheep) that you are going to raise on the farm.

As we explained in the previous chapter, there are 2 kinds of expenditures in a business: capital expenditure and operational expenditure. In the case of the land project that we talked about in Chapter 3, the capital expenditure will include all the long-term investments like solar panels, hydroponics machines, building the shed, etc.

Meanwhile, the operational expenditure will include day-to-day costs like buying seeds to grow fodder – both hydroponically (in area 3) and on land (in area 2), maintenance fees of the hydroponic and shed structure, vaccination of the livestock, transporting the livestock to and from the market, etc.

The money earned through the passive source of income, that is, selling potting soil, will be used to facilitate the operational costs on your farm. It will be used to aid daily operations on the farm until your primary source of income (earned through selling animal products) rolls in.

On your farm, certain elements require time to reach maturity, such as the fodder crops (cultivated in area 2), which require 3-4 months to fully mature, or livestock, which may take at least a year to reach maturity. The passive income received through the potting soil business will facilitate the functioning of your farm during this time.

That being stated, it's crucial to recognize that because this is a passive income source, it cannot demand the same level of attention or investment as the primary source. You need not dedicate excessive time to managing this venture. Your main focus should be raising the livestock and providing the best stress-free environment for them to flourish. You don't have to invest much in making the potting soil business grow; instead, focus on ways to optimize your animal husbandry practices as that is your main source of income.

BUSINESS IN MODERN TIMES

There are different kinds of options when selling a product. The old model of selling, which was prevalent before the advent of the internet, was physical stores. Before the internet changed how we shop, most people bought things from actual stores you could walk into, like grocery stores.

It was not only common but an absolute necessity to have a physical location to sell any product. This was because online shopping platforms like Amazon and Flipkart, or even individual shopping sites, were not widely practiced yet. So, one needed a physical location like a grocery store to sell products.

Shopping meant going out to those stores, seeing the products in real life, and deciding what to buy. It was a very different way of shopping compared to clicking and buying things online today.

Figure 193: Depiction of physical stores in older times

In today's time, with the expansion of the internet and technology and the wide availability of smartphones, selling and buying has turned into an online activity. Although online shopping apps like Amazon and eBay were founded way back in the 1990s, consumers had limited access to technology. Through the 2010s and into the 2020s, more and more people gained access to the internet.

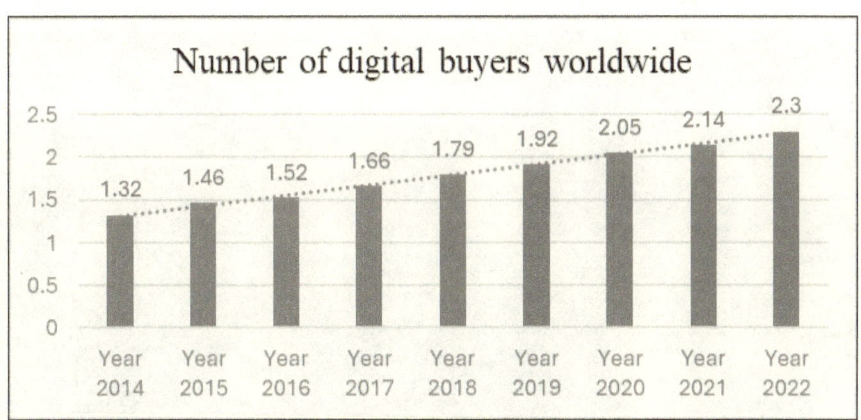

Figure 194: Graph depicting the increasing number of digital buyers from 2014-2022[274]

According to the International Telecommunication Union (ITU), approximately 5.4 billion people – or 67 per cent of the world's population – were using the Internet in 2023.[275]As internet access expanded, more customers could shop from online platforms, thus boosting their popularity and sales.

As of 2024, globally, the number of digital buyers stands at a whopping 2.71 billion[276]. That means that approximately 33.88% of the world's population is shopping online.

Figure 195: Depiction of the ease of online shopping where even groceries are delivered to your doorstep

Presently, anything and everything is available at the tip of your fingertips and delivered within days, regardless of your location.

Figure 196: Contrast between the growing use of shopping sites and reduction Number of customers at physical stores

Products manufactured in different parts of a country or even the world are easily accessible at the click of a button.

So, in today's world, where technology has become an integral part of our lives and affects every part of it, it would be foolish not to take advantage of it to grow your business.

THE DISADVANTAGE OF ESTABLISHING PHYSICAL STORES

In today's digital age, establishing a physical store can seem like a step backward, especially with the surge in online shopping. There are many reasons why it is not the best option to sell your product.

1. As we stated earlier, selling potting soil is a source of passive income. Investing in setting up a physical store to sell it will divert you from your main aim, that is, animal husbandry.

   The very meaning of a passive source of income is that it is an additional source apart from the main source. Since it's a secondary source, we cannot treat it like the primary in terms of investing capital, time or effort.

2. The cost of running the shop itself, including the rent, electricity bills, maintenance costs, etc., is an added cost on the producer. A physical store also requires someone to be there for at least 9-10 hours a day. Since our primary business is animal husbandry, your focus should be on taking care of the livestock, not spending an excessive amount of time on your secondary source of income. It is both capital – and time-intensive.

3. Operating a store that sells only one product is like putting all your eggs in one basket—a risky strategy that often leads to financial losses. The key to profit when running a shop is variety.

For example, a shop cannot just sell rice and expect profit. However, if the rice is not the only option but one among many options, the shop would work. This is why grocery stores have everything that can be included in 'grocery', ranging from food products like bread, milk, eggs to personal care products like shampoo, soap, etc.

The variety is what earns them their profits. Since we do not have either the variety or the time and capital to invest, this would result in only losses.

4. The product in question, that is, potting soil, does not have a brand value or name that is going to be on display. For example, tractors have a brand name and value; they run on the roads and are continuously on display.

Figure 197: Depiction of a tractor showroom of the Mahindra brand. Branding is important when your products are constantly on display and built for long-term use

The point we are trying to make with these examples is that if your product is going to be consumed immediately and not repeatedly used like clothes, it is unnecessary to set up a physical store to sell it.

Once out of the packet, the product no longer has any brand value. One cannot differentiate the soil based on its brand. In this case, the motto of the producer should be:

"Beyond the Brand: Quality that Speaks Volumes."

Figure 198: Once the soil is out of the packet, the branding is no longer important as it is a product that is consumed immediately and not constantly

5. In contrast to physical stores, online shops can quickly accumulate and display customer reviews, providing social proof that enhances brand value and trust without the need for a physical display.

The real value lies not in the recognizable name or logo, but in the product's ability to meet and exceed expectations in its application. The durability and efficacy of the product become the primary concerns once it serves its purpose, rendering the brand name a secondary consideration at best.

Because of this, having a physical store, which costs a lot to run, doesn't make much sense for this kind of product. It doesn't ensure that customers will be happy just because the product comes from a well-known brand. Instead, selling online is a better and cheaper way to tell customers about how good the product is, helping them see its real value."

THE STORY OF MAYA

In the quiet hours of dawn, in a small and peaceful town, Maya lived with a big dream. She had a garden, small but filled with all kinds of plants, and she wanted the whole world to know about it, not just her neighbors. Maya decided to use the internet to share her love for gardening, stepping into a world as vast and unknown as a dense forest.

When Maya decided to share her garden online, she ran into quite a few challenges. First off, figuring out all the new technology was really tough for her. The internet felt huge and complicated, like trying to find your way through a maze without a map. Then, there was the problem of setting herself up as a seller on different websites.

Each website had its own rules and steps to follow, and Maya wasn't sure which one was the best place for her plants. It was like trying to pick the perfect spot in her garden for a new plant, but without knowing where it would grow best. These first steps into selling online were really confusing and hard, like walking through a thick forest without a path.

But Maya wanted to share the beauty of her garden with others, so she kept going, even when it got tough. She started posting pictures and stories of her beloved plants, reaching out to others who shared her passion for gardening. Bit by bit, people began to notice. They were drawn to the beauty of Maya's garden and her adventures among the plants.

Maya faced challenges, like figuring out how to send her plants far away without harm, and learning how to make her garden stand out online. But she never gave up. With every problem she solved, her garden's fame grew.

Maya's story teaches us that with courage and hard work, even the smallest dream can bloom into something amazing. It's a reminder not to give up, no matter how daunting the world might seem. Maya's garden became more than a place to grow plants—it became a place where dreams could grow, too.

As we learn from Maya, facing challenges is part of the journey. The online world is always changing, but staying flexible and eager to learn can help us overcome any obstacle. Most importantly, Maya showed us that being true to ourselves is what connects us to others. Her genuine love for her garden and her commitment to sharing it authentically made her stand out. As we build our own dreams online, remembering to stay true to what we love is what will make us shine.

Joining Maya on this journey, we see that our passions can thrive in the digital world, just like plants in a garden, with a bit of patience and a lot of care. Let's nurture our dreams with the same love and persistence that Maya showed and watch as they grow into their full potential.

TYPES OF BUSINESS CONNECTIONS

Now that we have explained how selling and buying works in the world of the internet, we will now proceed to explaining the 3 types of business connections.

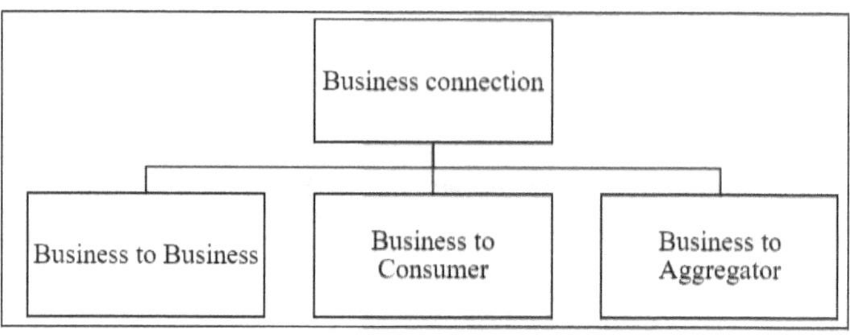

Figure 199: Types of business connections

1. B2B or BUSINESS TO BUSINESS

In this method, the producer can contact a local business to sell their product. For our product, the potting soil, the producer can contact their local nursery to sell the product.

This method is hassle-free. Since it is supplied to a business, the soil can be packaged in sacks weighing 5 kg. The sacks only need to have the business logo, contact number or email, MRP, manufacturing date, and the expiry date so the nursery person in charge would know which one to use first.

Because this soil will be without any chemical material and 100% organic, it will start developing bacteria in undesirable amounts in a month's time and should be used before that.

Figure 200: Depiction of a business-to-business connection. One business (the producer) selling products (potting soil) to another business (a nursery or an aggrotech shop)

The producer can ask the nursery staff to keep a few bags of potting soil with the brand logo out in the front for people to see and directly buy from the nursery itself. An agreement can be made with the nursery manager so that if someone is interested in buying a certain weight, for example, 10 kg, they can reach out to the producer through the nursery. The producer can provide the product, and the consumer can pick it up from the nursery.

2. B2C or BUSINESS TO CONSUMERS (DIRECT)

We are going to suggest 2 ways of doing this:

1. The first is through direct advertising, where the producers can reach out to local consumers through hawkers. The hawker can be asked

to take the products into the city on his vehicle for a fixed daily wage and advertise it through a loudspeaker and sell it.

Figure 201: A hawker selling potting soil and advertising it via a megaphone

2. Another way is to create one's own website or app. The major challenge here is how to advertise it so that whenever someone searches for the product online, your product is recommended and is on top of the list. Therefore, you will have to bear the cost of advertising it.

Figure 202: A person making an online website to sell their products

Figure 203: Making an app to sell your products

3. B2A or BUSINESS TO AGGREGATOR

An aggregator, in the most general sense, is a system or tool that collects and compiles data, information, or content from multiple sources into a single, consolidated format, making it easier to access, manage, and analyze.

In the context of online shopping, an aggregator can be defined as 'an internet company that collects information about other companies' products and services and puts it on a single website'[277]. Here, the aggregator is online platforms like Amazon, Flipkart, IndiaMart, etc.

The aggregator in this case provides logistical support, i.e. they tell you how to list your product, how to ship it, etc., and in return, they charge you a fee (for a detailed breakdown of fees charged by aggregators, see Chapter 11).

In the previous chapter, we explored the three options provided by online selling sites (that act as aggregators) to sellers – self-ship, easy ship, and fulfillment.

1. In self-ship, the seller is responsible for everything from producing to packaging to storing and shipping the product to consumers. The site will only showcase your products to the consumers.

Figure 204: The producer packaging packets of potting soil

Figure 205: In self-shipping, the producer is responsible for shipping the product to customers. They can either do it on their own or hire a courier service, as shown in the image.

2. In easy shipping, the site provides the service of shipping. You can produce and pack your product and the aggregator will pick the products from your location and ship them to consumers.

Figure 206: Depiction of easy shipping. The aggregator picks up your products from the given address and ships them to customers.

Figure 207: Depiction of fulfillment centers. The 3 sections show the different processes of packaging, storing, and shipping the products

3. The last option involves fulfillment centers. A fulfillment center acts as a central hub for all logistical operations required to transport a product from the seller to the customer.
It oversees the entire process of the order fulfillment journey, which includes tasks like picking up shipments, processing orders, as well as packaging and delivering items to the consumer.

Some aggregator apps provide the option of fulfillment where they pick products, store, pack, and ship them to the consumers.

You just have to do the primary packaging, and the aggregator will pick up the products to store them in the fulfillment center to be sold according to consumer demand.

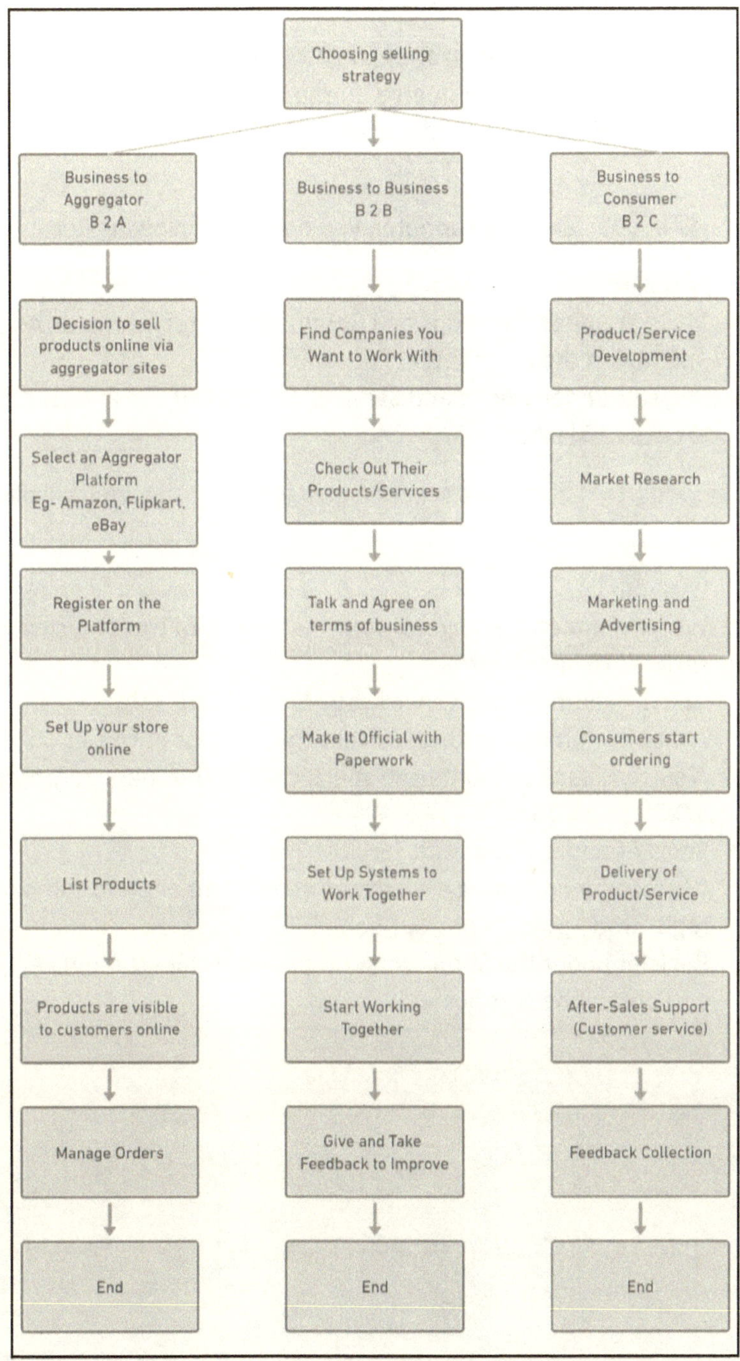

Choosing selling strategy
Business to Aggregator B 2 A
Business to Business B 2 B
Business to Consumer B 2 C
Decision to sell products online via aggregator sites
Find Companies You Want to Work With
Product/Service Development
Select an Aggregator Platform Eg- Amazon, Flipkart, eBay
Check Out Their Products/Services
Market Research
Register on the Platform
Talk and Agree on terms of business
Marketing and Advertising
Set Up your store online
Make It Official with Paperwork
Consumers start ordering
List Products
Set Up Systems to Work Together
Delivery of Product/Service
Products are visible to customers online
Start Working Together
After-Sales Support (Customer service)
Manage Orders
Give and Take Feedback to Improve
Feedback Collection
End
End
End

HOW TO REGISTER AS A SELLER ON AGGREGATOR SITES

To register yourself as a seller on an **aggregator** site, you must first understand your role in the world of e-commerce. In the field of e-commerce, you are a proprietor. A proprietor can be defined as the owner of a business, or a holder of property[278].

To register yourself as a proprietor, you need the following documents:

1. PAN card
2. Register under the Shops and Commercial Establishments Act, 1958 and obtain the certificate
3. Register under Goods and Services Tax (GST) if the annual turnover exceeds 20 lakhs

Afterwards, to register as a seller on an **aggregator** site, you will need the following:

1. PAN number
   We recommend going to your nearest E-Mitra or using online services to fill the form.
2. An email account used specifically for business purposes
3. A mobile number used specifically for business purposes
4. A current bank account used specifically for business purposes (Not a Savings account)
5. Register under Goods and Services Tax (GST)
   We recommend hiring a chartered accountant or CA to complete the registration process on your behalf.
6. Register under the Shops and Commercial Establishments Act, 1958 and obtain the certificate

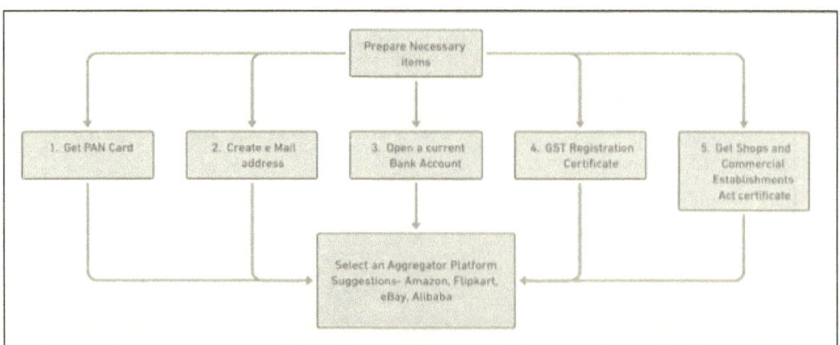

Figure 208: Flowchart of necessary documents to start selling online

We recommend hiring a company secretary or CS to complete the registration process on your behalf[279]. To fill the forms mentioned henceforth (for example – GST/PAN) you will have 2 options:

1. The first option is to go to the verified online site provided by the government of the respective document and fill it yourself. If you are not a tech savvy person and are not familiar with the process of filling forms online, this option can prove to be a difficult ordeal for you.

Figure 209: A person filling out an online form on their own

2. The second option is to go to the nearest E-Mitra and ask the person who runs it to fill the particular form for you. The said person will charge you a fee for filling the form on your behalf.
We recommend this method as it is hassle-free and quick. You will not have to involve yourself in the process at all. All you have to do is provide the documents required to fill the form, and the E-Mitra person will take care of the rest for you.

Figure 210: A person going to an E-Mitra to fill a form

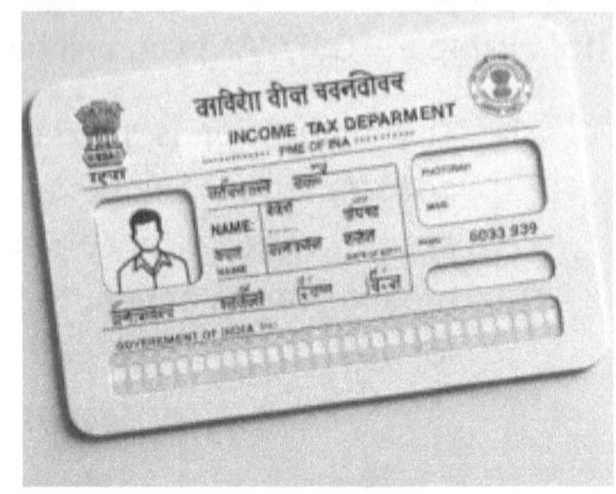

Figure 211: Reference image of a PAN card. This image does not depict the real document.

PAN CARD

To apply for a PAN card, you will need any one of the following documents-

1. Aadhaar Card issued by the Unique Identification Authority of India
2. Elector's photo identity card
3. Driving license
4. Passport

You can visit your nearest E-Mitra to apply for a PAN card.

EMAIL ACCOUNT

Follow these steps to create an email account for your business-

1. Download the mail app from Google Playstore (for android devices) on your electronic device (phone/laptop/computer).
2. Open the app and choose to create a new account.

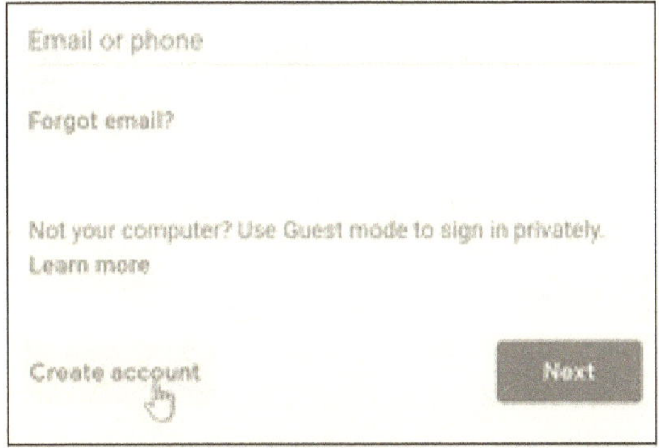

Figure 212: Step 1

3. **Write your company's name**

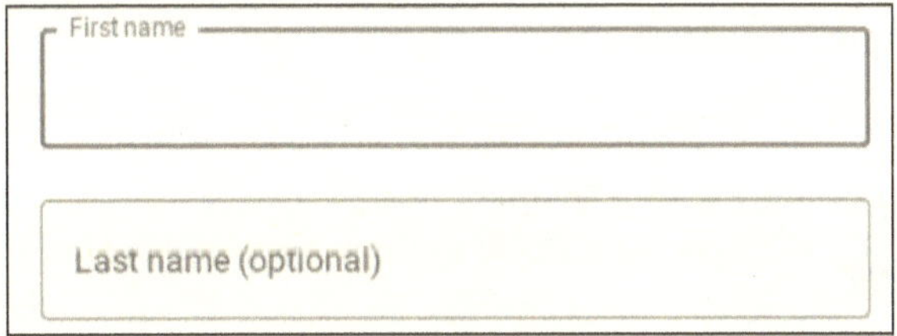

Figure 213: Step 2

4. **Fill in the basic information**

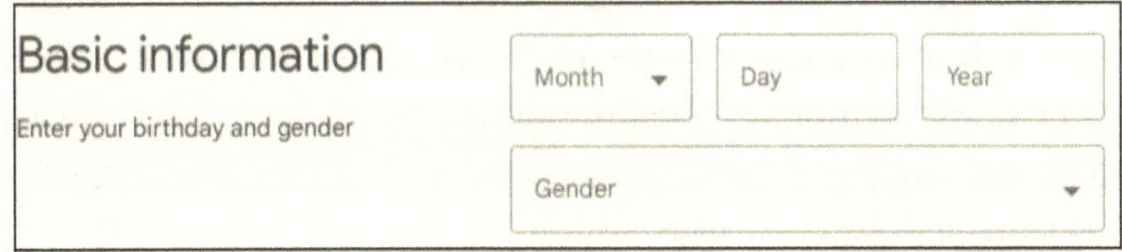

Figure 214: Step 3

5. **Create a username**

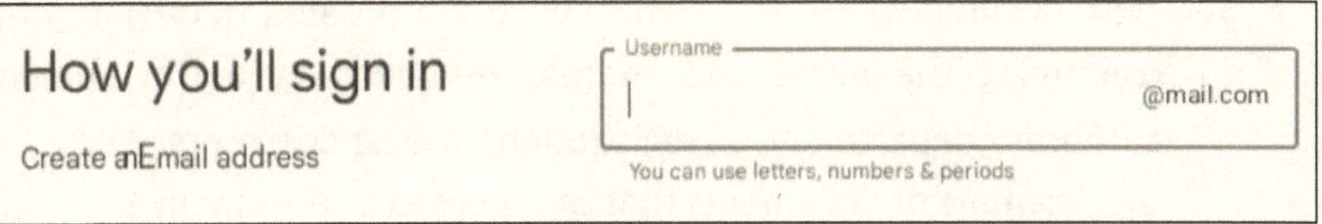

Figure 215: Step 4

Since this will be the mail printed on your products and used by customers to reach out to you, we recommend using a very short and simple email. For example, if your company's name is Organic Farm, your email could be farm. reach@gmail.com.

6. **Create a strong password for your mail**

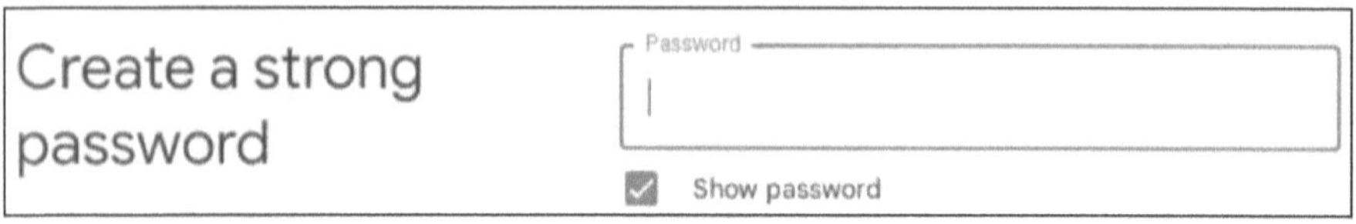

Figure 216: Step 5

A strong password is at least 10 letters long and consists of an uppercase letter, a lowercase letter, numbers, and symbols. For example, Organic@101.

After these steps are completed, you will have a Gmail account that you can use when registering as a seller.

BANK ACCOUNT

It is highly recommended to open a separate bank account for the purpose of transactions related to business. This account should be opened under your company's name. Keeping business accounts separate from personal accounts will ensure that business transactions remain separated from your personal transactions. It helps in having organized transactions. Since you are a business owner, it is recommended to open a 'Current account'. A current account is tailored for business owners and entrepreneurs conducting numerous transactions regularly.

In order to become a current account holder as a sole proprietor, the following documents must be submitted to the bank of your choice.[280]

1. Two documents in the name of the sole proprietorship firm confirming the name and address — issued by a Government authority/ department, as registration/ license document[281]
   a. Example of documents that can be used as document 1:
      - Valid Shops & Establishment Certificate/Trade License. Validity can be extended up to the grace period for renewal as mentioned in such a certificate.

   b.   Example of documents that can be used as document 2:
- Any one document from the following: the latest copy of the Electricity Bill, not more than 3 months old.
- Latest copy of Telephone Bill from the Telecom operator, not more than 3 months old
- True copy of the gas connection book in the name of the entity along with the latest gas receipt not more than 3 months old
- Gas bill in the case of a pipe connection
- Water Tax bill paid to Municipal Body/Corporations, not more than 6 months old, along with the Tax receipt, should stand in the name of the firm.
- Property Tax bill should not be more than one year old from the bill issuance date along with tax receipts for property tax paid to the Municipal Body/Corporations. The tax receipt should be in the name of the firm.

3. Permanent Account Number (PAN Card)
4. Latest passport-size color photograph of the sole proprietor.
5. Identity and address proof of the sole proprietor.
   - List of accepted documents – Aadhaar letter card issued by Unique Identification Authority of India (UIDAI), voter ID card, etc[282].
6. In case a Power of Attorney (POA) has been granted for account operations, the photograph, identity, and address proof of the POA holder should also be submitted.
   - List of accepted documents – Aadhaar letter card issued by Unique Identification Authority of India (UIDAI), voter ID card, etc[283].
7. Account opening cheque from an existing current account

GST NUMBER

Below are the list of documents you will need to register as a normal taxpayer.

   Constitution of Business – Proprietorship
   Nature of possession of premises – Own

Figure 217: Reference image of GST certificate.

Table 59: Documents required to register a GST number

Purpose	Acceptable Documents
Photo of Stakeholder (Promoter/Partner)	Photo of the Promoter/Partner
Photo of the Authorized Signatory	Photo
Proof of Appointment of Authorized Signatory (Any One)	Letter of Authorization
	Copy of Resolution passed by Board of Directors / Managing Committee and Acceptance letter
Proof of Principal Place of Business (Any One)	Electricity Bill
	Legal ownership document
	Municipal Khata Copy
	Property Tax Receipt

We recommend hiring a professional CA (Chartered Accountant) to carry out the registration process.

CERTIFICATE ISSUED UNDER THE SHOPS AND COMMERCIAL ESTABLISHMENTS ACT

To legally establish yourself as a proprietor, you will need to register under the Shops and Commercial Establishment Act and receive a certificate.

Every state in India has an individual site to register under this act, which comes under the Labor Department of that state.

Following below is a list of items that you will need when filling out the form online[284]:

1. Passport-size Photograph of Employer
2. Photo of shop along with the owner
3. List of Management Employees (MS Excel format)
4. Rates of Wages (MS Excel format)
5. Details of Employees working in the Establishment (MS Excel format)
6. Employee Weekly Holidays (MS Excel format)
7. Address proof of Establishment [Copy of shop's rent agreement (if on rent) or Shop's ownership document proof (if owner of the shop)
8. Affidavit (Declaration Form)
9. Photo ID (PAN Card/Driving Licence/Aadhaar Card/Passport)

The Excel format mentioned above is the format in Microsoft Excel in which you should provide all information regarding your establishment.

Following is an example of an XLS document of the number, name, age, gender, and date of joining information of employees:

	A	B	C	D	E	F	G
1		0 First Name	Last Name	Gender	Age	JoiningDate	
2		1 Dulce	Abril	Female	32	15/10/2017	
3		2 Mara	Hashimoto	Female	25	16/08/2016	
4		3 Philip	Gent	Male	36	21/05/2015	
5		4 Kathleen	Hanner	Female	25	15/10/2017	
6		5 Nereida	Magwood	Female	58	16/08/2016	
7		6 Gaston	Brumm	Male	24	21/05/2015	
8		7 Etta	Hurn	Female	56	15/10/2017	
9		8 Earlean	Melgar	Female	27	16/08/2016	
10		9 Vincenza	Weiland	Female	40	21/05/2015	
11							

Figure 218: Example of XLS format

Figure 219: Reference image of a certificate issued under the Shops and Commercial Establishment Act. This image does not depict the real document.

Here is a breakdown of the registration fee based on the number of employees you have:

Table 60: Fee for registration under the Shops and Commercial Establishment Act based on the number of employees

FEE FOR REGISTRATION			
S.No.	Number of Employees	Validity	Registration Fees (in Rs.)
1	0-10 Employee	Lifetime	₹5000/-
2	11-50 Employee	Lifetime	₹20000/-
3	51-100 Employee	Lifetime	₹50000/-
4	101 & Above Employees	Lifetime	₹150000/-

PROCESS OF REGISTRATION

1. To register as a seller on any aggregator site, create an account with the email you have just created and your phone number. Set a strong password for your account. A strong password is at least 10 letters long and consists of an uppercase letter, a lowercase letter, numbers, and symbols. For example, Organic@101.

Figure 220: Registering with your mail

2. Next, enter your GST number, which comes under your tax details. Once you enter your GST number, the site will verify it by sending an OTP to the registered mobile number under the GST number.

Figure 221: Entering GST details

3. After the verification is done, choose a store name. This name will represent your business on the site and will be visible to customers.

Figure 222: Choosing a store name

4. Next, submit the pickup address. This is the address from which the aggregator will pick up products. Thus, fill in the address of wherever you are storing your products and from where you want the aggregator to pick up your product.

Figure 223: Choosing a pickup address

Figure 224: Choosing a method of shipping

5. Next, choose a shipping method. As we explained earlier, most sites offer 3 options for shipping-

   a. Self-ship
   b. Easy ship
   c. Fulfilment centre

We recommend choosing the option of fulfillment as it is hassle-free.

The process of fulfillment provided by aggregator sites can be summarized as:

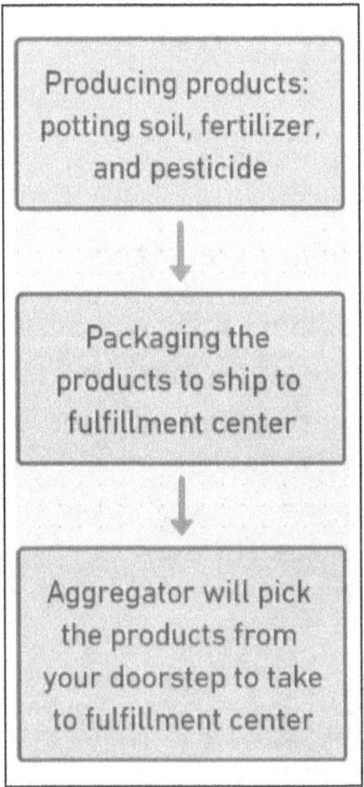

Figure 225: Process of Fulfillment

The production process is explained in detail in Chapter 11. Let us focus on the primary packaging. Following below is a list of items to be included on the shipping invoice of your product when sending it to the fulfillment center:

1. Specialized barcode for each individual product
2. Specialized number for each individual product
3. Company logo
4. Product MRP
5. Product manufacturing date
6. Product expiry date (month/year)

When you ship a product to fulfillment centers, the aggregator creates a label with these details that you can then print and stick. It is recommended to print these details on adhesive sticker labels for easy application.

Once you choose the option of fulfillment, you will have to add a warehouse of the aggregator (where your products will be stored) as an additional place of business with the tax authorities. In order to do this, you will need to fill an APoB (Additional Place of Business) form.

You can either hire a third party to carry out the process for you, do it yourself, or ask the aggregator to do so. To fill the APoB form, you will need the following documents:

  a. GST login and password
  b. No Objection certificates
  c. Business Solutions Agreement

6. After filling out the fulfilment form, add your bank account (current account) which will be used for business transactions. You will receive money from the aggregator in this account.

Figure 226: Entering bank account details

7. Select the GST rate or Product Tax Code (PTC) that will apply to your product based on the percentage of GST on different categories issued by the government. For example, for potting soil, the GST rate is 5%.

Figure 227: Choosing GST rate or Product Tax Code (PTC)

8. The last step is to list your products. Here, you will have to enter the description of each individual product along with its characteristics like MRP, weight, pictures, etc.

Figure 228: Listing your products

9. Once you have created a listing, you can launch your product. Your product is now available on aggregator sites and can be purchased online.

Figure 229: Launching your products

CONCLUSION

This chapter concludes with essential insights into the transformative journey from traditional stores to the expansive digital marketplace of e-commerce, highlighting the power of the internet to revolutionize business practices.

The narrative underscores that determination, adaptability, and authenticity are key to transitioning a passion into a flourishing online venture. It teaches us the significance of embracing digital platforms, learning from obstacles, and forging genuine connections with customers.

The transition from physical stores to online selling isn't merely a trend but a strategic adaptation to meet modern consumers' expectations for convenience, variety, and swift service. We've explored the practical steps for establishing an online presence, emphasizing the advantages of reaching wider audiences without the geographical limitations and significant expenses tied to physical stores.

Moreover, the discussion on different types of business connections, from business-to-business (B2B) collaborations to direct consumer interactions and utilizing aggregator platforms, offers a clear roadmap for budding e-commerce entrepreneurs.

Detailed guidance on how to register as a seller on online marketplaces demystifies the process, encouraging individuals with limited online experience to venture into e-commerce. As the digital environment continues to evolve, the importance of staying informed, flexible, and true to one's values cannot be overstated.

The story here, although hypothetical, illustrates the limitless opportunities the internet provides for transforming a simple idea into a global business.

In wrapping up, this chapter isn't merely informational; it's a motivational push for aspiring business owners. It serves as a reminder that in today's digital age, the resources for success are more accessible than ever. With the appropriate strategy, a small idea can bloom into a vast enterprise, reaching customers worldwide and making visions a tangible reality.

In this chapter, you learned:

Conclusion

I can assure the reader of this book that should you follow the steps and information shared in this book, it is a blueprint to a successful and respectful livelihood. You must have heard from your grandparents and forefathers about how rich they were or perhaps how full of struggles their life was. Either way, if you follow the book and don't experiment the first time, I can guarantee success!

Just remember, patience and practice give good experience, and using experience positively will bear positive fruits.

Happy Farming... and those who wish to learn more, you're welcome to write to me at sangam@dauraiwala.com.

Yes! One acre is enough.

Yours Sincerely,
Sangam
MBA, B.E (Hons.) Computer Science

Endnotes

1. Since we have not had a census in 2021, we are forced to quote as per the census of 2011. To make up for the missing data, we are stating data from renowned and recognized institutions.
2. Source: Annual Report 2022-23, Department of Agriculture and Farmers' Welfare Link to PDF: https://agriwelfare.gov.in/Documents/annual_report_english_2022_23.pdf
3. Source: Press Information Bureau
   Link-https://pib.gov.in/PressReleaseDetailm.aspx?PRID=1590395#:~:text=The%20per%20capita%20availability%20of,of%20lands%20in%20the%20Country.
4. The unit of bigha is not standard and varies from state to state. Here we have taken the acre to bigha conversion as prevalent in the state of Rajasthan, where 1 acre is approximately equal to 1.613 bigha.
5. As per the survey conducted by the National Sample Survey Office (NSO), Ministry of Statistics and Programme Implementation (MoSPI) in 2019. Source: The Press Information Bureau (as of 09/02/2024). Link: https://pib.gov.in/PressReleaseIframePage.aspx?PRID=1910357
6. Source: World Bank Open Data
   Link-https://data.worldbank.org/indicator/SP.RUR.TOTL.ZS?locations=IN&most_recent_value_desc=false
7. Source: Agricultural Statistics at a Glance 2022
   Link – https://www.desagri.gov.in/wp-content/uploads/2023/05/Agricultural-Statistics-at-a-Glance-2022.pdf
8. Source: Press Information Bureau, Government of India, Ministry of Agriculture & Farmers' Welfare (as of 09/02/2024). Link: https://pib.gov.in/newsite/PrintRelease.aspx?relid=199780#
9. The current estimated population of Rajasthan is approximately 8.36 Crores. Source – Population Census Link-https://www.census2011.co.in/census/state/rajasthan.html#:~:text=no%20correct%20answer.-,The%20last%20census%20of%20Rajasthan%20was%20done%20in%202011%20and,population%20is%20approximately%208.36%20Crores.
10. Source – United Nations Population Fund (UNFPA) (as of 09/02/2024) Link – https://www.unfpa.org/data/world-population/IN
11. Source: United Nations Population Fund (UNFPA) (as of 09/02/2024) Link: https://www.unfpa.org/data/world-population/IN

12 Source: Rural Development Department, Government of Haryana
    Link – https://haryanarural.gov.in/mahatma-gandhi-national-rural-employment-
    guarantee-scheme-mgnregs/#:~:text=The%20Government%20of%20India%20
    passed,to%20do%20unskilled%20manual%20work

13 Source – Press Information Bureau
    Link – https://pib.gov.in/PressReleasePage.aspx?PRID=1887438

14 The MGNREGA Job Card (JC) is a document that is issued to an applicant once he
    or she is registered with the local Gram Panchayat under the MGNREGA scheme.
    Source: Ministry of Rural Development
    Link – https://nregastrep.nic.in/netnrega/homestciti.aspx?state_code=27&state_
    name=RAJASTHAN

15 Source – Demand for Grants 2023-24 Analysis: Agriculture and Farmers Welfare,
    PRS (as of 09/02/2024) Link –
    https://prsindia.org/budgets/parliament/demand-for-grants-2023-24-analysis-
    agriculture-and-farmers-welfare#:~:text=The%20share%20of%20landless%20
    agricultural,1951%20to%2055%25%20in%202011.&text=The%20Standing%20
    Committee%20on%20Agriculture,not%20receive%20income%20support%20
    benefits.

16 Source – Tokyo Metropolitan Government Census 2020 (as of 09/02/2024)
    Link – https://www.metro.tokyo.lg.jp/english/about/history/history03.html#:~:
    text=Population%20Summary&text=The%20ward%20area%20is%20
    home,as%20of%20October%201%2C%202020.

17 Source – NYC Department of City Planning Census 2020 (as of 09/02/2024)
    Link – https://www.nyc.gov/site/planning/planning-level/nyc-population/nyc-
    population.page

18 Source – National Population and Talent Division (NPTD) 2023 (as of 09/02/2024)
    Link – https://www.singstat.gov.sg/modules/infographics/population

19 Source – US Census Bureau, Census 2020 (as of 09/02/2024) Link to PDF –
    https://www.bostonplans.org/getattachment/c55502f3-3a70-4772-a894-
    0c51c325b216#:~:text=Boston's%20population%20reached%20675,647%20

20 Source: Food and Agriculture Organization of the United Nations (as of
    09/02/2024) Link: https://www.fao.org/3/cb6033en/cb6033en.pdf

21 Source: Food and Agriculture Organization of the United Nations (as of 09/02/2024)
    Link: https://www.fao.org/sustainability/news/detail/en/c/1274219/

22 Source: Food and Agriculture Organization of the United Nations (as of
    09/02/2024) Link: https://www.fao.org/sustainability/success-stories/detail/
    en/c/1295695/

23 Source: Aquaman, from DC Comics ...

24 pH scale ranges from 1 to 14, where 1 is highly acidic, 7 is neutral, and 14 is highly
    alkaline.

25   Source – All for a good harvest: Addressing micronutrient deficiencies, September 2019, PwC India (as of 10/02/2024). Link to PDF – https://www.pwc.in/assets/pdfs/research-insights/2019/all-for-a-good-harvest.pdf

26   Source – tractor junction (as of 10/02/2024) Link – https://www.tractorjunction.com/blog/wheat-farming-in-india/

27   Source: Farmers' portal, link – https://farmer.gov.in/mspstatements.aspx

28   Source-tractor junction (as of 10/02/2024) Link – https://www.tractorjunction.com/blog/wheat-farming-in-india/

29   Source – Press Information Bureau (as of 10/02/2024) Link – https://pib.gov.in/PressReleaseIframePage.aspx?PRID=1896134

30   Source – Press Information Bureau (PRS)

31   Source – Food and Agriculture Organization of the United Nations (as of 10/02/2024) Link – https://www.fao.org/3/cb6033en/cb6033en.pdf Note: the percentage change for the Russian Federation and Ukraine has been measured since 1992.

32   Sources: Food and Agriculture Organization of the United Nations; PRS Link – https://prsindia.org/policy/analytical-reports/state-agriculture-india

33   Link to PDF – https://mospi.gov.in/sites/default/files/Statistical_year_book_india_chapters/ch12.pdf

34   Source: Press Information Bureau (PRS) (as of 10/02/2024) Link – https://prsindia.org/policy/vital-stats/status-water-availability-agriculture-india

35   Source – ResearchGate Link – https://www.researchgate.net/figure/Location-map-of-Marathwada-region-of-Maharashtra-state-India-Selected-grids-at-the_fig3_358294380

36   Source – https://www.iasgyan.in/daily-current-affairs/monsoon

37   Source – Article from Down-to-earth (as of 10/02/2024) Link – https://www.downtoearth.org.in/news/natural-disasters/marathwada-s-dry-story-53792

38   Source – Article from 'The Deccan Herald' (as of 10/02/2024) Link – https://www.deccanherald.com/india/maharashtra/685-farmer-suicides-in-marathwada-so-far-in-2023-divisional-commissioner-report-2682458

39   European Commission – World Atlas of Desertification (as of 10/02/2024) Link – https://wad.jrc.ec.europa.eu/irrigations

40   Link to the article (as of 10/02/2024): https://timesofindia.indiatimes.com/city/ahmedabad/guj-has-countrys-highest-area-of-land-affected-by-salinity/articleshow/86538525.cms

41   Climate resilience is the ability of a system to cope with climate change effects, such as increased or irregular rainfall.

42   Food security means having consistent access to enough safe and nutritious food to lead a healthy life. It's not just about having enough food but ensuring that the food is nutritious and safe to eat.

43 By marginalised farmers, we are referring to households that own 1 acre of land, which makes cultivation just a source of survival for them.

44 Source – *National Geographic*

45 By Andreas Lederer Link – https://commons.wikimedia.org/w/index.php?curid=8372772

46 By M. Gurven: Link-https://tsimane.anth.ucsb.edu/tsimaneinfo.html#:~:text=The%20Tsimane%20are%20an%20Amazonian%20group%20that%20relies%20on%20fishing,%20hunting,%20gathering,%20and%20occasional%20wage%20labor.

47 Source – Britannica Link – https://www.britannica.com/topic/Inuit-people#/media/1/192518/232536

48 For reference, you can watch the movie 10,000 BCE. It is fiction but will give you an idea of what was.

49 Source – National Geographic (as of 10/02/2024) Link – https://education.nationalgeographic.org/resource/domestication/

50 Credit – By Trish Mayo from New York, US – P1250552, CC BY 2.0, Link – https://commons.wikimedia.org/w/index.php?curid=6923484

51 Credit – By Miya.m – Bombay, Prince of Wales Museum, CC BY-SA 3.0, Link – https://commons.wikimedia.org/w/index.php?curid=7020208

52 Credit – By Kim Foster – originally posted to Flickr as Sisters-llamas6, CC BY 2.0, Link – https://commons.wikimedia.org/w/index.php?curid=6876409

53 Referred from Asterix and the Soothsayer, a comic by R. Goscinny and A. Uderzo.

54 By Front view: Marten Kuilman Side view: Antonio Milena/ABr – This file has been extracted from another file, CC BY 3.0 br, Link – https://commons.wikimedia.org/w/index.php?curid=89615264

55 Image available in the public domain.
    Link – https://en.wikipedia.org/wiki/File:Ekapada_shiva.jpg

56 Oinochoe, 520–500 BC, from Vulci. Link: https://en.wikipedia.org/wiki/Nemean_lion#/media/File:Herakles_Nemean_lion_BM_B621.jpg

57 By Hunefer – image available in the public domain. Link: https://commons.wikimedia.org/w/index.php?curid=79229218

58 Attributed to the Priam Painter – Marie-Lan Nguyen (2011), CC BY 2.5, Link – https://commons.wikimedia.org/w/index.php?curid=13879854

59 By Metropolitan Museum of Art – Metropolitan Museum of Art Provided under Public Domain licence, CC BY-SA 4.0, Link – https://commons.wikimedia.org/w/index.php?curid=139233642

60 By Gary Todd Link-https://commons.wikimedia.org/w/index.php?curid=97154620

61 By Nittavinoda – Own work, CC BY-SA 4.0, Link – https://commons.wikimedia.org/w/index.php?curid=70559192

62 By Babel Stone Link — https://commons.wikimedia.org/w/index.php?curid=18869637

63 By Kaiserlich Deutsches — image available in the public domain, https://commons.wikimedia.org/w/index.php?curid=18996437

64 Image available in public domain Link-https://en.wikipedia.org/wiki/Ashvamedha#/media/File:Asvamedha_ramayana.JPG

65 Note: Cholas of India are amongst the longest-ruling dynasties. Their mention is found in Sangam literature from the 3rd century BCE. Inscriptions, Ashoka edicts, *Megasthenes*; Pliny the Elder all mention the Chola dynasty. So, they perhaps ruled for a thousand years.

66 Made in Kota, Rajasthan, India — image available in the public domain. Link: https://commons.wikimedia.org/w/index.php?curid=18860382

67 By Sailko — CC BY 3.0 Link — https://commons.wikimedia.org/w/index.php?curid=64295817

68 By Kaidor — CC BY-SA 4.0 Link-https://commons.wikimedia.org/w/index.php?curid=71237789

69 Source: Google's English dictionary provided by Oxford Languages.

70 Source: Collins Dictionary

71 Source — Article from The Paperclip (as of 10/02/2024) Link — https://thepaperclip.in/the-love-story-that-gave-us-terror-of-bengal/

72 It was built by Arnoraja (alias Ana), the grandfather of Prithviraj Chauhan, in 1135-1150 AD and is named after him.

73 Source — Petruzzello, Melissa. "6 Animals We Ate Into Extinction." Encyclopedia Britannica Link — https://www.britannica.com/list/6-animals-we-ate-into-extinction

74 By BazzaDaRambler — Oxford University Museum of Natural History Link-https://en.m.wikipedia.org/wiki/File:Oxford_Dodo_display.jpg

75 Source — Goldring, James, and Anderson (1998)

76 Source — History Channel (as of 10/02/2024) Link — www.history.com/news/industrial-revolution-negative-effects

77 Source: Economic Observatory, Lessons from History (as of 10/02/2024). Link — https://www.economicsobservatory.com/what-can-we-learn-from-the-role-of-coal-in-the-industrial-revolution

78 The measuring unit of the thickness of a plastic carrier bag is a micron. One micron is equal to a unit of length of one-millionth of a meter.

79 Source: Article from The Economic Times (as of 10/02/2024) Link-https://economictimes.indiatimes.com/defaultinterstitial.cms

80 Source — ICSID (as of 10/02/2024) Link — www.icsid.org/uncategorized/can-of-coke-production-cost/

81 A thermoplastic is a class of polymer that can be softened through heating and then moulded into any shape. It solidifies after cooling.

82 Source: United Nations Environment Programme (as of 10/02/2024). Link: https://www.unep.org/interactives/beat-plastic-pollution/

83 Source: United Nations Environment Programme (as of 10/02/2024) Link: https://www.unep.org/interactives/beat-plastic-pollution/

84 Source – Space.com (as of 10/02/2024) Link – https://www.space.com/mountain-discarded-clothes-chile-satellite-photo

85 Source – Space.com (as of 10/02/2024) Link – https://www.space.com/mountain-discarded-clothes-chile-satellite-photo

86 Source: Space.com (as of 10/02/2024) Link-https://www.space.com/mountain-discarded-clothes-chile-satellite-photo

87 Image credit – SkyFi Link – https://www.space.com/mountain-discarded-clothes-chile-satellite-photo

88 By Chris Jordan (via U.S. Fish and Wildlife Service Headquarters) / CC BY 2.0 – Link – https://commons.wikimedia.org/w/index.php?curid=26762401

89 By Rhododendrites – Own work CC BY-SA 4.0, Link-https://commons.wikimedia.org/w/index.php?curid=131682882

90 Source – Keep Britain Tidy (as of 10/02/2024) Link – https://www.keepbritaintidy.org/get-involved/support-our-campaigns/plastic-challenge/impact-wildlife

91 By Sébastien Stradal for MDC Seamarc Maldives CC BY-SA 4.0, Link – https://commons.wikimedia.org/w/index.php?curid=34858268

92 Source: United Nations Environment Programme (as of 10/02/2024) Link: https://www.unep.org/news-and-stories/story/plastic-planet-how-tiny-plastic-particles-are-polluting-our-soil

93 Source – Article from India Today (as of 10/02/2024) Link – https://www.indiatoday.in/magazine/special-report/story/20210510-declining-camel-population-in-rajasthan-1796990-2021-05-01

94 Source – Article National Geographic (as of 10/02/2024) Link – https://www.nationalgeographic.com/animals/article/india-five-million-stray-cattle

95 Source – South China Morning Post (as of 10/02/2024) Link – https://www.scmp.com/news/asia/south-asia/article/3217392/india-loves-its-cows-5-million-strays-thats-becoming-problem

96 By Ibama from Brazil – Operação Hymenaea, July/2016, CC BY 2.0, Link – https://commons.wikimedia.org/w/index.php?curid=51685896

97 By Ibama from Brazil – Terra Indígena Porquinhos, Maranhão, CC BY 2.0, Link-https://commons.wikimedia.org/w/index.php?curid=74323984

98 By Cnes – Spot Image Link-http://gallery.spotimage.com/product_info.php?products_id=1255

99 Source – https://repositorio.comillas.edu/jspui/bitstream/11531/26603/1/Roman Gaztanaga%2CDavid.pdf

100 Source: Earth.org Link – https://earth.org/desertification-in-china/

101 Source – https://wikipeacewomen.org/wpworg/en/?page_id=2619

102 Source: YouTube.com, Channel: Euronews Green (as of 10/02/2024). https://www.youtube.com/watch?app=desktop&v=424XT4tqzis

103 Source: US Department of Energy
Link-https://www.energy.gov/eere/bioenergy/biofuel-basics#:~:text=Ethanol%20(CH3CH2OH)%20is%20a%20renewable%20fuel%20that%20can%20be%20made%20from%20various%20plant%20materials%20and%20used%20as%20an%20alternative%20to%20petrol%20(gasoline)%20in%20internal%20combustion%20engines%20to%20reduce%20greenhouse%20gas%20and%20other%20smog%2Dcausing%20emissions.

104 Source: World Wildlife Fund (as of 10/02/2024). Link: https://www.worldwildlife.org/industries/cotton#:~:text=Donate-,Overview,textiles%20are%20made%20of%20cotton.

105 Link: https://agritech.tnau.ac.in/agriculture/agri_costofcultivation_cotton12.html

106 *Grasim* Industries Limited is India's pioneer in Viscose Staple Fiber (VSF)— a man-made, biodegradable fibre that is fast emerging as a sustainable alternative to cotton.

107 In olden times, draught animals, i.e., animals used for labour like oxen, horses, donkeys, and camels, were more prevalent. With the advent of technology, they were replaced by machines and presently are not used by the majority of people.

108 The process of extracting IMO from the rumen is a complicated process and can be carried out by a trained veterinarian only. More accessible alternatives to IMO include fermented rice water along with molasses or jaggery.

109 Source – BRAI
Link to PDF: https://brai.in/wp-content/uploads/2017/07/Land-Measurement-Units-in-India-new.pdf

110 1 square foot means the area of a square with sides 1 foot in length.

111 There are projects where you could buy trees that are a year old and transplant them. You do not have to grow them as saplings.

112 Around 75% of the world's flowering plants and about 35% of global food crops depend on animal pollinators, with bees being among the most important.

113 Government nurseries have a wide variety of plants available at significantly lower prices than privately owned nurseries.

114 Seeds of all crops listed above can be found on www.indiamart.com or other aggregator sites.

115 Definition from the Oxford Dictionary

116 Minerals do not contain carbon atoms; hence, they are considered inorganic.

117 Note that excessive levels of added fat can have a negative impact on fibre digestion

118 Find your nearest KVK at this site – https://kvk.icar.gov.in/KVK_selection_ddl.aspx

119 A genetically modified organism (GMO) is an animal, plant, or microbe whose DNA has been altered using genetic engineering techniques. (Source: National Geographic Society)

120 We cannot say GMOs are bad in all cases, but we should ensure that we only use them where necessary.

121 Arid regions are characterised by minimal precipitation, typically receiving less than 25 centimetres (250 millimetres) of rainfall annually.

122 Semi-arid regions receive a moderate amount of precipitation ranging from 25 to 50 centimetres (250-500 millimetres) per year.

123 Link to PDF – www.nddb.coop/sites/default/files/pdfs/Animal-Nutrition-booklet.pdf (as of 10/02/2024)

124 Seed cost on the basis of ₹150/kg ($2/kg) It is advisable to irrigate the crop instead of depending on the rains. Seed application in ¼ acre – 4kg
Seed cost in ¼ acre – ₹600 ($7.22)
Dollar conversion on the basis of 1$= ₹83.12 as of 20/01/2024
Source – https://g.co/kgs/exTGava

125 Seed cost on the basis of ₹550/kg.
Seed application in a ¼ acre – 1 kg
Seed cost in a ¼ acre – £550 ($7)

126 Seed cost on the basis of ₹600/kg.
Seed application in a ¼ acre – 1 kg
Seed cost in a ¼ acre – £600 ($7.22)

127 Seed cost on the basis of ₹1000/kg.
Seed application in a ¼ acre – 1 kg
Seed cost in a ¼ acre – £1000 ($12)

128 Detailed explanation can be found here – www.masterclass.com/articles/neem-oil-for-plants

129 Detailed explanation can be found here – www.thegarlicfarm.co.uk/blogs/news/make-your-own-all-natural-garlic-sprays-1-

130 Ecosystem – A biological system composed of all the organisms found in a particular physical environment, interacting with it and with each other. (Definition from Oxford dictionary)

131 Also known as

132 Definition from the Oxford Dictionary

133 Definition from the Oxford Dictionary

134 Source – Government Schemes India Link – https://govtschemes.in/fertilizer-subsidy-scheme-2022 (as of 12/04/2024)

135 Exchequer refers to the government department that controls public money. This department is now called the Treasury. Definition from Oxford Dictionary.

136 Definition from ClearTax (AS OF 10/02/2024) Link – https://cleartax.in/glossary/fiscal-deficit/

137 Source: The Economic Times
Article-https://economictimes.indiatimes.com/news/economy/agriculture/govt-approves-rs-60939-crore-subsidy-for-pk-fertilisers-for-april-september/articleshow/91127459.cms?from=mdr

138 Source:www.agrifarming.in/the-best-fertilizer-for-rice-crop-organic-npk-and-schedule-for-paddy

139 Source: International Fertilizer Society – Energy Consumption and Greenhouse Gas Emissions in Fertiliser Production (as of 10/02/2024)
Link – https://fertiliser-society.org/store/energy-consumption-and-greenhouse-gas-emissions-in-fertiliser-production/
Flue gas – a mixture of gases produced by the burning of fuel or other materials in power stations and industrial plants and extracted via ducts. Definition from Oxford Dictionary.

140 Source: Oxford Dictionary

141 Source: Oxford Dictionary

142 Lactic acid is a naturally occurring preservative, present in various food items, including pickled vegetables and yogurt. In soil, lactic acid bacteria improve soil structure, control diseases, and promote growth.

143 Source – Oxford dictionary

144 Source: Oxford Dictionary

145 Source: United Nations Food and Agriculture Organization (as of 10/02/2024)
Link – www.fao.org/3/y5104e/y5104e05.htm

146 Source – Deep Green Permaculture: How to Make Compost In 18 Days Using the Berkeley Hot Composting (as of 10/02/2024) Method. Link – https://deepgreenpermaculture.com/2010/05/08/hot-compost-composting-in-18-days/

147 Source: Deep Green Permaculture: How to Make Compost in 18 Days Using The Berkeley Hot Composting Method (as of 10/02/2024)
Link – https://deepgreenpermaculture.com/2010/05/08/hot-compost-composting-in-18-days/

148 Density – The mass of a substance per unit of volume (definition from the Oxford dictionary).

149 Source – CHEMICAL AND PHYSICAL PROPERTIES OF COMPOST – El-Sayed G. Khader Link – https://www.researchgate.net/publication/275407706_Some_Physical_and_Chemical_Properties_of_Compost

150 To compact means to press something tightly together (definition from the Oxford dictionary).

151 Buy at www.amazon.in/Earthworms-Eisenia-fetida-vermicomposting-Earthworm

152 Buy at www.indiamart.com/proddetail/lumbricus-rubellus-live-earthworms

153 Source – Youtube.com, Channel – Acorn Land Labs Link – https://youtube.com/shorts/PBXUR_AWmXc?si=XTWiMNseTy5-PQmy(as of 10/02/2024)

154 The holes should be clean and properly drilled with no rough edges or it can cause injury to the worms.

155 The organic waste should have a very small amount of moisture to ensure successful composting.

156 If using cow dung, soften it with water for 2-3 days before putting it in the bucket.

157 The advisable amount of worms is double the amount of organic waste.

158 Buy at – https://www.amazon.in/Real-Trust-Compost-Fabric-12ftx4ftx2ft/dp/B08N T8X5HL/

159 Buy at-www.amazon.in/Earthworms-Eisenia-fetida-vermicomposting-Earthworm/

160 Buy at www.indiamart.com/proddetail/lumbricus-rubellus-live-earthworms

161 Detailed video explanation on YouTube.com, Channel – Road to Organic Link – https://youtu.be/YSy2lUhPd7c?si=FXV5XeF-hax87aYJ (as of 10/02/2024)

162 Volume = Length × Width × Depth

163 Additional height of 90 cm

164 Source-www.thepharmajournal.com/archives/2020/vol9issue1/PartB/8-12-30-670.pdf

165 Weight = Volume x Density

166 Source – https://agritech.tnau.ac.in/agriculture/agri_Nutrient_mainfeild_%20 Organic_biofertilizers_Rice.html

167 A sample can be taken to a Soil Testing Laboratory.

168 Bio Enzymes refer to proteins created by microorganisms like bacteria, fungi, and yeast.

169 Citrus fruits include oranges, lemons, tangerines, grapefruits, etc.

170 An airtight container is a sealed container that doesn't let air in or out, thereby maintaining a closed environment inside.

171 Can be purchased on – www.amazon.in/beatXP-Multipurpose-Portable-Electronic-Weighing/

172 The pH scale ranges from 0 to 14, with 0 being highly acidic, 7 being neutral, and 14 being highly alkaline.

173 HDPE – High-Density Polyethylene – a thermoplastic polymer

174 When yeast is added, the bioenzyme will be ready in one month. In the absence of yeast, the bioenzyme will take three months to be ready.

175 Source: Journal of Agriculture and Food Research: Recent Trends in Utilization of Citrus Fruits in Production of Eco-Enzyme

176 The residual syrup that remains after the sugar crystals are extracted.

177 Palm sugar is a sweetener derived from any variety of palm tree.

178 We are taking 1 kg as an example. The reader may decrease or increase the quantity according to their convenience, but the ratio of fish waste to molasses/ palm sugar should remain 1:1.

179 1 tablespoon = 15 grams

180 1 gallon = 3.7 litres

181 Biomagnification is the process by which certain substances, such as pollutants or toxic chemicals, become more concentrated in the tissues of organisms as they move up the food chain.

182 Source–https://www.blue-growth.org/Plastics_Waste_Toxins_Pollution/Biomagnification_Bio_Accumulation.htm

183 One ppm is equivalent to 1 milligram of something per litre of water (mg/l) or 1 milligram of something per kilogram of soil (mg/kg)

184 Source – Healthline: Should You Avoid Fish Because of Mercury? Link to article – https://www.healthline.com/nutrition/mercury-content-of-fish

185 **Humic acid** is a natural substance found in soil, formed from the breakdown of dead plants and animals. It is dark brown or black and plays a crucial role in improving soil health and plant growth.

186 Read the full article on – https://www.indiatoday.in/india/story/farmer-hangs-himself-from-tree-gurugram-land-dispute-with-family-2385410-2023-05-28

187 Etymology – the study of the origin and history of words and their meaning (Definition from the Oxford dictionary)

188 This fable is disputed among historians because of the complexities involved in building a 'hanging garden', and its exact location is still not known.

189 Source: Gathera Link – https://gathera.com/blogs/learn/william-f-gericke-the-inventor-of-hydroponics

190 Source – Gathera Link – https://gathera.com/blogs/learn/william-f-gericke-the-inventor-of-hydroponics

191 By Anusha

192 'Controlled environment' means that every element within the structure can be controlled by the farmer. This includes humidity, sunlight, movement of air, etc.

193 As long as due process is followed.

194 By Anusha

195 Image source – RASHTRIYA KRISHI VIKAS YOJANA GOA STATE CO-OPERATIVE MILK PRODUCERS' UNION LTD Link – https://rkvy.nic.in/static/download/RKVY_New_Success_Stories/goa/4.pdf

196 Link to the product – https://www.amazon.in/Metal-Plastic-Hydroponic-Germination-Light/dp/B07J2PF3RG/ref=sr_1_9?keywords=hydroponic+trays+100+piece&qid=1706500155&sr=8-9

197 If this is not done, once the plants mature, they will outgrow the tray and disintegrate, hence ruining the plant mat.

198 Image source – RASHTRIYA KRISHI VIKAS YOJANA GOA STATE CO-OPERATIVE MILK PRODUCERS' UNION LTD Link – https://rkvy.nic.in/static/download/RKVY_New_Success_Stories/goa/4.pdf

199 Image source – RASHTRIYA KRISHI VIKAS YOJANA GOA STATE CO-OPERATIVE MILK PRODUCERS' UNION LTD Link – https://rkvy.nic.in/static/download/RKVY_New_Success_Stories/goa/4.pdf

200 Image source – RASHTRIYA KRISHI VIKAS YOJANA GOA STATE CO-OPERATIVE MILK PRODUCERS' UNION LTD Link – https://rkvy.nic.in/static/download/RKVY_New_Success_Stories/goa/4.pdf

201 Governmental Aid
On a small scale, it requires much less capital investment than what is required for big hydroponic stations. (exact amount?) In India, the government aids the construction of hydroponic setups. It provides credit-linked back-ended subsidy at 20% of the total project cost, limited to Rs 25 lakh per project in general areas and Rs 30.00 lakh in the NE Region, Hilly, and Scheduled areas. The said support is available for projects spanning an area of more than four hectares (ten acres) in open cultivation and more than 1000 square meters in protected cultivation.

202 By Danish

203 By Danish

204 Elevation reduces but does not completely eliminate the risk of soil-borne diseases. Proper hygiene and regular cleaning are still necessary to ensure health.

205 By Danish

206 By Danish

207 Image source – https://www.dynamic-engineering.co.th/products/slats-nova

208 By Anusha

209 By Anusha

210 By Anusha

211 Formula for conversion: (°C × 9/5) + 32 = °F
For example: (1°C × 9/5) + 32 = 33.8°F

212 By Anusha

213 By Anusha

214 By Danish

215 By Danish

216 By Anusha

217 By Anusha

218 By Danish

219 By Anusha

220 By Anusha

221 By Anusha

222 By Anusha

223 Solute – a substance that has been dissolved in a liquid (= made to become part of the liquid) so that together they form a solution. (Definition from Oxford dictionary)

224 Solvent – the liquid in which a solute is dissolved to form a solution. (Definition from Oxford dictionary)

225 RO water purifiers cannot completely remove all solutes from the water. They can only decrease their level of concentration. The purest form of water (without

any solutes) is distilled water. To distil is to make a liquid pure by heating it until it becomes a gas, then cooling it and collecting the drops of liquid that form (definition from Oxford dictionary)

226 Osmosis-a process by which molecules of a solvent tends to pass through a semipermeable membrane from a less concentrated solution into a more concentrated one. (Definition from Oxford dictionary)

A less concentrated solution means a lower concentration of solutes and a higher concentration of water.

A highly concentrated solution means a high concentration of solutes and a lower concentration of water.

227 Semi-Permeable – allowing certain substances to pass through it but not others, especially allowing the passage of a solvent but not of certain solutes. (Definition from Oxford dictionary)

228 Reverse osmosis – a process by which a solvent passes through a porous membrane in the direction opposite to that for natural osmosis when subjected to a hydrostatic pressure greater than the osmotic pressure. (Definition from Oxford dictionary)

229 Source: Fresh Water Systems
Link – https://www.freshwatersystems.com/blogs/blog/what-is-tds-in-water-why-should-you-measure-It

230 Situated in Pisangan village in Ajmer district, Rajasthan, India.

231 1 gallon = 3.78541 litres

232 Source: University of California Division of Agriculture and Natural Resources
Link – https://ucanr.edu/sites/placernevadasmallfarms/files/197793.pdf

233 Increasing this number will have a negative effect on the optimal functioning of the shed.

234 By Danish

235 By Danish

236 By Danish

237 Gable – the upper part of the end wall of a building, between the two sloping sides of the roof, that is like a triangle in shape (definition from Oxford dictionary)

238 By Danish

239 By Danish

240 Net metering definition from Paradise Energy Solutions.
Link – https://www.paradisesolarenergy.com/blog/difference-between-off-grid-and-on-grid-solar-energy
Please check the net metering laws in your area/country as they may differ.

241 Solar panel efficiency is a measurement of how much of the sun's energy a certain panel can convert into usable electricity. Source: solar.com
Link-https://www.solar.com/learn/solar-panel-efficiency/#:~:text=Solar%20panel%20efficiency%20is%20a,cells%20inside%20a%20solar%20panel.

242 1000 watt = 1 kilowatt or kW.

243 This is an approximate number. It may vary based on factors like the presence of clouds, intensity of sunlight, etc.

244 Warranty differs based on the company that is providing solar panels.

245 Consecutively – following one after another in a continuous series (definition from Oxford dictionary)

246 Concurrently – at the same time (definition from Oxford dictionary)

247 Volt – a unit for measuring the force of an electric current (definition from the Oxford dictionary)

248 Voltage – electrical force measured in volts (definition from Oxford dictionary)

249 Although it will be a loss in the long run, low-quality solar panels are less efficient in converting solar energy to electrical energy.

250 Definition from the Oxford Dictionary

251 Definition from the Oxford Dictionary

252 By Anusha

253 Jay Scott's collection Link – https://jayscotts.com/blog/pot-shapes-for-plants/

254 1 gallon = 3.785 litres

255 One pound (lbs) is equal to 0.453 kg. One kilogram (kg) is equal to 1000 grams (g).

256 Definition from the Food and Agriculture Organization of the United Nations

257 By Anush

258 By Anusha

259 By Anusha

260 By Anusha

261 Definition from the Oxford Dictionary

262 By Anusha

263 Source: Investopedia
Link-https://www.investopedia.com/ask/answers/112814/whats-difference-between-capital-expenditures-capex-and-operational-expenditures-opex.asp#:~:text=Capital%20expenditures%20are%20a%20company's,%2C%20utilities%2C%20and%20property%20taxes.

264 Source: Investopedia
Link-https://www.investopedia.com/ask/answers/112814/whats-difference-between-capital-expenditures-capex-and-operational-expenditures-opex.asp#:~:text=Capital%20expenditures%20are%20a%20company's,%2C%20utilities%2C%20and%20property%20taxes.

265 Link to site – https://printo.in/

266 Definition from Investopedia.
Link-https://www.investopedia.com/terms/f/finders-fee.asp#:~:text=A%20finder's%20fee%20or%20referral,or%20seller%20in%20the%20deal.

267 Link – https://sell.amazon.in/fees-and-pricing

268 Volumetric weight is calculated as Volumetric Weight (kg) = (Length x Breadth x Height)/5000 where LBH are in cm.

269 This is just a remote price and not generalised.
Conversion: 1 Indian Rupee equals 0.012 United States Dollars.
As of 19 February 202

270 Conversion: 1 Indian Rupee equals 0.012 United States Dollars
As of 19th February 2024

271 Link to site – https://www.mudra.org.in/

272 Link to site – https://www.nabard.org/content1.aspx?id=599&catid=23&mid=23

273 Definition from Oxford Dictionary

274 Source: Statista

275 Source: International Telecommunication Union (ITU) (as of 06/03/2024)
Link – https://www.itu.int/en/ITU-D/Statistics/Pages/stat/default.aspx

276 Source: Oberlo (as of 06/03/2024)
Link – https://www.oberlo.com/statistics/how-many-people-shop-online

277 Definition from Oxford Dictionary

278 Definition from Oxford Dictionary.

279 We are mentioning a site where you can hire people and pay them to fill forms of the Shops and Commercial Establishments Act, GST, and any other legal document when starting your business. Using a third party ensures a hassle-free process with a minimum risk of errors. This is just an example; you can use other sites, whichever best suits your needs.
Site – IndiaFilings
Link – https://www.indiafilings.com/company-annual-filing?matchtype=p&device=c&campaign=20048225270&keyword=company%20secretarial%20services&matchtype=p&network=g&position=&location=1007805&gad_source=1&gclid=CjwKCAiAopuvBhBCEiwAm8jaMWxvSxi9IFQi4yVi0V1jL5vBEAsgUr1Wf_C4fAQD10fHpCUCoOaxPhoCyOkQAvD_BwE
Caution: Please beware of fraudsters when looking for online sites to fill out forms.

280 Source: ICICI Bank
Link – https://www.icicibank.com/business-banking/current-account/documentation#faqaccordion-2

281 For more information regarding other documents that can be used, please visit – https://www.icicibank.com/business-banking/current-account/documentation/list-of-documents-table-a

282 For more information regarding other documents that can be used, please visit- https://www.icicibank.com/business-banking/current-account/documentation/list-of-documents-table-b

283 For more information regarding other documents that can be used, please visit- https://www.icicibank.com/business-banking/current-account/documentation/list-of-documents-table-b

284 E-filing of applications, e-payment, and e-submission of documents are mandatory; no hard copies are required. Approved certificates are issued online.